U.S FOREIGN POLICY
IN THE CARIBBEAN, CUBA,
AND CENTRAL AMERICA

U.S. FOREIGN POLICY IN THE CARIBBEAN, CUBA, AND CENTRAL AMERICA

James N. Cortada
James W. Cortada

PRAEGER SPECIAL STUDIES • PRAEGER SCIENTIFIC

New York • Philadelphia • Eastbourne, UK
Toronto • Hong Kong • Tokyo • Sydney

Library of Congress Cataloging in Publication Data

Cortada, James N.
 U.S. foreign policy in the Caribbean, Cuba,
and Central America.

 Bibliography: p.
 Includes index.
  1. Caribbean Area—Foreign relations—United States.
2. United States—Foreign relations—Caribbean Area.
3. United States—Foreign relations—1981–
I. Cortada, James W. II. Title. III. Title:
US foreign policy in the Caribbean, Cuba and
Central America.
F2178.U6C67 1985   327.730729   84-26629
ISBN 0-03-002119-7 (alk. paper)

Published in 1985 by Praeger Publishers
CBS Educational and Professional Publishing, a Division of CBS Inc.
521 Fifth Avenue, New York, NY 10175 USA

© 1985 by Praeger Publishers

56789 052 987654321

Printed in the United States of America on acid-free paper

INTERNATIONAL OFFICES

Orders from outside the United States should be sent to the appropriate address listed below. Orders from areas not listed below should be placed through CBS International Publishing, 383 Madison Ave., New York, NY 10175 USA

Australia, New Zealand
Holt Saunders, Pty, Ltd., 9 Waltham St., Artarmon, N.S.W. 2064, Sydney, Australia

Canada
Holt, Rinehart & Winston of Canada, 55 Horner Ave., Toronto, Ontario, Canada M8Z 4X6

Europe, the Middle East, & Africa
Holt Saunders, Ltd., 1 St. Anne's Road, Eastbourne, East Sussex, England BN21 3UN

Japan
Holt Saunders, Ltd., Ichibancho Central Building, 22-1 Ichibancho, 3rd Floor, Chiyodaku, Tokyo, Japan

Hong Kong, Southeast Asia
Holt Saunders Asia, Ltd., 10 Fl, Intercontinental Plaza, 94 Granville Road, Tsim Sha Tsui East, Kowloon, Hong Kong

Manuscript submissions should be sent to the Editorial Director, Praeger Publishers, 521 Fifth Avenue, New York, NY 10175 USA

*For Shirley
and Dora*

PREFACE

The purpose for writing this book is to offer specific suggestions on the formulation of U.S. foreign policy toward Cuba, the Caribbean, and Central America. Although the reader will see a great deal of historical and economic data presented below, this book is not intended to be a history of U.S. foreign relations. History does not repeat itself directly although behavioral patterns of nations become observable and therefore useful. We examine those in light of what is possible. We identify elements of predictability and apply those to the development of strategic considerations for the United States. The authors are convinced that an understanding of these patterns can contribute to the development of U.S. policies in that part of the world in which the United States today lacks direction.

What is proposed in some cases may not be new because of the limits inherent in foreign policy. However, by heavily relying on the history of contemporary relations with the area, examination of economic realities, and squared against what constitute the best interests of the United States, one can develop a rationale for the suggestions made, taking into account the interests of the United States as reflected both in the political realities of the twentieth century and the Preamble of the Constitution. Furthermore, the primary focus is on twentieth century developments.

The regions selected for this study constitute an area of significance today to the general security and welfare of the United States. The complexity of the issues involved are broad and constitute a challenge to policymakers who currently do not have as well-developed policies for this area as they do for the Soviet Union, Western Europe, China, Japan, and the Middle East. It will encompass the impact of history, economics, and anthro-sociological considerations in the formulation of specific ideas—factors seldom given importance by U.S. policymakers worrying about Central America, the Caribbean Basin, and especially Cuba.

The general plan followed in this book is initially a short discussion of the significance of this part of the world to the United States. Chapter 1 defines what constitutes the basis for U.S. self-interest within the context of the Constitution. Chapter 2 discusses some of the most important foreign policy instruments available to the government of the United States for use in this area today, highlighting aspects that lessen their strength and efficacy in our judgment. Special attention is devoted to the matter of human rights since this consideration seemed to outweigh the realities of situations "out there" particularly during the Carter Administration. Basic assumptions are made that affect the logic of succeeding chapters.

In respect to the Central American situation, a key ingredient necessary for future peace and stability is the use of past experiences with treaty arrangements. To develop that argument fully and explore its past performance, Chapters 3 and 4 are devoted to recent historical developments in the area and the relations of the United States with key countries. An important element of our view is the significance of democracy as a stabilizing force in Central America. Promoting democracy abroad is looked into because first, it has long been a desirable objective of the U.S. people and second, because the gap between the ideal and what can actually be achieved is generally very broad. We hold the firm belief that in countries where this political philosophy is alien, a viable Western democratic political institution cannot develop unless there exists a broadly based rural landowning middle class, as well as one in urban centers.

The point is crucially important because aid programs designed for Central America and the Caribbean Islands in recent years do not specifically highlight this necessity. Hence, the U.S. experiences disappointments when a nation which has received substantial aid explodes with Uncle Sam as the whipping boy. Nevertheless, U.S. assistance to Latin America, beginning with the Lend-Lease programs in World War II, and in the subsequent decades helped the entire continent to achieve very considerable economic improvement, and indirectly to the development of urban middle classes. As retired veteran Ambassador and former Assistant Secretary of State for Inter-American Affairs Robert F. Woodward (whose experience in Latin America began in 1933) reminded the authors, "it has been U.S. policy to try to help develop such a middle class in all of the countries. All kinds of methods and funding have been tried, and gradually these developed on a large scale and were carried out surprisingly consistently from Administration to Administration by a fairly well-convinced element in Congress and a great deal of real continuity in the levels of the Executive Branch just below the elected authorities. A really careful analysis of what has happened in Latin America in all of the principal branches of human endeavor (perhaps divided up in much the manner of the goals in the Alliance for Progress documents) may show that there has been truly surprising changes in living standards for a large percentage of the populations in the past 40 years, say since World War II. At the same time, the *dramatic proliferation of population has resulted in even larger numbers who are living in poverty.*"[1]

Chapter 5 reviews current economic and political realities and makes suggestions about U.S. policy options applicable both in Central America and in the Caribbean. Chapter 6 does the same for Cuba. The final chapter summarizes recent circumstances and possible realities in the political-economic fortunes of U.S.-Caribbean, Cuban, and Central American relations in general. Because of the importance of treaties in bringing peace to Central America in the past, the most important ones are reprinted as appendixes.

For those who wish to examine further aspects of the topics discussed, a limited bibliography with occasional comment is included. It is assumed that specialists are familiar with the literature in their own fields; therefore, no encyclopedic listing is attached.

A number of people have been helpful to us during the preparation of this book whom we would like to thank. Professor Lester Langely, of the University of Georgia, gave us advice on organization; Professor Lawrence S. Kaplan, of Kent State University, carefully critiqued our historical discussions; Professor Fredrick B. Pike, of the University of Notre Dame, went over the manuscript very carefully offering us his wisdom and knowledge about middle classes and Latin American political conditions. Several retired U.S. diplomats with decades of experience in the areas discussed in this book generously helped with facts, comments, and judgments: Ambassador Philip W. Bonsal (served in Cuba); Ambassador Robert F. Woodward (served in a variety of capacities both in Washington D.C. and in the area). Richard C. Brown, currently working within the Department of State on matters dealing with the Caribbean Basin helped us appreciate contemporary situations. These specialists kept us from making even more mistakes and caused us to think long and hard about our recommendations. We are grateful to each of them for their interest and kind assistance.

Librarians were helpful at several institutions. Those at the Orange County Public Library in Orange, Virginia found a large number of materials through inter-library loans. The resources of the library at the University of Virginia also proved extremely useful. Other materials were examined at Vassar College, U.S. Library of Congress, and at the U.S. Department of State. Final bibliographic work was done with the help of librarians at Vanderbilt University.

We are also grateful to those organizations that gave us copyright permissions to use their material in this book. For the preparation of the manuscript and its many modifications, we are indebted to Mrs. Doris Oveissi. Lori Siskind copyedited the manuscript, improving it with her sensitivity and thoroughness. Our wives, to whom we have dedicated this book, tolerated us as we bored them with details of the topic and spent time away from more important responsibilities. Our publisher has shown faith in our project and provided efficient services leading to publication. Any weaknesses the reader may detect are our sins for which we ask understanding.

James N. Cortada
James W. Cortada

CONTENTS

LIST OF TABLES AND MAPS

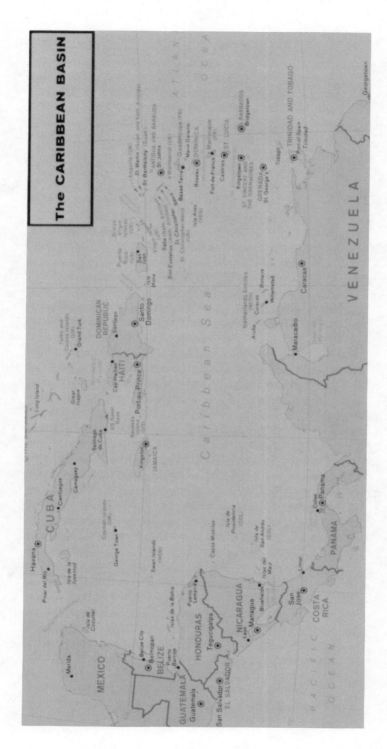

The CARIBBEAN BASIN

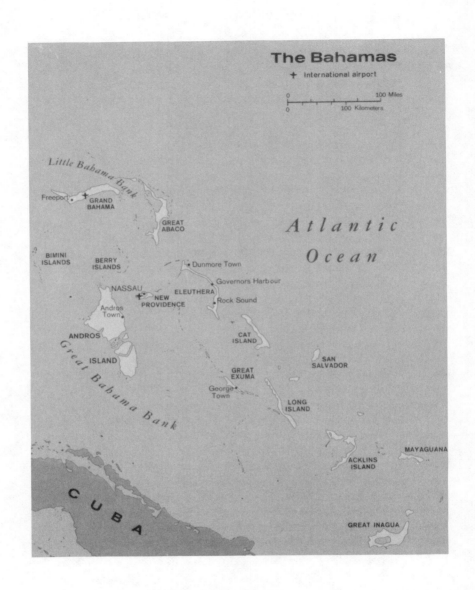

The Bahamas

+ International airport

0   100 Miles

0   100 Kilometers

Little Bahama Bank

Freeport + GRAND BAHAMA

GREAT ABACO

Atlantic Ocean

BIMINI ISLANDS

BERRY ISLANDS

• Dunmore Town

NASSAU

ELEUTHERA

+ NEW PROVIDENCE

• Governors Harbour

• Rock Sound

Andros Town

ANDROS

CAT ISLAND

SAN SALVADOR

Great Bahama Bank

ISLAND

GREAT EXUMA

George Town

LONG ISLAND

MAYAGUANA

ACKLINS ISLAND

C U B A

GREAT INAGUA

U.S FOREIGN POLICY
IN THE CARIBBEAN, CUBA,
AND CENTRAL AMERICA

1

INTRODUCTION

> To forsee danger is better than to sorrow.
>
> *Old Spanish Proverb*

The application of common sense to the foreign policy of the United States in Central America, the Caribbean Islands, and in Cuba has to begin with a clear understanding of their importance. In May 1982, the U.S. Department of State put the issue bluntly: the area's "shipping lanes are vital to U.S. defense and prosperity." Nearly one-half of U.S. trade, two-thirds of our imported oil, and many strategic minerals pass through the Panama Canal or the Gulf of Mexico.[1] In short, this is modern language for a condition that has always existed; namely, the objective that territories nearest the United States remain friendly to us.

The Caribbean Basin security issue is one which cannot be ignored. It is easy to fall back on history and argue that military concerns were a mark of the nineteenth and early twentieth centuries. Invasions of Cuba and Central America in the 1800s by guerrilla bands from the United States and later marine landings in Central America in the early 1900s seem like ancient history. But recall that during World War II, German submarines sank some 560,000 gross tons of Allied shipping in the Caribbean. In 1962 the Cuban missile crisis nearly brought the United States and the Soviet Union to the brink of war. And in 1965 over 20,000 U.S. troops landed in the Dominican Republic.

With Cuba bristling with armaments, a Soviet brigade of sorts in the island, Cuban military aid to Nicaragua and to the guerrillas in El Salvador, while the Reagan administration furnishes military advisors and aid to El Salvador and other countries in the immediate area, it would be naive to rule out defense considerations. Harking back to Cold War tactics reminiscent of the Cuban missile crisis, the Soviets supplied Nicaragua with shiploads of material, while the United States held intensified naval

1

exercises in the area. Clearly, the military significance of the Basin has not diminished with time.

The significance of the area politically and economically warrants the most serious consideration. It is one of the points of this book that unlike such areas as the Soviet Union, Western Europe, the Middle East, or Japan, as a nation we have little understanding of the countries examined nor do we have foreign policies concerning them, as clearly understood as we have elsewhere. If we do not develop a more sophisticated awareness of neighbors so close to the United States, we run the threat of events leading to our playing a military card—an unnecessary and costly option.

A step in the right direction involves appreciating some other reasons why the entire Basin should be of concern to us. The United States in 1981 imported some $30 billion in goods from the area. In return it sold just over $31 billion. As much as $13 billion is invested by U.S. firms and citizens in the region while tourists to the area are increasing each year.[2] The United States has a commonwealth status with Puerto Rico which, should it ever become a state, would simply highlight Washington's commitment to the Basin. Politically, as the following chapters will suggest, the range of friendship and mistrust for the United States is broad, complicating our relations. Hence, these political realities must be accounted for in the development of rational U.S. policies for the region.

The economics of the area are also of particular concern to the United States. The standard of living ranges from a high level of Puerto Rico and Jamaica, for example, to very low depths in Haiti and the Dominican Republic. The highest population density in the New World is in El Salvador and much lower in some of the island republics. Economic concerns impact the United States in several ways. First, there is the trade alluded to before and which will be discussed more in subsequent chapters. The problems associated with the Haitian boat people searching for jobs after landing on U.S. shores are other by-products of economics. A similar problem exists with Mexicans crossing into the southwestern part of the country for similar purposes. Perhaps economics also influenced Fidel Castro's decision to allow over 125,000 Cubans to leave the island for Florida during the Mariel boat lift of 1978.

Yet there is an even greater consequence of economics. Throughout this volume it is suggested that one of the primary ways the United States can insure its political and military security in the general area is to encourage the development of a broadly based middle class. To do that requires the dramatic improvement of the economic wellbeing of each of these nations, particularly in Central America. The solution proposed is thus complicated and will take a great deal of time but represents in our opinion a real fix to the problem of communist infiltration into the area. It also offers the economic and political stability necessary to foster additional trade with the United States. Thus, one of the central points of focus in this book is how to marry international economic programs to foreign policies. Put in other, more blunt terms, the United States has to edge these nations into a standard of living with appropriately enhanced levels of education and health that will motivate them to maintain political stability and friendship with North America. Implied in this assumption is that democracy in this part of the world needs to be encouraged by concrete U.S. actions as part of the long-term strategy to stabilize the area, and thereby make it more secure for the interests of the United States.

The strategy of developing a rural-based middle class that has an economy enhanced with industrialization and that can acquire the characteristics of a stable, democratic society is not without precedent. Studies conducted on democracies in a variety of cultures that today have middle classes suggest strongly that land distribution and democracy go hand-in-hand. Concentration of land in too few hands (as is frequently the case in Central America today) does not represent fertile ground for democracy. Where land is concentrated, the owners also control power, knowledge, and status. Moreover, such a small elite have more in common than not and thus are not inclined to quarrel among themselves. In a more economically equitable system—one that has a middle class and industrial-ization—more varied groups exist (both political and economic), social mobility is more obvious, and interests become highly diversified. These are conditions that lend themselves to democratic systems. By strong implica-tion, we will suggest that such an environment is not a fruitful one for communism and therefore the possible enemies of the United States.[3]

POLITICAL AND ECONOMIC REALITIES

While the temptation to carry the reader through a long and tedious discussion of theories of modernization, and discussions about economic and political development is great, suffice it to say that common sense dictates that the United States encourage its neighbors to embrace political attitudes as close to ours as is practical. The caveat is that these can never be quite the same since the cultures differ significantly. But there are some thoughts that need to be aired. And at the risk of oversimplification or offending those who study political behavior in great detail, several observations of political actions are in order which have influenced the arguments presented in this book.

First, a democratic political system permits implicit emphasis on the development of service trades, light industries, and successful farming. This is because of the built-in flexibility present in the private sector economy in a democratic system. This economic flexibility is essential to the continuous creation of employment opportunities, capital formation, and improving standards of living. In contrast, the rigidity characteristic of Marxist-Leninist totalitarian societies hampers severely the prospects of adequate growth in the service, light industry, and agricultural sectors of an economy. A by-product of this situation is the need for large conscripted standing armies to sop up unemployment. This phenomenon is all too common, for example, in the Soviet Union, Cuba, and throughout Eastern Europe.[4]

Second, right-wing authoritarianism through "half-way house" measures does not freeze private sector economies and farming to the same extent as is evident within Marxist-Leninist structures. Neither does it allow for full growth in these economic sectors because of tight government controls. Furthermore, such a system freezes oligarchies in control of governments, leading to acute disequilibrium in income distribution. This imbalance sooner or later results in massive labor discontent with attendant political and subversive actions. Ultimately, revolution and alternative Marxist-Leninist solutions gain high visibility.

If the government and economy follow a communist pattern in which there is growing unemployment and declining capital formation, then the need for extensive security (police) forces emerges. The ultimate result is a growth in conscription which shifts even greater amounts of available economic resources out of the private economy and into the hands of the government (taxes, responsibility for manufacturing, employment, etc.). The internal security forces are required to deal with domestic political dissatisfaction. The rise in military conscription, as a mechanism for solving the unemployment problem, can in turn also lead to increased military activities. The formula, unfortunately, is too well known to ignore. It was evident in pre-World War II Germany and Italy, between 1939 and 1975 in Franco's Spain, in Nicaragua under Somoza, in the Dominican Republic under Trujillo, and in Peron's Argentina.[5]

Third, survival and stability in democratic regimes appear to require that the majority of both the rural and urban populations reflect a high literacy rate and be in a substantial middle income category relative to a nation's wealthy and poor.[6] In short, the development of a middle class such as is evident in Western Europe, the United States, Canada, and Costa Rica suggests the significance of this requirement. The experiences of the twentieth century indicate more often than not, that political stability can be enhanced, and economic growth encouraged with the existence of a broad-based middle class. The apparent and sometimes momentary exceptions leading to dictatorships may be as a consequence of events and circumstances unique to an era (as in pre-World War II Germany for example).

Fourth, insufficient national income both in absolute terms and in satisfying internal needs saps the basis of democracy. At the risk of oversimplification, Uruguay, for example, once the showplace for democracy and well-being in Latin America, overlooked the sharply growing cost of the social welfare of its society, which, outpaced by declining exports and internal income, eroded a standard of living necessary to support democracy. The democratic structure collapsed (and pressed by the radical leftist *Tupamaros*), chaos ensued, and a military government emerged.

Indirectly related to the process of modernization and to the political structure of countries seeking extensive economic improvement is the view of Marxist-Leninist revolutionaries concerning the middle class. The issue is of immense importance to the Central American scene and for the societies of Cuba and other Caribbean nations. The concern is highlighted significantly by developments in Nicaragua and by civil war in El Salvador. Marxist-Leninist revolutionaries have no sympathy for the middle class or for the bourgeoisie. These classes are considered far more dangerous to the prospects of a Marxist-Leninist regime than the upper classes, which are small and not too difficult to eliminate if a communist government is in control.

Castro, for example, recognized early in the Cuban revolution the danger inherent in the middle classes to his regime and consequently evolved policies, either intuitively or by design, which practically removed the entire Cuban middle class. This was in effect done by creating a hostile atmosphere for the survival of this class. The result was mass migration abroad, mostly to the United States. In an earlier period the Bolshevik revolutionaries wiped out the Kulak landowning peasant class by brutal liquidation.

These patterns of behavior lead to the assumption that permanent control of the Central American or Caribbean nations by communist governments will result in the demise of the incipient urban middle class by design. With this action a communist regime can remove the primary danger to itself. An obvious consequence would be the delay in the development of democracy and, if history serves us right, economic stagnation would result as occurred in Cuba overlaid by a tight security mechanism.

The impact of the Cuban experiment on Central American thinking cannot be overlooked or underestimated. Castro has succeeded in two ways important to the Central Americans. First, he has practically eradicated illiteracy and second, he has instituted quite effective free medical facilities throughout the island. In developing U.S. policy in Central America, the United States can and should help facilitate the development of these benefits in the area. Either it is done by democratic means or by communist forces since dramatic demand for these two public facilities exists. Furthermore, by having the United States take the initiative in helping and urging local governments to implement educational and medical improvements, an important argument in favor of communist rule is diminished.

As we argue throughout this book, the United States has—at the same time—to develop economic policies in the area that dramatically affect the standard of living and economic health of these nations. The reason for this is simple: it is precisely in the economic sector that Castro and his Soviet supporters have failed. This failure can be attributed to the rigidity of the Marxist-Leninist system they have adopted as it affects those sectors of an economy concerned with services, trade, industry, and farming. The failure is also attributable to the loss of access to substantial U.S. and Western European investment and development capital. In Central America at least, and to varying degrees in other Caribbean nations, availability of capital must be of sufficient magnitude to assure constant forward movement. The mechanism of the Central American Common Market provides an important vehicle for this help, in addition to bilateral relations and assistance from such nations as the United States.

Thus, understanding what truly is exportable from Cuba on the one hand, and what on the other cannot be, can contribute to a better appreciation of the strengths and weaknesses of the enemies perceived by the United States in this part of the world. Complicating the process even further, however, is a host of issues regarding what constitutes the best interests of the United States. Before any assessment of the history of our relations with Central America and policy recommendations can be made for this area and the Caribbean in general, one must establish a clear understanding of what constitutes our self-interests (*quid pro quo* to use diplomatic language). It is to that issue that we must now turn.

ROLE OF NATIONAL SELF-INTEREST

Basic to an effective foreign policy is a perception of what is national interest. This appreciation can range from the narrow extreme of only military considerations to the opposite pole of idealistic purposes messianic in character. The issue can be likened to the traditional tale of the five blind men and the elephant in which each had a different description of what the animal looked like based on what part of the body each examined. In a democracy such as that of the United States the description can take on a multitude of hues. The net results are zigzags in interpretation with negative consequences from one administration to another. But one reality is certain. If no general national consensus is reached concerning the nature of national interest, the United States will continue to be a divided nation on issue after issue, weakening, if not paralyzing, our ability to respond.

This is a lesson so painfully revisited recently during the Viet Nam War. While many people may feel that it is perhaps too much to hope that leaders will emerge in the two major political parties, with the wisdom and knowledge, who could foster the flowering of bipartisan postures in international affairs regardless of which party is in power, there is hope. The hope is a simple one, that whoever formulates foreign policy can subscribe to a method for defining national interests and policies that should emerge to defend these interests.

A proposition advanced in this book is that we can focus on the Preamble of the Constitution of the United States for fundamental guidance and inspiration. Throughout the history of this nation during periods of grave crisis U.S. citizens have intuitively turned to consideration of the purpose for which the nation was founded. This view places the efforts reflected in this book in the camp of those who call for realism in foreign policy and excludes utopian propositions. It is our belief, supported by history, that this approach makes sense and is practical in that foreign policy so based can be sold to the U.S. public.

It follows logically from this stance that self-interested (*quid pro quo*) thinking should underlie all diplomatic thrusts. Keen awareness of the connection between the contents of the Preamble and the approach suggested has several important consequences. It would force more careful thought on the major premise of U.S. actions, making it easier for political leaders to explain lucidly and cogently to voters and their representatives in Congress the "whys" and "wherefores." The U.S. public is too sophisticated to accept superficial or simplistic explanations for specific important U.S. foreign policy moves and positions; hence, the nation's divisiveness on many key issues today. On the other hand, explanations and pleas for support tied explicitly to national interest as defined in the Preamble would go a long way toward marshaling popular consensus.

It may seem that we are belaboring the point about self-interest (*quid pro quo*) too much, that in fact it should be obvious to all. It may also appear ridiculous to presume that government officials do not always follow this maxim. Yet as diplomatic historians have proven and political scientists argue, that is not always the case. The blind men and the elephant come to mind again. As this book will argue, complicated circumstances, political pressures, and ignorance often make it difficult if not impossible to understand what constitute the national interests of the United States. It is not always obvious in any one period what does make sense given the political realities of our lives and the art of the possible.

The future by definition always appears hazy and confusing. Yet the marriage of history and diplomacy do provide strong indications of what does make common sense for the United States and what can be accomplished.

It is not our puprose to provide a highly esoteric treatise on the art of diplomacy or of the origins of *quid pro quo* in international affairs but rather a practical guide to what we should do over the next five to twenty years, given the experiences of what we have learned as a nation. The reader might well wonder, as this book is read, whether or not Washington D.C. is filled with incompetents when in reality that is not the case. The story is complicated and the subject vast but some suggestions and observations are possible.

The Preamble was drafted and argued about in the eighteenth century in an era when nations felt committed ruthlessly to self-interest regardless of the collective good of all nations. Subject communities in the form of either client states (those dominated by another nation) or colonies formed clusters of states often not bound by any messianic or utopian ideals but rather by self-interests of the dominant nations. Diplomacy was conducted to enhance the interests of a country regardless of the expense to another. There were no Geneva Conventions, League of Nations, or United Nations to temper the intensity of international adventures. Traditions of political behavior evolved and were inherited only modified as circumstances dictated. Thus when the 13 colonies broke from Britain, they assimilated the political traditions of the British. The Spanish colonies, when they broke from Spain in the early years of the nineteenth century, continued to practice diplomacy and political life as had their Mother Country.[7]

During the nineteenth century more rapid communications and the necessity for complex international markets of supply of raw materials and outlets for finished goods gave meaning and purpose to the Industrial Revolution, the race for colonies by the European states in Africa, the Pacific, and in Asia, and the creation of a frightfully complicated network of alliances that culminated in World War I. At the risk of oversimplification of history, the message is clear: issues took on new hues, interests shifted, and more people were involved in foreign affairs.

Indeed diplomacy grew complicated as the nineteenth century aged and the twentieth looked in sight. By the early 1900s no longer did a handful of people in a small number of cities direct international affairs. It was impossible to follow the precepts of political management as articulated by Niccolò Machiavelli (1469–1527) in his book, *The Prince*. The age of simplicity was gone. In the first place, as Chapter 2 illustrates, the globalization of international affairs made it more difficult for a government either to understand always and clearly what constituted its self-interests or how to defend and enhance them. The number of options and tools has grown. Also, from a cluster of several dozen states in the Western World in the early 1800s we have now gone to over 150 on our planet. Whereas, for example, in the early 1800s, Chinese diplomats could formulate and implement policies regarding Japan and what later became known as Viet Nam, to the total ignorance of Spain or the United States, such is not the case in the twentieth century. Newspapers, telephones, and now data processing communications systems, make it possible for actions taken in one remote part of the world to be appreciated almost instantaneously everywhere. In short, by the turn of the twentieth century the landscape was painted with complexity, picturing a crowded field of countries, diplomats, and people.

Historians have argued that the world got smaller as a consequence of better technology and expansion of international affairs to a global plane. There are no more colonies to chase down, Africa and Latin America no longer represent unchartered territories, and the U.S. West is populated. Consequently the frustrations that might have been met in one direction and which could be released through colonial activity or relations with nations in other parts of the world shrank or disappeared. Students of foreign affairs argue increasingly that international relations, like fish in a tank, have small fields of action. Because there is limited space and narrowing bands of opportunity (consider for example the restrictive effect atomic warfare has on policy formation), people in general, like fish in the tank, wanted and indeed were forced to pay greater attention to the world they lived in. One could not swim away from problems.

Consequently, and as the Industrial Revolution came into its own, diplomacy became increasingly socialized. Some have referred to this as the "democratization" of diplomacy. It is a phenomenon we will see in the pages of this book. As literacy rates went up, and the availability of information to the general public became more common, it became possible for large numbers of people to articulate what they perceived to be the self-interests of the state and to participate in the formulation and implementation of foreign policy. While interested individuals have always tried to influence diplomacy, the effort is more widespread today than 200 years ago. Select interest groups began to view international affairs from parochial perspectives as did a growing number of government agencies. Again we have the circumstance of the elephant and its five blind men. Narrow views are evident everywhere: nuclear freeze movements, Federal Reserve Board's concern with the international flow of money, those who advocate no contacts with South Africa and those who do, Jewish groups supporting Israel, or ultrapatriotic societies supporting "tougher" stands on communism. While we will selectively judge the merits of interests whose views impact our arguments, one should understand that the problem various groups present is that they complicate any definition of quid pro quo.

SOME LESSONS IN INTERNATIONAL RELATIONS

So what can we learn from the history of self-interest in U.S. and other foreign policies applicable to the problems of the United States in the Caribbean Basin? First, historians have proven that it has become more complicated to define our national interests over time and that implementation of foreign policies has also proven difficult, particularly since the eighteenth century. As will become evident in the chapters that follow, diplomats are a minority in the field of foreign affairs. They were crowded by politicians, interest groups, and government agencies all wishing to eat at the table of international affairs. Many voices spoke at the same time, making it difficult to hear distinct lines of conversation. That problem is still with us today. The Caribbean and Central American areas are not exempt from the influence of this phenomenon.

We have hinted at the bureaucratization of foreign policy. While more of its characteristics and consequences will be illustrated later, the idea is an important one worth discussing now. As the number of people involved in the development and implementation of foreign policy increased (particularly since World War II), diplomacy acquired its own set of procedures that became almost bureaucratic in nature, actions that too infrequently were questioned. In short, to steal from the language of accountants, increasingly we did less "auditing" of why we did certain things in foreign policy and found it difficult to do any "zero-based budgeting" in international affairs. Critics, because they formed small groups, could, but large government institutions staffed with thousands of people found this self-questioning more onerous. Agencies have lives of their own autonomous of individuals. Turning the ship of state in another direction has become increasingly complex. The magnitude of difficulty can be compared to sailing a small boat as opposed to a large oil tanker. This analogy was frequently used throughout the late 1970s and early 1980s by Charles Brown, Chief Executive Officer of AT&T, in describing how he felt as the company changed from a regulated utility into a marketing business. And that company is much smaller than the U.S. government.

Therefore, the lesson is that questioning diplomats and their actions and policies is easy, but marshaling the energies of diverse and important numbers of people for different considerations, while not impossible, simply becomes more difficult. Hence, diplomacy and policies frequently become processes. Things were done because they had always been done that way or because too infrequently key decision makers had failed to realize that circumstances had changed sufficiently to warrant a complete review of a situation, as was the case with Central America over the past three years. Challenging the mentality of the status quo, however, is possible; history suggests that it has happened in the past, and it must happen again.

In a useful study of international affairs covering the past century, two scholars interested in diplomacy reminded us of some well understood circumstances in international relations. F.S. Northedge and M.J. Grieve concluded their work with several observations. First, diplomacy is at its best when a nation understands its self-interests, realizing that the purpose of diplomacy is to further those interests as well as possible. We need to understand our adversary's interests and what complex options he or she has to deal with. Do this and one begins to understand the motivations of other nations and our possibilities. Thus we ask the reader to wear the shoes and walk the path of Soviet diplomats, U.S. politicians, and the leaders of such diverse nations as El Salvador, Nicaragua, and Cuba to understand what is happening as it affects the United States and what possible options exist. This book will be a tour guide.

Northedge and Grieve point out one other lesson, namely, that "foreign policy is best conducted perhaps in a spirit of realistic and cautious optimism." They further argue that the history of diplomacy proves "that hopes are never quite perfectly fulfilled; but neither are all fears realized."[8] With this thought in mind, let us see what is possible in U.S. foreign policy.

2

REALITIES AND ASSUMPTIONS IN U.S. FOREIGN POLICY

> Perseverance is more prevailing than
> violence; and many things which cannot
> be overcome when they are together,
> yield themselves up when
> taken little by little.
>
> Plutarch's *Lives*, Sertorius

THE STAGE

Since the end of World War II, the United States has scored only four successful far-reaching foreign policy objectives, all achieved more than a quarter of a century ago. The remarkable recovery of Western Europe as a result of the Marshall Plan, the structuring of the NATO shield, the Truman Doctrine in the case of Greece, and the emergence of Japan as a powerful economic ally of the West unquestionably represent landmarks in U.S. diplomacy. Noticeably, all four are directly related to our common defense and general welfare, two of the reasons cited in the Preamble of the Constitution of the United States justifying the creation of our nation. Also, the three achievements are solidly based on quid pro quo considerations, that is, on a clear understanding of mutual commitments of specific benefit to ourselves and the other powers. Not to be overlooked as a spinoff of these successes was, and still is, our intense preoccupation with the Soviet threat and the related issue of communist penetration in the Third World as a Soviet instrument, important determinants in our foreign policy moves. This concern has led the nation to consider Third World relations during the past 30 years or so mainly under the shadow of this spinoff, practically to the exclusion of other considerations.

Over the years there has been a sharp departure in U.S. diplomacy from a quid pro quo approach in favor of strategies and tactics undefined both in terms of precise goals and of direct relevance to the unequivocal definition of our national interest. As a consequence, we have drifted into patronizing or paternalistic roles, particularly in connection with Third World countries, exacting no precise obligations of direct importance to our national welfare and security, as a counterpart to U.S. diplomatic, military, and economic aid efforts.

Thus, despite the expenditure of enormous sums and grave military conflict our current influence in the East Asian theater is minimal and negligible in the Asian subcontinent and Africa. In Latin America the net loss of Cuba as a trading and political partner and its conversion into a Soviet satellite, and strained relations with the rest of the southern continent attest to acute shortcomings in U.S. foreign policy. In the Middle East the situation is chaotic, aggravated by the Iraq-Iran conflict and Soviet intervention. The Egyptian-Israeli peace treaty is a frightfully fragile affair, of questionable durability until some formula can be found to solve the Palestinian refugee issue. The threat of disintegration in Lebanon portends ominous prospects for the area. In Iran the disaster for U.S. foreign policy defies description and prediction. With the possibility for dwindling Soviet oil supplies during the current decade, despite current reports to the contrary, the Soviet Union's assault in Afghanistan is a possible indication of the move eventually contemplated, meaning easy access to Arabian and Iranian oil supplies. With Canada a longtime friend and "relative" we find ourselves at odds regarding oil and foreign investment policies. Should Canada fall apart through the secession of its French-speaking section, there is no telling what new problems will arise inches across our northern border.

Our relations with the Soviet Union remain strained. Efforts at detente, energetically promoted by the Soviet Union, considered sympathetically during the Kissinger period and also by the Carter administration, could be of no benefit to the United States unless the standoff included cessation of Soviet initiatives in Third World countries. Furthermore, detente without the removal of Cuban troops from Africa and the Middle East would be equally meaningless. Hence, our policy, strategy, and tactics toward the Soviet Union must be based on quid pro quo considerations. Yet, approaches by President Reagan's Administration in this direction, backed by a growth in U.S. military capability at home and in Europe, a must if negotiations with the Soviet Union are to have real meaning and results, have met with tremendous opposition in Congress, and in Western European and U.S. intellectual and ecclesiastical circles.

With respect to our relations with Western Europe and Japan, there is clearly no room for complacency. The props underlying our interdependence require the closest examination.

It is essential that alternatives to U.S. foreign policy be constantly under review.

POLICY OR POLICIES

For our foreign relations to rest on a firm base, there must be an unequivocal understanding of what constitutes our national interest. Definition of the latter is impossible if not measured against a fundamental yardstick. That need can be met only by the preamble of the Constitution of the United States, because it explains very clearly the purposes for which the nation was founded:

> We the people of the United States, in Order to form a more perfect Union, establish justice, insure domestic Tranquility, provide for the common defense, promote the general Welfare, and secure the Blessings of Liberty to ourselves and our Posterity, do ordain and establish this Constitution for the United States of America.

It will be noted from the preamble that the United States was thus established for the benefit of our forefathers and their posterity. There is no reference in the preamble to any messianic mission for the new nation. Nothing is said about overthrowing the monarchies of Europe or elsewhere, nor making the world safe for democracy, nor guaranteeing food for the world's poor, nor proposing that other colonies strike their independence and make themselves into the image and likeness of the United States. The terms of the preamble are specific. The national interest should, therefore, be defined as applicable solely to the purposes for which the nation was founded. Should the U.S. people share a different vision of the reasons for which our country exists, a change in the Constitution would be required modifying the thinking of the nation's progenitors. Yet it is doubtful that the vast majority of the U.S. citizens would permit such tampering with our basic charter.

Our foreign policy is and should be one of the means by which the felicity of the nation can be assured. For such policy or policies to be fruitful in terms of the national interest as here defined, it is inevitable that they be based on quid pro quo considerations. Particularly since the end of the last century, our dealings with foreign situations have all too frequently been marked by either unrealistic idealism or quite crass materialism, with little or no direct relationship to the national interest as defined in the Preamble.

Governmental assistance to an earthquake-shattered country, international sea or earth rescue missions, and food for the needy in Africa are examples of international activities stemming from the historic natural reactions of the U.S. people to the misfortune of others. But these efforts should not be confused with foreign policy instruments. It is irrelevant whether they generate good will or respect toward people of the United

States as donors. These actions should stand on their own and it would be unworthy for the nation to anticipate gratitude or any other reward than the satisfaction of having performed in a civilized and humanitarian fashion. In fact, there are some foreign cultures in which the wealthy are expected to give to the poor as a matter of obligation with no thanks due.

It would be useful to recall that in general foreign policy instruments are those actions our government can take which hopefully will bear certain specific desirable results beneficial to the national interest. Traditionally among these instruments are the exchange of diplomatic and consular relations; bilateral and multilateral agreements and treaties; commercial, cultural, scientific and military exchanges; promotion of imports and exports; encouragement of U.S. private enterprise in the field of foreign trade and investments abroad; international alliances; official exchange of visits by heads of state; promotion of two-way tourist travel; arms sales; economic, military, and technical aid programs; support of international organizations, to name but a few.

Regarding foreign policy instruments, a definition is in order regarding the meaning of policy, strategy, and tactics as technical terms because generally U.S. policy formulation inclines toward loftiness of expression, while our troubles stem from flawed strategy and, frequently, awkward or poor tactics. Policy in a diplomatic context can be considered as the general conduct to be pursued by a government with respect to international relations. In this sense the maintenance of a strong defense capability to deter foreign aggression comes within the purview of the concept. How to implement this policy with its diplomatic component falls within the scope of strategy or strategies and tactics.

Strategy may be considered as a term borrowed from military thinking. In the latter sense in dictionary language it is defined as "generalship; the science or art of combining and employing the means of war in planning and directing large movements or operations."[1] Applied to foreign affairs strategy refers to the management or use of foreign policy instruments, including war in case of extreme gravity, to achieve specific diplomatic aims considered essential to the national welfare. For example, if U.S. policy accepts, or is committed to, the premise that expanding world trade is basic to the nation's economic prosperity, strategy would involve the negotiation of multilateral and bilateral trade concessions.

Tactics are the actual means of achieving policy and strategy objectives. They involve the specifics of implementation and rely heavily on the caliber of negotiators or on-the-scene "managers." In the foreign trade example thoroughness of preparation and negotiating skills of our representatives are at a premium. Individual personality, imagination, and language skills play a vital role in tactics, since detailed planning cannot foresee the on-the-spot situations that arise and which must be dealt with adroitly, but within the limits of basic policy and strategy.

FRAGMENTATION OF EMPIRES

With more than 150 independent nations now in existence in addition to functional and geographic regional groupings, formation and implementation of policy in the traditional sense is impossible. Classic diplomacy calls for relations among or between a rather small number of sovereign states. The United Nations Organization's membership initially totalled 26. By the end of 1979, 153 countries belonged to the world body. In the balmy days of European supremacy, woefully weak or badly divided nations in Africa or Asia fell under colonial blankets and were thus eliminated as actors in the concert of nations. Furthermore, the rules included only a limited number of policy instruments, and critical situations arising from colonial competition could be settled in Paris, London, Rome, or Berlin. Public opinion in the areas affected as well as the colonies' basic interests could be ignored or relegated to secondary considerations.

The breakup of the French, British, Dutch, Portuguese, Belgian, Italian, and U.S. colonial holdings after World War II led to developments that are still in a state of evolution with no end in sight. Witness, for example, the quite recent liquidation of the Portuguese colonial empire. Oddly enough the Soviet Union, long a strident critic of European colonialism kept intact the vast non-Slavic Siberian colonial empire inherited from Holy Mother Russia, increased its colonialist reach in Eastern Europe and in the Baltic Region, advanced its holdings at the expense of the Japanese, and is attempting to absorb Afghanistan through military means. The Soviet Union thus remains as the only true major colonial power on the globe. Yet a substantial number of nations attending the nonaligned nations' conference in Havana in September 1979 voiced strong support for pro-Soviet sympathies! It is this kind of paradoxical phenomenon that adds considerable complications to modern-day diplomacy.

Among the more serious consequences of the fragmentation process is the revival of precolonial antagonisms in many new nations and the creation of new rivalries. This reality contributes enormously to regional armed conflict such as those in the Middle East and the India-Pakistan war, posing a grave threat to world peace because of relevance to Soviet U.S. tensions.

A further contributing factor to intraregional problems stems from the artificial boundaries established by the European Powers during the colonial era in their Asian, African, and Middle Eastern colonies or protectorates. A case in point is the situation created in the Mesopotamian valley by the British and French. At the time of Turkish sovereignty in the area, the people in the valley spoke a common language marked only by dialectal differences, professed the faith of Islam with the exception of small Christian or Jewish enclaves, and in general shared a broad, similar cultural outlook. Weak Turkish rule was the order of the day while tribal government and organization played an important role in the life of the region. Whatever clashes occurred concerned these and were generally settled in traditional tribal fashion without serious consequence beyond the area's natural limits.

With the partition of the region after World War I, the British and French with mandate authority following the Treaty of Versailles occupied the region and established modern-day Syria and Lebanon under French aegis and Iraq under British tutelage. Natural boundaries based on age-old considerations were swept aside.

We have relatively normal relations with Syria, but marked by a position of little influence, while the latter's reliance on Soviet arms is of considerable value to the Soviet Union. Our relations with Iraq are tense with both countries represented in each other's capital through national interest sections in Third Country embassies. But, both the Soviet Union and the United States failed to establish strong zonal positions of decided influence in the Mesopotamian valley. Apologists for the lack of U.S. success point to the development of Arab-Israeli conflicts as the complicating factor in view of U.S. support for Israel. But if this rationale is valid, why did the pro-Arab Soviets also stub their toes?

To detail the variety and nature of intraregional stresses around the globe and how they influence world events specifically is beyond the scope of this work. Suffice it to say that every corner of the world is plagued with "neighborhood" rivalries with the result that there is no such phenomenon as a homogeneous Third World, just as there never existed a monolithic Communist World, as evidenced by the Sino-Soviet rivalry. In fact, even the designation Third World is probably inappropriate and misleading. The division of the globe into three oversimplified categories is unrealistic for the reason that relationships are still based on bilateral considerations among 150 nations or so. There is no such thing as a "Soviet bloc" settling affairs of the world with the "industrial West and Japan" and a "Third World" which includes over 100 nations. The latter are split in each and every direction and reflect a myriad of social, political, and economic characteristics. Hence, a U.S. policy for the Third World, for example, is not a viable concept. What is required is an ample stock of policies to deal with about 150 nations bilaterally and several regional groupings of varying strengths and philosophies. Hence, the need for a quid pro quo approach in our foreign policy tied to a commonly understood definition of the national interest for which the Preamble of the Constitution offers the most logical anchor.

ASSUMPTIONS

It is not fruitful for the United States, or any other nation for that matter, to develop reasonably realistic policies, strategies, and tactics relative to foreign affairs without postulating certain basic judgments regarding world conditions and prospects. These will vary from country to country in view of particular assessments, aspirations, and internal political realities. What is most predictable about future international events is the probability that the unexpected will occur! Furthermore, wars, technological breakthroughs in communications, transportation, and weaponry, for instance, are ever present likelihoods affecting assumptions continuously.

It follows that unless the Congress and the executive branch have a clear perception of the world as it is, and what U.S. interests really are as well as our financial and military limitations, we will continue to find ourselves repeatedly in dreadful messes abroad. If we keep along the path of the last 20 years or so, we will not only run the risk of exhausting our patrimony but possibly face a nuclear confrontation with the Soviet Union. The arsenal of nuclear weaponry possessed by the two superpowers and to a lesser extent scattered around the globe no longer allows amateurish bungling in our international relations. The public and our top political figures in and out of government must somehow be made to realize this fact.

Cross-cultural understanding is essential to the effective formulation of policies, strategies, and tactics. The Iranian crisis, for example, reflected starkly a situation derived from colossal misreading on the one hand of U.S. motives, mentality and reactions by the Iranian mullahs and revolutionaries, and on the other by the top U.S. leadership on predictable Iranian behavior following the Shah's departure. Skill leading to successful diplomacy consists to a great extent in the foreseeing of problems ahead, the taking of timely and orderly measures to deal with issues, always within the framework of caution by hedging against the possibility of failure. Risk taking for fear of offending foreign shaky governments is unacceptable diplomatic practice. All too often the U.S. government maintains substantial diplomatic and support personnel in highly unstable areas or tolerates offensive actions against our embassies abroad without adopting immediate retaliatory actions. Quid pro quo would require in those circumstances rapid and effective responses. We should be able always to identify realistically in precise terms where our national interest lies. We should be fully cognizant of the psychology and aspirations in terms of national goals of other nations. We should be knowledgeable and tolerant of the foibles and inevitable human weaknesses inherent in all governments and aware at the same time that our own postures are too often flawed by venal special interests, internal considerations, and energetic, emotional ethnic minority pressures.

One extremely important consideration must be reckoned with. It does not follow automatically that friendship with particular nations leads to mutually reinforcing actions in times of international crises. Even precisely worded pacts may be brushed aside. Illustrations of this truism flood the pages of history. For example, the Kaiser in 1914 considered Germany's solemn commitment to respect Belgian neutrality as a scrap of paper. The United States left the British and the French in the lurch during the 1956 Suez War, just as these two old friends did to us during the Vietnam conflict, to a lesser extent. In recent years we unilaterally denounced our treaty arrangements with Taiwan after the Carter administration decided to engage in normal diplomatic relations with mainland China. At the start of World War II the Soviet Union signed its famous nonaggression pact with Hitler's Germany and not long after both were locked in a life-and-death struggle. The list could go on interminably and sadly.

The point is that nations team up only when their national interests coincide. Reality dictates that all countries, friendly or not, will pursue their national interests as they see them regardless of formal agreements and sentimental considerations. The ancient diplomatic dictum that the friend of today may be the enemy of tomorrow and vice versa is as valid today as when first enunciated. These views are not a form of latter-day Machiavellianism, but judgment of a most imperfect world often guided by paranoic leaders or short-sighted governments, even if well meaning. Examples of the former were Stalin, Hitler, and Mussolini, and of the latter the French and British in the period between the two world wars. Let us recall that in the Iranian crisis, Japan, the United Kingdom, France, and Germany were initially far more concerned with the international flow of oil than in the grave and provocative violation of U.S. diplomatic rights in the seizure of the embassy personnel by the Iranian militants with the approval of Ayatollah Khomeini.

Although not inclusive by any means, the following nevertheless appear to be key factors in the global scene of direct importance to the United States for the formulation of policies, whether for Latin America or elsewhere. Without broad assumptions about world conditions, regional or particular country policies would be developed without rationale:

1. The military standoff and world-wide political and ideological competition between the United States and the Soviet Union will continue into the indefinite future.
2. Third party and intraregional conflicts will periodically create flash points exacerbating Soviet-U.S. relations.
3. Fossil fuel availability will continue to influence profoundly the foreign policy of all producing countries as well as major consumers.
4. The Soviet Union will continue to experience sporadic wheat shortfalls.
5. The Soviet Union will continue to seek a position of greater military strength relative to the United States and Western Europe, thus rendering significant disarmament negotiations extremely difficult of success.
6. For the foreseeable future internal situations in both Eastern and Western Europe can be expected to remain in their present state of internal and external uneasy equilibrium.
7. U.S. relations with Western Europe will remain dominated by economic and European defense considerations.
8. Japanese-U.S. relations for the relatively near future should continue quite stable. However, if Japan feels that the United States is unable or unwilling to protect Middle East oil essential to its survival, relations between the two countries will weaken. Japan predictably would gradually develop substantially increased military capability, seek greater self-reliance, and move closer to China.
9. Positive relations between mainland China and the United States will continue to develop in a gentle and gradual manner as both nations warily avoid stepping on each other's toes, but with occasional pitfalls; Taiwan will remain a "dark cloud."
10. There is no such thing as a "China" card in the Soviet-U.S. rivalry. China would not jeopardize its independence from the Soviet Union by placing trust in any U.S. commitment, nor will it allow either of the two superpowers to use China for their own ends.
11. Events in Africa and Asia, as well as in the Middle East, will continue to be plagued by frequent crises and intraregional stresses. Political and economic instability in these areas will be more often the rule than the exception, at least for a generation to come.
12. In time, economic realities will force many of the underdeveloped nations to seek regrouping in federations or associations linked in turn to one of the major industrial powers, while retaining individual sovereignty.

13. Central and South America will continue to edge forward toward economic and social improvement, marked by frequent internal national and regional political instability and periodic tensions with the United States. Recognition of this prospect could lead to smoother relationships with the nations south of the border. These Hispanic nations with cultural heritages drastically different from those of the United States neither desire, nor will evolve into, the image and likeness of the United States. Prospects for durable democracy in these countries are remote until strong, broadly based urban and rural middle classes emerge.

14. The United Nations as a world body concerned with technical and health responsibilities will become increasingly useful. Correspondingly, as an instrument capable of effective use in the resolution of grave international political and military conflicts, its value will remain questionable despite occasional minor successes.

15. The United States specifically will develop greater skill and care in developing more fruitful relations with Mexico and Canada. Economic realities will tone down whatever animosity exists toward the United States as circumstances force mutual accommodations.

16. Scientific advances in space and communications will force closer cooperation among most nations.

17. The magnitude of past, present, and future lending operations to Third World countries by the private Western European, Japanese, and U.S. banking systems will continue to exceed repayment capabilities creating grave tensions between lenders and borrowers.

18. The general health of socioeconomic conditions in the underdeveloped world will depend largely on the economic-social health of the developed world.

19. The kind of massive redistribution of international wealth associated with the Third World's "new economic order" is not realistic and will therefore not occur.

Blending general assumptions with broad policy, strategic, and tactical considerations, and tailoring the amalgam to specific and/or regional application is a very complex exercise. It is with this aspect of foreign policy that years of experience in the diplomatic profession remain at a premium. But in our system, career diplomats have little if any effective or determinative say in the formulation of basic policies and overall plans of action. Since key decisions are made in the White House or by the political appointees of an administration, the professional foreign service officers are implementers of policy, not creators.

Inherent in our system is that the president and many of his senior political appointees are rarely foreign policy experts and, therefore, at a disadvantage in knowing which experts' advice should be followed. This fact was dramatically thrown in high relief in the early days of the Iranian hostage crisis when President Jimmy Carter sought advice from all. With no first-hand knowledge about Iranian characteristics, one wonders about his guesswork in the selection of the path to follow. In so complex a field as foreign affairs, key policymakers must know enough about the matter in their own right in order to be in a position to select appropriate alternatives. For the same reason, President Reagan must depend on his Secretary of State.

Apart from the problem of a usual lack of expertise at the top levels of government, long a characteristic of our nation with regard to international relations, there is the additional problem of a penchant in higher echelons to thrive on and actually enjoy a crisis atmosphere. At such times a feeling of exhilaration sharpened by anxiety permeates the atmosphere in the White House and concerned Executive Branch departments, accompanied by a sense of infectious self-importance among both career and appointed officials involved, merely adding unnecessary complications to already difficult situations. Actually, the reverse should be the norm in the business of foreign affairs. The mixture of assumptions and procedures ideally ought to point in the direction of achieving a comfortable position for the United States. Such a goal is not so impossible to attain as it seems at first glance. Setting realistic sights, avoiding unnecessary risks, being clearly aware of alternatives in the establishment of particular policy targets will almost automatically lead to more stable international relationships.

Attempts to force ill-suited or emotional policies into acceptance by other countries unsympathetic to such inevitably lead to unforeseen stresses and strains, if not worse. Predictably, situations occur which, when combined with the crisis-prone atmosphere in Washington and fanned by a press equally anxious for exciting headlines, cause minor issues to be blown up to serious proportions.

A well-accepted principle in connection with international affairs is that any political, economic, or military action by one nation will automatically cause a reaction in countries affected. Carried to negative extremes war could be the result. At the opposite end of the spectrum alliances could flourish. Most situations emerge somewhere between extremes. But it is the blend of assumptions, goals, and diplomatic action that influences actions and reactions. Diplomacy must be based on a judicious mixture of moral force and the exercise of power, a formula determined by developments as they affect the well-being of the nation.

The one without the other results in either foolhardy or blatantly contra-productive policies.

DIPLOMATIC INSTRUMENTS AND DOCTRINES

As already indicated, the range of foreign policy instruments is very broad. Special comment is warranted regarding some that figure promi-nently in the implementation of U.S. foreign policy, since these are among the more important means of achieving quid pro quo objectives:

Human Rights

The issue of human rights as a matter of world interest belongs to the same high plane of important international concerns as international law, population control, law of the sea, world peace, save-the-children movements, food-for-all doctrines, etc. These matters warrant the closest attention and support of any country that considers itself civilized and worthy of sitting in the concert of nations. That the United States should press in favor of the positive aspects of these issues is proper and desirable.

Official U.S. commitment to human rights as an ingredient in our foreign policy as related to aid programs dates back to the Foreign Assistance Act of 1961, since amended but retaining its main thrust. The statutory provisions established by Congress "require reports on human rights practices in countries receiving economic assistance under Part I of the Act or proposed as recipients of security assistance."[2] Under the 1961 Act, "The Secretary of State shall transmit to the Speaker of the House of Representatives and the Committee on Foreign Relations of the Senate, by January 31, of each year, a full and complete report regarding . . .

> (1) the status of internationally recognized human rights, within the meaning of subsection (a) in countries that receive assistance under this part.

Thus an annual report to Congress on the subject has been an established requirement. Congress further requires that:

> The Secretary of State shall transmit to the Congress, as part of the presentation materials for security assistance programs for each fiscal year, a full and complete report, prepared with the assistance of the Assistant Secretary for Human Rights and Humanitarian Affairs, with respect to practices regarding the observance of and

respect for internationally recognized human rights in each country proposed as a recipient of security assistance. In determining whether a government falls within the provisions of subsection (a) and in preparation of any report or statement required under this section, consideration shall be given to . . .

(1) the relevant findings of appropriate international organizations, including non-governmental organizations, such as the International Committee of the Red Cross; and

(2) the extent of cooperation by such government in permitting an unimpeded investigation by any such organization of alleged violations of internationally recognized human rights.[3]

Pursuant to the congressional requirement Douglas J. Bennet, Jr., Assistant Secretary for Congressional Relations of the Department of State, submitted to the Chairman, Committee on Foreign Relations, United States Senate, under cover of a communication dated January 31, 1979, enclosures entitled *Country Reports on Human Rights Practices*.[4] Under the caption *Internationally Recognized Human Rights* in the Introduction to the Country Reports, there is the following statement:

Reflecting the statutory directive and Administration policy, these 'Country Reports' address the status of internationally recognized human rights in the countries reported upon. These rights have been formally recognized by virtually all governments and by the United Nations in the Universal Declaration of Human Rights. This international consensus is also reflected in the treaties deriving from the UN Declaration—the international Covenant on Civil and Political Rights and the International Covenant on Economic, Social and Cultural Rights. These rights can be grouped into three broad categories:

First, the right to be free from governmental violations of the integrity of the person—violations such as torture, cruel, inhuman or degrading treatment or punishment; arbitrary arrest or imprisonment; denial of fair public trial; and invasion of the home. Second, the right to the fulfillment of vital needs such as food, shelter, health care and education.

Third, the right to enjoy civil and political liberties, including freedom of speech, of press, of thought, of assembly, and of religion, the right to participate in government and the right to travel freely within and outside one's own country.[5]

One hundred and fifteen reports were submitted which included countries with excellent human rights performance by the standards indicated and others with poor records. Several countries were not included which reportedly have been the subject of inquiry or action by the United Nations Human Rights Commission or the Inter-American Commission on Human Rights such as Cambodia, Equatorial Guinea, South Africa, Uganda, Argentina, and Chile.

As is apparent from the foregoing, U.S. concern for human rights as an international issue has a lengthy history. However, until the advent of the Carter Administration the doctrine received somewhat selective support from previous administrations, with special emphasis regarding the Soviet Union and its satellites. Under President Carter the Department of State created a full-blown bureau headed by an Assistant Secretary with a substantial staff organized on a geographic basis in terms of a world-wide survey. The effect has been to convert human rights considerations from a factor in our international dealings into a major foreign policy instrument. President Ronald Reagan's administration continued compliance. In its Report for 1982, dated February 1983, the Department of State reflected the caution required in applying the mandate.[6]

Well meaning as is the congressional intent in its human rights legislation relative to aid programs, there is a serious contradiction with other aspects of U.S. foreign policy. For example, the General Policy enunciated by Congress with respect to development assistance authorizations emphasizes four points:[7]

1. The alleviation of the worst physical manifestations of poverty among the world's poor majority.
2. The promotion of conditions enabling developing countries to achieve self-sustaining economic growth with equitable distribution of benefits.
3. The encouragement of development processes in which individual civil and economic rights are respected and enhanced.
4. The integration of the developing countries into an open and equitable economic system.

Taken in conjunction with the third item in the Introduction to the Country Reports, which specifies the right to enjoy civil and political liberties, etc., the General Policy postulates logically would mean that recipients are free to move in whatever political and economic direction they wish. But in many African and Latin American nations there are strong Marxist movements with marked anti-U.S. anticapitalist overtones calling for the expropriation and expulsion of U.S. interests. Congress and the Department of State in line with the Congressional language morally would have to acquiesce to such prospects and continue U.S. aid support, if the Marxist elements reached power through the electoral process, even if in a clear minority position, provided civil rights, freedom of speech and of the press were respected!

On the other hand, in other parts of the international development legislation Congress encourages the mobilization and participation of United States private capital and skills "in the economic and social development of less developed friendly countries and areas" in authorizing the creation of the Overseas Private Investment Corporation.[8] Still further Congress requires that aid be suspended if the government of a country "has nationalized or expropriated or seized ownership or control of property owned by any United States citizen or any corporation, partnership or association not less than 50 per centum beneficially owned by United States citizens, or, . . . et cetera," barring speedy compensation or clear intent to do so.[9]

In brief what Congress really says is that countries can do what they feel like so long as human rights as defined in the references mentioned in the Introduction are adhered to. The logic of the Congressional mandate implies that Congress would not be disturbed if anti-U.S. elements came into power, even if they were to make life as miserable as possible for U.S. economic and political interests. Congress also seems to say that it encourages private capital participation, but woe to the country that dares eliminate it from the scene by nationalization or some such means without compensation, even if it arrived in control of the situation as a freely elected government. Certainly one should not extend aid to a country that willy nilly expropriates U.S. property without just compensation. But, there is apparent serious contradiction in the congressional language. If a Marxist-Leninist regime came into power via free elections, nationalized U.S. assets and paid compensation, would Congress authorize aid to that country?

The problem is that most countries do not have societies and scales of values compatible with those of the United States and Western Europe. In Latin America, country after country views the U.S. system as a threat to its traditional culture and seeks alternatives to both our completely free enterprise approach and that of the socialist nations. That is why there is no end of trouble for us in Central America and why we are constantly in conflict of some kind or another with Argentina, Brazil, Chile, Peru, Ecuador, Paraguay, Uruguay, Bolivia, Columbia, and even semidemocratic Venezuela and Mexico. As we move farther from the Western Hemisphere the contrast with our way of life becomes ever so sharper.

The strong emphasis on human rights as a yardstick in our aid programs, and to some extent in our relations with other countries, places the United States in a Catch-22 situation by pursuing single-mindedly a particular goal regardless if it should lead to the destruction of our crucial world ties. Carried to a further logical conclusion we would have to limit relations to a handful of nations. How can we possibly consider favored nation treatment to Communist China, or credits to Russia before the

Afghanistan caper, while bearing down on Brazil because it will not accept our approach to human rights? Under the human rights doctrine on the books, how can we have denied Somoza's Nicaragua arms while supplying them to El Salvador, Guatemala, and Honduras? The fact is that the linking of human rights criteria, as legislated by Congress with specific country relations, is unworkable.

At the same time we should under no circumstances underpin regimes obviously and widely recognized as commiting atrocities. In the interest of common sense and in recognition of the foibles of humankind, Congress should retain reference to violations of human rights as indicated in the first category listed in the Introduction to the Country Reports, but change the yardstick nature of items second and third instead to an expression of hope that one day perhaps they can be achieved. The second item should be dealt with in this manner, that is, the one which refers to the fulfillment of vital needs, because it is beyond our capability as a nation to make no more than a dent in this unhappy problem. In fact, bringing the issue home, let us with a bit of humility remember that we are very far as yet from solving the problems of housing and vital needs in the core of our major cities. If we ever find a solution to these problems and if in our country at all levels we reflect respect for human values, and cordiality and trust in our interrelationships, the world will sit up and take notice and perhaps adopt higher standards of social and personal morality in government and civic affairs. Preaching and congressional legislation will not bring this about.

Aid Programs

One of the most powerful diplomatic instruments developed in the post-World War II era by the major industrial nations is the resort to economic, cultural, and military assistance to foreign countries. Particular recipients have been many of the former colonial areas under control of the British, French, Dutch, Portuguese, and Japanese. In a similar vein most of Latin America has been the object of vast U.S. help. A latter development is the emergence of multilateral financial institutions as a means of furnishing capital for developmental purposes in the less economically advanced countries. Since the erstwhile European colonies included areas in Asia and Africa rich in raw materials or possessing geopolitical importance, many of the new countries quickly became ideological battlegrounds in the Soviet-U.S. rivalry for the "hearts and minds of men." The struggle continues with no abatement in sight, for which broad comment is in order.

Differences in policy, strategy, and tactics between the United States and the Soviet Union surfaced clearly from the inception of the Cold War conflict. Quite cynically, had it not been for the threat of the Soviet Union to Western Europe there probably would have been no Marshall Plan. Carrying this postulate further, in absence of continued efforts by the Soviet Union to subvert as many less developed nations as it can for its own purposes, there probably would be very tepid U.S., Western Europe, and Japanese interest in pouring vast sums into the Third World. Certainly, reliance would have remained on private capital efforts with negligible governmental participation.

With fewer economic resources at its command and an economy based to a considerable extent on remaining indefinitely on a wartime footing, the Soviet Union selected a few targets having strategic value in its continuing conflict with the West. Soviet assistance and that of its satellites preferentially concentrated on massive, showy capital projects and equally large scale shipments of arms. Whether such assistance was or is basic to the recipient country's needs and to what use the arms would be put constituted lesser concerns for the Soviet Union in the pursuit of establishing foci of influence and domination. Such is still the policy of the Soviet Union.

In contrast the United States and the West in general swung to an opposite extreme. The assumption underlying U.S. aid policy has been, and still is, that economic development on a world-wide basis leads to greater economic interdependence and that somehow solid benefits accrue to the United States as a result.

In its general policy statement in the Foreign Assistance Act of 1961, as amended, currently valid, Congress stated that:

> The individual liberties, economic prosperity, and security of the people of the United States are best sustained and enhanced in a community of nations which respect individual civil and economic rights and freedoms and which work together to use wisely the world's limited resources in an open and equitable economic system. Furthermore, the Congress reaffirms the traditional humanitarian ideals of the American people and renews its commitment to assist people in developing countries to eliminate hunger, poverty, illness and ignorance.
>
> Therefore, the Congress declares that a principal objective of the foreign policy of the United States is the encouragement and sustained support of the people of developing countries in their efforts to acquire the knowledge and resources essential to development and to build the economic, political, and social institutions which will improve the quality of their lives.[10]

In its statement regarding specific development assistance policy in the same Act, the Congress further states:

> Bilateral assistance and United States participation in multilateral institutions shall emphasize programs in support of countries which pursue development strategies designed to meet basic human needs and achieve self-sustaining growth with equity.
>
> The Congress declares that the principal purpose of United States bilateral development assistance is to help the poor majority of people in developing countries to participate in a process of equitable growth through productive work and to influence decisions that shape their lives, with the goal of increasing their incomes and their access to public services which will enable them to satisfy their basic needs and lead lives of decency, dignity and hope.[11]

Two very important omissions are evident in the aid philosophy enunciated by Congress which, of course, is binding on the Executive Branch in the structuring and implementation of U.S. foreign aid programs. One is that no reference is made to the fact that we are in the aid business partly because of Soviet and communist threats. The other ignores that the cultural mores, political and social philosophies, religious beliefs, national aspirations of recipient nations, as well as intraregional conflicts, may skew thoroughly whatever congressional intent is implicit or explicit in the policy advocated.

Furthermore, congressional policy taken at face value, or literally, means that Congress is really supporting a type of massive philanthropy on a world-wide scale, without a clear conception of how such a policy will specifically benefit the United States. Under the circumstances it makes it very difficult for the Department of State to develop programs that tie in closely with clear and specific U.S. foreign policy objectives. The very vagueness of congressional intent makes the process of submission of aid programs to the congressional subcommittees for assessment and approval that much more difficult. The end result is the working at cross-purposes by both Congress and the Executive Branch to the greater confusion of recipient nations and multilateral banking institutions.

Another problem with congressional policy is an apparent lack of understanding of the effects of economic development on stability, even in the light of the U.S. experience—a unique event in any circumstance. One important reason for the destruction of the monarchy in Iraq in 1958 was that King Faisal's government followed U.S. and British advice and concentrated on major projects with oil revenues. The vast mass of poverty stricken Iraqis were not about to wait for a generation before benefits drifted down to them and thus the country exploded with terrible violence. In Iran a contributing factor to the collapse of the Shah's regime was again the instance of great oil wealth helping create an urban middle class with little or no advantage to the underpaid and underemployed rural proletariat. Congress disregards the fact that development resulting in industrial expansion will automatically attract the rural poor to urban centers creating huge slums in the great cities of the Third World, thus encouraging political and social instability. Also, in this sense Congress overlooks a similar phenomenon in our own country where the plight of New York, Philadelphia, Detroit, Cleveland, Chicago, and other important urban centers has been aggravated by the migration of rural poor from the southern states seeking a better life.

Congressional interest in feeding the poor of the world and criticism from time to time of assistance programs for not achieving greater success represents shallow thinking. On the one hand, Congress does not differentiate between the use of food programs as diplomatic instruments versus acts of compassion. On the other, it ignores that the United States simply does not have the resources to feed the poor of the entire world, that the assistance voted by Congress is a tiny fraction of what would be needed, and that there are severe limitations to U.S. know-how in helping foreign countries develop agricultural techniques capable of increasing food output on the scale required to register dramatic impact.

Both developmental economics and agricultural assistance can be most positive in raising standards of living, but both the Congress and Executive Branch officials must know what they are doing, respond affirmatively to the wishes of recipient countries, and carefully estimate the impact on U.S. interest at home and abroad.

The point that must be made is that economic development by itself without taking into consideration the myriad of factors involved is not necessarily conducive to stability, internally, regionally, or globally, or of direct advantage to the United States. We should certainly continue to participate substantially in foreign aid programs, but with a clear vision of why we are doing so and specifically what we expect to achieve either bilaterally or regionally. Hence, the need for quid pro quo considerations.

The congressional statement that economic development is a good thing for the United States is not enough. The general policy position spelled out in the Foreign Assistance Act of 1961, as amended, should also explain explicitly why such development is beneficial to the United States militarily, socially, politically, economically, and culturally; the factor of rivalry with the Soviet Union should be openly acknowledged, since this would make it clear to recipient nations that they cannot expect the United States to cover indirectly their financial obligations to the Soviet Union or its satellites. The Congress should reflect in such a statement awareness of the internal political and social circumstances in countries receiving aid and that the Executive Branch must take them into account in the development of programs.

These views do not rule out the wisdom and reasons of compassion for helping the poor of the world and in supporting multilateral approaches in this regard, but let us make sure we know what the likelihood of success is, predict impact on a recipient country, and show respect for how it wishes problems resolved—not how Washington experts think it should be done.

Foreign aid is a valuable instrument of foreign policy and diplomacy. Let us use it as such.

A feature of U.S. aid policy which warrants some clarification concerns the role of the Export-Import Bank. The principal function of this institution is to promote U.S. exports through a credit policy which enables U.S. private enterprise to compete effectively in the international market. It is not essentially an aid instrument although indirectly under certain circumstances it could serve as such.

Diplomatic Exchanges

Agreements with foreign countries leading to the exchange of diplomatic and consular representations are valuable traditional instruments for the furtherance of national interests. Ordinarily the presence of ambassadors and consuls signifies a desire by both the sending country and the host nation to maintain open, full government-to-government lines of communication. In theory such arrangements should permit the gradual strengthening of mutual relationships to the benefit of both. Traditionally as a sign of displeasure one or the other country or both would recall an ambassador and leave a charge d'affaires to look after the embassy. If matters worsened further "diplomatic relations would be broken" through the total withdrawal of all embassy and consular personnel by both countries. Such extreme action does not necessarily signify a declaration of war, although obviously in times of armed conflict the missions, as embassy and consular establishments are sometimes called, would be closed and personnel interned until exchanges could be arranged for return to their home countries.

In recent years the major powers have become quite thick-skinned in tolerating abuse in some of the newly independent countries; such abuse prior to World War I or even World War II would have been *casus belli*. As far as the United States is concerned a very disturbing practice has emerged. Full embassy staffs and their families often are permitted to remain in highly unstable circumstances for fear of offending a host government. The result has been tragic at times without any positive benefits. Thus, waiting until the last minute in Saigon to evacuate families and personnel was inexcusable. A similar situation occurred in Teheran in the fall of 1979 triggered by admission of the deposed Shah to the United States for medical treatment. Less than a year before, embassy immunity had been violated by revolutionary mobs with the apparent concurrence of the highly unstable government. For the U.S. government to have maintained a considerable staff in Teheran under the volatile circumstances, particularly with the knowledge that the Shah's entry into the United States carried the risk of acute Iranian reaction, was also inexcusable. Given unstable situations, regardless of what interpretation may be reached by a host government, embassy staffs should be reduced to a bare minimum and consist only of volunteers thoroughly familiar with the language and customs of the area. Families under those circumstances should either not be permitted to join personnel or be evacuated if already there.

Nevertheless, diplomatic exchanges and negotiations are still basic tools essential to the conduct of our international relations. Every effort should always be made to maintain in times of crisis core staffs of seasoned foreign service personnel. Governments never know when an opening might unexpectedly occur which can be taken advantage of if a staff is still in place.

Investment and Commerce

The long established policy of the U.S. government to encourage high levels of international trade through elimination or modification of import tariffs in all countries is eminently sound and time has proven its worth. Efforts in this direction should and probably will continue unabated. In this respect every encouragement should be given to further strengthening the role of the government's Export-Import Bank, as a guarantor of payment for private sector shipments. The Overseas Private Investment Corporation (OPIC) also insures U.S. private investments in underdeveloped countries.

U.S. private investment abroad is another matter and one which warrants careful reassessment as a matter of public policy. One problem concerns the establishment in other countries of U.S.-owned industries which will compete with those in our country at an advantage because of cheap labor, resulting in sectoral unemployment in the United States. The other relates to the fact that the predominance of foreign-owned businesses in an underdeveloped nation will predictably trigger, sooner or later, antiforeign political agitation. If these interests happen to be of the

United States, the violence will be directed against the United States giving rise to sharp tensions with the country concerned. Thus, years of diplomacy and perhaps economic aid may be nullified by the excessive presence aspect. A similar situation will occur if the single largest company is a U.S. company, particularly if engaged in mining or oil production.

Fortunately, U.S. investors are becoming increasingly sensitive to these dangers and have been developing formulas that tend to leave control and majority ownership either in private local hands or in association with a foreign government. Incidentally, the United States is not immune to worry over foreign investments in our country. Witness the following language from Executive Order 11858 of May 7, 1975 (Fed. Reg. 20263) regarding monitoring of foreign investments in the United States through the creation of the Committee on Foreign Investment in the United States, composed of representatives of the Departments of State, Treasury, Defense, Commerce, the Assistant to the President for Economic Affairs, and the Executive Director of the Council on International Economic Policy:

> (b) The Committee shall have primary continuing responsibility within the Executive Branch for monitoring the impact of foreign investment in the United States, both direct and portfolio, and for coordinating the implementation of United States policy on such investment . . . et cetera.[12]

Hence, Congress would be well advised to inject in its aid legislation some element of caution in the encouragement of private capital to venture abroad.

One other phase of U.S. overseas investments which sooner or later will create broad discussion with far-reaching consequences is the role of multinational companies. The ability of these companies to operate beyond the reach of individual countries, to affect currency holdings and values, as well as international prices of the products produced is worrisome to most lesser developed nations. They do not quite know how best to deal with them, although it appears likely that national legislative actions will be adequate for the situation (oil in Venezuela, for example).

Arms Sales and Military Assistance

The issue of arms sales and military assistance to Third World countries has long been one of controversy within the Congress and from administration to administration. Apart from considerations of a geopolitical nature, the question of morality also enters the picture. While the furnishing of weapons to nations that clearly have no business in diverting energy and resources for their acquisition, when problems of food may be paramount, the fact remains that the world is both a continuing scene of intraregional disputes, and one of contention between the Soviet Union and the Western bloc. From U.S. viewpoint the matter of national security and reasonable relations with all countries is fundamental. Hence, a balance must be struck between scruples and the reality of international life.

The Soviet technique of penetration is usually to focus on a poor and militarily weak country which has a history of potential or actual conflict with a neighbor or neighbors. A treaty of friendship and economic assistance or commercial exchange is sought. If accepted, arms generally follow under extremely liberal terms. From that point on a determined effort is made by the Soviets or their allies to secure the sympathy of key elements in the military establishment and thus undermine any anti-Soviet official activities. Sometimes the effort fails but on others it is successful. Afghanistan was softened up for Soviet penetration somewhat along this pattern. Thus, the source of arms and the purpose for which they may be destined can be of vital importance to U.S. diplomacy.

To establish a reasonable policy or doctrine regarding the sale and/or grant of arms, it is helpful to outline briefly the circumstances that govern generally the desire of a Third World country to develop military capability and acquire arms for this end. Independent nations, regardless of size, tend to obtain arms either through domestic manufacture or from a foreign source for the following reasons:

1. Symbols of sovereignty.
2. National defense.
   a. "just in case" situations
   b. under conditions of threat by armed, seemingly bellicose neighbors
   c. response to direct or indirect foreign aggression
3. Suppression of internal revolutionary movements.
   a. aided and inspired from abroad
   b. completely indigenous
4. Normal, nonmilitary urban and rural police functions.

Since international suppliers, principally the industrial nations, both from the Eastern and Western political blocs, are also motivated by prospects of commerical gain, use of arms as a means of establishing positions of influence, interference in the outcome of civil conflict or rebellion, or particularly in the case of the Soviet Union for subversion, basic U.S. policies must take these situations into account.

Arms sold as symbols of sovereignty should be made available under normal commercial terms and recognized international practice. The same criteria should apply to "just in case" situations. Venezuela and Brazil would fall into these two categories.

Nations subject to genuine threats from well-armed neighbors such as Israel should be given ample facilities for the acquisition of U.S. arms. The same doctrine should apply to countries under attack. Afghanistan conceivably would qualify under that circumstance.

In the case of countries desiring arms for the suppression of extreme revolutionary activity inspired and armed from abroad, and clearly not widely supported by the populace at large, arms should be made available easily and quickly to the government of the country concerned, regardless of whether civilian or military. This would be a situation in which thoroughly documented evidence of Soviet involvement or that of one of its satellites would justify U.S. assistance. However, in such cases there should be no U.S. military presence in the involved country either for training or any other purposes, since most countries in the Third World are ultrasensitive to foreign military on their soil. Furthermore, since the Viet Nam conflict the U.S. public has become skittish about supporting any policy involving the prolonged presence of U.S. military personnel in any civil strife outside of the United States. Also, local military commanders will tend to lean increasingly on the United States to fight their internal war. If necessary, training should be conducted in the United States. North Yemen could be an example of a nation in such a situation. Oman or El Salvador could be another.

Should the rebellion or internal disorder be entirely indigenous, with negligible or no help from abroad, the United States should under no circumstances furnish any military equipment either to the government or the revolutionary factions. The purpose of this policy should be to prevent the United States from taking sides in what would be essentially a civil war, regardless of political affiliation. The theory in such an event is that if the government in power enjoys wide respect it should be able to restore law and order with its normal military resources. If it should have lost the confidence of the majority of the nation, no amount of massive military help will enable its forces to break the revolutionary thrust.

The supply of normal police equipment, arms, and training should be on a straight commercial basis. If training is required it should be conducted in the United States and not in the acquiring country. The United States under those circumstances should avoid giving the impression of imposing its police system through the presence of a training mission. Thus, should internal disorder develop at some unforeseen time, the United States would not find itself in the uncomfortable position of being possibly accused of playing an actor's role.

There are of course factors of judgment which must enter in any arms transactions for which common sense and a feeling of proportion are important, if not, crucial. It would be inadvisable to become a party to arms purchases, even for cash and carry, of such a magnitude that sooner or later internal vital developmental projects, health and food considerations would suffer.

Promoting Democracy

Practically from its inception as a nation, the United States has drawn on the promotion of democracy abroad as an important diplomatic weapon. Benjamin Franklin's actions and the birth of our Republic influenced the course of events in France which destroyed the Bourbon Monarchy. The U.S. example had a profound effect on the Spanish colonies south of the Rio Grande, and the conception of a democratic republic contributed to the Latin American independence movement, even affecting the wording of the new constitutions. As late as 1917 our troops went into war in Europe with the ideal of "saving the world for democracy." Even today, the United States presses the principle of political democracy forward at every opportunity.

That the United States continues to sponsor and support so glorious an ideal both as a matter of principle and one of practicality is understandable. Clearly there is less likelihood of war when governments are subjected to the checkrein of an electorate than when the decision rests in the hands of one man or a small oligachy. Furthermore, under a democratic process with freely elected governments the dignity of man is more apt to be respected than in totalitarian or despotic regimes supported by force.

What is puzzling is the surprise of U.S. leaders when they discover the extent to which lip service is paid to the democratic ideal throughout the world, and how little to its reality. Perhaps part of the reason for this lack of understanding is insufficient knowledge of why our system and that of Western Europe function the way they do. The chagrin at the failure of democracy, as understood in the United States, in a score of countries affects our diplomacy toward those nations. Conversely, there is little comprehension of why progress toward an acknowledged ideal, often sanctified in loftily worded constitutions, is so slow in most countries throughout the world. There is no reason why the United States should not continue to advocate the principles of democracy as part of its diplomatic arsenal of instruments. But it is quite another thing when adoption of the U.S. democratic ideal is required specifically in *quid pro quo* international dealings in areas or countries where, by virtue of their cultural mores, including religious institutions, achievement of such goals are very much in the far distant future, if ever.

That human basic behavioral patterns are slow to change is evident even in the case of the Philippines, where after 50 years of intensive U.S. cultural colonization, a steady return to traditional and "undemocratic" structures and attitudes has been readily apparent since the islands acquired their independence after World War II. The English evolution toward political democracy was a long, often stormy and tedious process, which extended over many centuries. Our own system, based primarily on our English inheritance, has itself been in continuous evolution since the beginnings of the Republic, a phenomenon marked by a tragic civil war and periodically by landmark U.S. Supreme Court decisions down to this day. Hence, a great deal of sophistication is required of our foreign policymakers in bantering about standards of democracy in the international arena. To do otherwise is to raise questions abroad about our credibility and possibly force potential friends and allies into the arms of totalitarianism as a long-term fate.

There is another crucial consideration which must be taken very much into account in dealing with the issue of promoting democracy abroad. This concerns the historic bases of democracy in those countries in which this political philosophy has flourished as a going proposition. Mainly, one must be limited in this regard to Western Europe, although the record of post-World War II Japan is extraordinary, and of course among others, our country, Canada, New Zealand, and Australia.

It appears that throughout the history of democracy in these countries one important common denominator stands out dramatically: the emergence of a strong urban and rural middle income group linked to the great flexibility inherent in liberal capitalism. Without question the growth of service industries supplementing commerce and industry has afforded a continuous expansion for that group.

If valid, the implication of this thesis for Third World countries is very far reaching and should be an extremely important factor in the structuring of U.S. economic assistance policies. Thus, if these policies should have as a clear target the objective of helping substantially and realistically in the creation of middle income classes in countries where today the disparity between rich and poor is vast, the probability of sowing the seeds for democracy would be greatly enhanced.

It is no accident that the principal objective of Marxist political action groups is the destruction of the bourgeoisie and the creation of a proletariat. The former requires political and economic freedom to survive and is by definition opposed to the rigidity of Communist dogma.

In contrast the proletariat structure can be subjected to the tight control characteristic of a Marxist state. This reality was readily recognized by Dr. Fidel Castro when he allowed over 500,000 Cubans, almost the entire middle class in the Island to migrate to the United States and elsewhere in the early days of the Cuban Revolution. A restless class constantly clamoring for political and economic liberty represented a fearful danger to the Communist regime in Cuba. Hence, it had to be eliminated. In Russia the agrarian Kulak class was ruthlessly slaughtered for the same reason. In brief, wherever a Communist regime has been established the bourgeoisie and its penchant for democracy has been removed by one form or another.

What is called for in U.S. aid legislation is recognition that U.S. objectives require the creation or strengthening of both urban and rural middle income classes. It is not enough to build up only the urban sector.

SUMMARY

It would be too much to expect that Congress and the political appointees in the Executive Branch who really make key foreign policy decisions will do so on rational and knowledgeable grounds. Inexperience about foreign matters, all too frequent an occurrence at the highest levels of policymaking, combined with sensitivity in Congress about domestic special interests and ideological positions preclude such a utopia.

In addition, presidential elections every four years usually result in shifts of foreign policy emphasis and attention; a circumstance that encourages intractable opponents to wait out administrations with which they find it difficult to deal. In other situations, problems are impossible to fix with short-term solutions. For example, recall the Arab-Israeli issues, Russia and Afghanistan, the Cuban complex, China and Taiwan, etc. Nevertheless, improvements must and can be made which will permit a more comfortable position for the United States in the world scene. To achieve this end a common understanding of fundamental considerations on which our foreign relations rest must be reached, not only within government circles but also by the U.S. people in general. Hence, the attempt in this chapter is to propose the Preamble as a cornerstone for the definition of our national interest, and the concept of *quid pro quo* strategies and tactics as basic formulae in pursuing international objectives. This philosophy is not only viable, but can be easily understood and accepted by most of the nation as consistent with both our past and present way of life. Precisely because of the complexities involved, Central America and the Caribbean Island Republics, and Cuba specifically, have been selected for purpose of illustration. Perhaps ideas may be found in this work which will lead to greater consistency in U.S. foreign policies, and to their expression in a manner easier for the U.S. public to support with confidence.

3

ROOTS OF U.S. CONCERNS FOR CENTRAL AMERICA, FROM THEODORE ROOSEVELT TO WARREN HARDING, 1901–1921

> Many a slip 'twixt the cup and the lip.
>
> *Old Proverb*

A brief survey of U.S. diplomacy in Central America from the beginning of the present century to recent times is helpful for two important reasons. Until the formal emergence of President Franklin Roosevelt's Good Neighbor policy, during the 1930s, Central America served as a minilaboratory for the application of U.S. policy concepts, particularly in the pre-World War I years. These, modified by experience and Latin American reactions, as well as specific contributions by the Central Americans, related importantly to ideals and mechanisms that later became reflected in the formal creation of a genuinely representative inter-U.S. system at Bogota in 1948, through the emergence of the Organization of American States.

The new body succeeded the Pan-American Union which in turn had been the outgrowth of official International Conferences of American States, the first of which was held in Washington in 1889–90. Although headquarters for the renamed Organization remained in Washington, its officials were drawn from all the Latin American nations as well as the United States, and the board of governors reflected appointees other than the Latin American ambassadors accredited to Washington. The choice of the first secretary general was Alberto Lleras Camargo who served from 1948 to 1954. A distinguished Colombian, Lleras Camargo ably and vigorously led the new entity and contributed greatly to the high regard in which the Organization is held throughout the two continents.

In another aspect the review furthers a better understanding of U.S. diplomacy and consequences in Central America, the effects of which are evident in the area to this day. It also helps place in perspective suggestions and recommendations advanced in this book relative to the region.

The genesis of U.S. concern for the Caribbean Basin stemmed from two very important events. Victorious in the Spanish-American conflict in 1898, the United States found itself in occupation of two islands, Cuba and Puerto Rico, and not quite sure about their future destinies. But, the confidence engendered by the success of the recently expanded U.S. navy gave the United States public a sense of euphoria and power bound to affect a region through which the future isthmian canal would be built. It should be remembered that by February 1902, President Theodore Roosevelt could announce ratification by the Senate of the final Hay-Pauncefote Treaty which permitted the United States to build the canal on its own without strings from the British.

An incident of far-reaching consequences for U.S. policy in the Caribbean involved the blockade of Venezuelan ports by British, German, and Italian warships arising from irresponsible behavior by Venezuelan President Cipriano Castro toward obligations due nationals of these and other countries, as well as damage to foreign owned properties. The European action developed between late 1902 and the spring of 1903. The United States, to a great extent because of public opinion, intervened in the matter and pressured the Venezuelan dictator to accept arbitration, a solution agreeable to the European powers. The matter was referred to the Hague Permanent Court of Arbitration. In time President Castro disappeared from the scene, Venezuela apportioned a percentage of customs receipts to satisfy the debts, and the incident dissipated. However, the issue highlighted the fact that under international law a creditor nation could enforce collection of a debt in the case of irresponsible behavior by a debtor nation, even if necessary to the extent of occupation.[1]

For the United States with the canal project in the background, the issue posed a serious dilemma. If the repeat of Venezuela's behavior somewhere in the region resulted in an extraterritorial power seizing a port for the purpose of collecting on an obligation, not only could there be a violation of the Monroe Doctrine, since the foreign occupier might not be in a hurry to leave, but a threat to the proposed canal would have developed.

In the pre-World War I years there was every reason to be concerned about the possibility of a European power trying to establish a toehold somewhere south of the U.S. border, using debt collection as an excuse. It was an era when a Europe hungry for empire was busy carving up Africa and trying its best to establish special positions in China.

One consequence derived from the Venezuelan incident was the obvious need for President Roosevelt to develop a posture, consistent with the Monroe Doctrine, designed to prevent the eventuality of European intervention in the Americas in connection with nonpayment of debts. Thus, in his 1904 State of the Union he stated what since has become known as the Roosevelt Corollary to the Monroe Doctrine:

> Chronic wrongdoing, or an impotence which results in a general loosening of the ties of civilized society, may in America as elsewhere ultimately require intervention by some civilized nation, and in the Western Hemisphere the adherence of the United States to the Monroe Doctrine may force the United States, however reluctant, in flagrant cases of such wrongdoing or impotence to the exercise of an international police power.

It should be noted that on November 3, 1903, Panama, with the blessings of the United States, declared its independence from Colombia, and the way was cleared for the construction of the canal following a treaty between the United States and Panama signed on November 18, 1903. U.S. recognition of Panama as an independent state took place three days after revolt in Panama City. From the date on which the canal's construction began until the present, the security of the canal has been a major factor in the evolution of U.S. foreign policy in the Caribbean region. Announcement of the Roosevelt Corollary was the first effort in this respect, one which eventually led to repeated military interventions in Central America, Haiti, Dominican Republic, and Cuba.

Initially Washington viewed the entire Basin as the object of uniform attention. But the internal turmoil in Central America, stemming from ambitious and unscrupulous military tyrants in their quarrels with each other in the different countries, combined with attempts by one leader or another to impose his will on the region, and reconstitute the defunct unified republic, soon caused the U.S. government to seek means with which to cope with the situation. This evolution led to a Central American policy somewhat different in detail from the approach to the island republics. The latter by virtue of their isolation from one another, except on rare occasion Haiti and the Dominican Republic, could not meddle seriously in each other's affairs.

Thus, in examining basic aspects of U.S. diplomatic approaches in the Caribbean Basin, the Central American Republics must be dealt with as a group, and the islands somewhat separately. However, Haiti, the Dominican Republic, and the Central American countries had in common heavy indebtedness to foreign powers. They suffered from internal instability and lacked a sense of governmental responsibility toward foreign financial obligations.

In the early 1900s, for all intents and purposes, the U.S. public, and the government almost as much, viewed the policy evolving in the Caribbean as based on principles applicable to all Latin America. Hence, it is interesting to examine the instructions issued by President Theodore Roosevelt to the U.S. delegation attending the Second International Conference of American States which met in Mexico City from October 22, 1901 to January 22, 1902. Particularly important was the following admonition:

> The chief interest of the United States in relation to the other Republics upon the American continent is the safety and permanence of the political system which underlies their and our existence as nations—the system of free self-government by the people. It is therefore to be desired that all the American Republics should enjoy in full measure the blessings of perfect freedom under just laws, each sovereign community pursuing its own course of orderly development without external restraint or interference. To this condition of security, the peace and prosperity of all our neighbors will materially contribute. Every failure on their part to maintain social order, every economic distress which might give rise to domestic disturbance, every discord between them which could impede their industries, menace their stability, or bring upon them the calamity of foreign interference would be a misfortune to us. It should therefore be the effort of this commission to impress upon the representation of our sister Republics of Central and South America that we desire above all, their material prosperity and their political security, and that we entertain toward them no sentiments but those of friendship and fraternity.[2]

In another paragraph the President further instructed that:

> With respect to political differences subsisting between the States of Central and South America it is important for the commission to proceed with caution. The general principle should be to enter as little as possible into these questions. At the same time it will be useful to impress upon all the deep interest which the government of the United States has in the peace and tranquility of all the American States in their territorial integrity.[3]

Regarding U.S. assistance to help the Latin American states achieve material prosperity, the instructions included the following:

> With reference to questions of a commercial and industrial character, it is important to lay special stress upon the growing desire in the United States to secure the largest mutuality of interest and to avoid even the semblance of an attempt to obtain unfair advantages for ourselves. The true interest of our people, it is being more and more generally admitted, lies in helping the Latin American countries with our more advanced industries and our characteristic forms of energy to expand

into strong and flourishing communities, and not in seeking to aggrandize ourselves at their expense. In developing closer relations with them we should be most careful of their autonomy.[4]

In another section of the instructions, support for the principle of arbitration as a way to settle international financial differences was shown by endorsement of the idea for the establishment of "an organized tribunal for the adjustment of indemnity claims."

A close assessment of the references cited, which cover only a small part of the total instructions, reveals that practically all of the ingredients of basic U.S. foreign policy toward Latin America were stated. By support for holding the Inter-American Conference, the U.S. government instinctively moved in the direction of encouraging the creation of an inter-U.S. political and economic system, reflected 46 years later in the establishment of the Organization of American States. Encouragement for democracy in the continent, territorial integrity (Monroe Doctrine), rule of law as a basis for stability, nonintervention from abroad, interdependence, economic development with the assistance of investment by U.S. private capital, material prosperity as an essentiality, and arbitration to settle international commercial disputes are factors which implicitly were recognized as important for the security of the United States.

The Third International Conference of American States was held at Rio de Janeiro from July 21, 1906 to August 26, 1906. The instructions from President Roosevelt to the U.S. representatives were practically unchanged from those given the delegates to the Conference of 1901–02, except for procedural and peripheral items. However, by this time the U.S. government had been experiencing the facts of life in Central America. In fact in 1907 together with Mexico the United States convoked a peace conference in Washington to stop a regional war involving three of the Republics, and threatening to become further generalized. Thus, Secretary of State Elihu Root traveled to Rio de Janeiro to address the Third International Conference of American States, a reflection of the importance given the developing events in Central America, even though the Conference was supposedly concerned with the whole of Latin America.

It is interesting to contrast the lofty tone of the basic instructions to the U.S. delegations attending both the Second and Third Conferences with Secretary Root's address. Among other points, Root stated that:

The first fruits of democracy are many of them crude and unlovely; its mistakes are many, its partial failures many. Its signs not few. Capacity for self-government does not come to man by nature. It is an art to be learned, and it is also an expression of character to be developed among all the thousands of men who exercise popular sovereignty.[5]

In this statement, Root, and presumably President Roosevelt, recognized the great difficulties inherent in the evolution of democracy in areas where this philosophy, except as a distant and imperfectly understood ideal, had not planted roots. Root continued as follows:

> To reach the goal toward which we are pressing forward, the governing multitude must first acquire knowledge that comes from universal education, wisdom that follows practical experience, personal independence and self-respect befitting men who acknowledge no superior, self-control to replace that external control which a democracy rejects, respect for law, obedience to the lawful expressions of the public will, consideration for the opinions and interests of others equally entitled to a voice in the State, loyalty to that abstract conception—one's country— as inspiring as that loyalty to the personal sovereigns which has so illumined the pages of history, subordination of personal interests to the public good, love of justice and mercy, of liberty and order. All these we must seek by slow and patient effort; and how many shortcomings in his own land and among his own people each of us is conscious.[6]

With respect to U.S. policy, Secretary Root said:

> We wish for no victories but those of peace; for no territories except our own; for no sovereignty except the sovereignty of ourselves. We deem the independence and equal rights of the smallest and weakest member of the family of nations entitled to as much respect as those of the greatest empire, and we deem the observance of that respect the chief guaranty of the weak against the oppression of the strong. We neither claim nor desire any rights or privileges, or powers we do not freely concede every American Republic. We wish to increase our prosperity, to expand our true way, to expand our trade, to grow in wealth, in wisdom, and in spirit, but our conception of the true way to accomplish this is not to pull down others and profit by their ruin, but to help all friends to a common prosperity and a common growth, that we may all become greater and stronger together.[7]

From the Report of the Conference it appears that Root's comments were very well received and applauded. There is no reason to question even remotely the integrity of Root's belief in the statement he made. The question is how did the statement square with U.S. actions in the Caribbean, developments which were to haunt U.S.-Latin American relations to the present. Root's address was delivered in 1906, one must note. But in 1903 the United States had played the canal card which resulted in lopping off land belonging to the Republic of Colombia. In 1905 President Roosevelt concluded an agreement with the Dominican

Republic for appointment of an U.S. customs collector who would pay off foreign creditors with the balance going to the Dominican affairs, even if meant to forestall European intervention over the issue of indebtedness. In 1902 when Cuba's independence was recognized, the island had to accept the Platt Amendment, which in effect gave the United States a certain degree of supervision or veto over Cuba's foreign relations, particularly financial. It also provided for U.S. intervention in the event of certain internal disorder.

The answer rests on two considerations. One relates to the fact that in that period it was accepted international practice to intervene to protect a creditor nation's rights or those of their nationals if the debtor country acted irresponsibly. The other concerned the view that U.S. actions protected the territorial integrity of the nation in question by forestalling any extracontinental power intervention, since the United States would abandon the "intervened" nation once the debts were paid. The matter involving Colombia and Panama, and the "ditching" of Nicaragua as the alternative route, is a murky one with respect to the U.S. role, particularly since Roosevelt reportedly crowed in 1911 that "I took the isthmus." In all probability, Root regarded the security of the United States as overriding, and therefore saw what had happened relative to the outcome of the civil war in Colombia, as a not clear-cut issue in any event.

Historically, it is unique that despite repeated interventions in the Caribbean and Central America, and at times intense provocation by Mexico, the United States honored Secretary Root's dictum about not adding to the national territory.

An interesting aspect of the U.S. policy of not absorbing permanently weak neighboring states is that galling as the U.S. interventions have been, rarely was there ever a generalized feeling in the countries affected that in time the United States would not once again depart from the scene. Inevitably the U.S. interference would be accompanied to a greater or lesser degree by financial benefit to the affected country and an easing of turmoil, for which reasons there were always influential elements agreeable to U.S. tutorship. The large mass of peasantry, which carried the brunt of suffering during the interminable civil conflicts, since they were forcibly dragged off their fields or peonage and forced into partisan military service, were either indifferent to the intervention or welcomed the resulting tranquility.

It is curious that the most energetic protests about U.S. actions in the Caribbean came from the extreme end of the southern continent. Certainly, within the time frame under discussion the possibility of the United States' occupying Buenos Aires was not within U.S. capability. Some explanations have variously been advanced to explain the Argentine alleged fear of the United States. In the early 1900s Argentina itself was heavily in debt to European creditors, and was concerned about the U.S. precedent in the Caribbean encouraging European powers to follow suit.[8]

Another suggests that Buenos Aires at the height of prosperity viewed itself as the leader of South America and a competitor of the United States, and considered the latter an aspirant to this role. A traveler who visited Buenos Aires frequently in the pre-World War I era explained to one of the authors that Buenos Aires looked almost exclusively to Europe for inspiration and cultural patterns, particularly France. The traveler, who also was familiar with Paris, stressed the strong anti-U.S. mood of the French who regarded U.S. people as crude and naive, but exaggeratedly ambitious. Since France still considered empire building a national goal, many of these sentiments probably rubbed off on the Argentines frequently traveling to Paris for study or pleasure. Importantly for the United States, the Argentine leadership made little impact on the Central Americans placed by destiny under the shadow of a giant nation.[9]

Throughout the second half of the nineteenth century in particular, as a result of innumerable dealings with foreign creditors and problems arising from nonpayment and border problems among themselves, all of the Central American countries acquired familiarity with arbitration as a means of solution or postponement of the inevitable. They had also learned at the hands of the European powers and the United States about the significance of treaties. By 1902 there had been about 14 to 16 clearly defined attempts to renew the ill-fated confederation, in addition to frequent internal strife or occasional war with a neighboring state. The result had been devastation of their economies and increasing danger of occupation by a foreign power.

CORINTO PACT

In 1902 another of the many military encounters between several of the states again raised the specter of a serious intraregional war. In an unprecedented move the "executives" of Costa Rica, Honduras, El Salvador, and Nicaragua met at Corinto, Nicaragua, and on January 20, 1902, signed a treaty requiring obligatory arbitration as a means for the peaceful solution of differences between the nations of Central America. The U.S. Minister at San Jose, Costa Rica, William Lawrence Merry, also accredited to El Salvador and Nicaragua, who transmitted to the Department of State a translation of the Spanish version of the treaty text as it appeared in the Managua, Nicaragua, newspaper, *El Comercio*, January 30, 1902, reported to Washington that President Iglesias of Guatemala who had arrived in San Jose informed him that Guatemala also agreed to sign the treaty.[10]

In a dispatch dated March 1, 1902, from the Legation at San Jose, Costa Rica, Minister William Lawrence Merry informed Secretary of State John Hay that the President of Guatemala "has joined in the arbitration treaty signed at the Corinto conference on January 20, 1902, by the Presidents of Nicaragua, Costa Rica, Salvador and Honduras, in accordance with his promise to President Iglesias. 'The peace of Central America now appears assured in the near future.'"[11]

It will be noted in the Corinto treaty that the foreign ministers were all civilians and the presidents all generals. The latter were under no compunction to abide by what they had signed other than their own inclinations, since all power was centered in their hands. Also noteworthy was the lack of reference to any movement toward confederation, a recognition by the omission of the grave political obstacles in the path of reunification.

CENTRAL AMERICAN PEACE TREATY OF 1902

The Corinto convention was followed by a treaty of nonintervention and arbitration among Guatemala, Nicaragua, Honduras, and El Salvador. In a dispatch from the Legation at Guatemala, May 18, 1902, to Secretary of State Hay, by Secretary of Legation Philip M. Brown, who was accredited to both Guatemala and Honduras, reference was made to a peace treaty "recently ratified by the National Assembly of Guatemala, wherein the principles of noninterference in the domestic affairs of each other and compulsory arbitration of disputes between the signatory governments were recognized."[12]

The text enclosed by Brown in his dispatch is as follows:

Central American Treaty of Peace

The Governments of the Republics of Guatamala, Honduras, and Nicaragua, invited by His Excellency the President of El Salvador to hold an international conference with the object of assuring peace and harmony between the Central American republics, have commenced their deliberations through their representatives, and have agreed to the following stipulations:

First. The Governments of Guatemala, Honduras, Nicaragua, and El Salvador take upon themselves the obligation to maintain peace between the Republics here represented. Consequently, as an inviolable principle of conduct, they establish the nonintervention of any one of them in the domestic affairs of the other sister Republics.

Second. The cultivation of good relations being one of the most efficacious means of maintaining peace, the four Governments compromise* themselves to reciprocally accredit consuls-general with the character of charge d'affaires, with their residence in the capitals of each of the Republics.

Third. To adjust the disputes that may arise between the nations signing, the principle of obligatory arbitration, already recognized, is hereby confirmed.

Fourth. The questions that arise between any of the Republics signing, that are not bound between themselves by former conventions of arbitration, shall be dissolved** in accordance with the principles and regulations set forth in the Pan-American treaty entered into at Mexico on January 29, 1902.

Fifth. In case of a serious difficulty between two or more of the Republics signing that makes armed strife probable the parties interested oblige themselves to ask for and the neutrals to interpose their friendly mediation for the peaceful adjustment of the pending difficulties.

Sixth. This treaty being of general interest to Central America, and the sister Republic of Costa Rica not being represented in this conference, it is decided to invite Costa Rica, in order that, if she deems it convenient, she may accept and sign the stipulations set forth herein.

Seventh. Once the present convention shall have been approved by the President of each republic, it will at once go into effect, without the necessity of previous exchange, it being sufficient for its effect the reciprocal notification of the high contracting parties to the convention that it has been approved in the prescribed form.

In witness whereof we sign in quadruplicate, in the city of San Salvador, this second day of November, one thousand nine hundred and three.

> Manual Maria Giron
> F. Davila
> Adolfo Altamarino
> Manuel I. Morales
> Executive Palace,
> Guatemala, November 9, 1902

The constitutional President of the Republic decides:
To approve the Central American peace convention signed by the

---

Note: * Mistranslated. *Comprometer* in Spanish in the sense used is to obligate or obligated.
    **Probably resolved instead of dissolved (Authors' comments).

delegates of the Republics of Guatemala, Honduras, Nicaragua, and El Salvador the 2nd day of the present month in the capital of the latter Republic.
Let this be communicated.

Estrada C.

Secretary of State in the office of foreign relations.

Juan Barrios M.[13]

The reference in item "Fourth" to the Pan-American treaty entered into at Mexico on January 29, 1902 concerns the proposals advanced at the Second International Conference of American States regarding arbitration, a matter of considerable interest to the United States. Because of problems that all the Latin American nations had experienced either with creditor nations or in boundary disputes among themselves, or with extraterritorial powers concerning disputed borders, the matter of arbitration had long been of continental interest.

After rather spirited debate, all 19 Republics represented at the Conference agreed on acceptance of The Hague convention. The United States and Mexico were empowered to "negotiate with the other signatory Powers to the Convention for the Peaceful Adjustment of International Differences, for the adherence thereto of the American Nations so requesting and not now signatory to the said Convention."[14] The date of the Protocol of Adherence to the Conventions of The Hague was January 15, 1902.

However, at the Second International Conference of American States a project for a treaty of obligatory arbitration to which only ten of the attending nations subscribed was also drafted. Of the Central American countries only Guatemala and El Salvador concurred with this project, which was dated January 29, 1902. The invitation for the conference concerning the cited 1904 Central American Treaty of Peace was issued by El Salvador and the Republic of Guatemala quickly accepted; both signatories to the January 29th project drafted in Mexico City during the Second International Conference of American States.

Also important in connection with the two peace treaties of 1902 and 1903 was the lack of provision for ratification by the respective assemblies of the countries concerned. The authority of their presidents was sufficient. Therein lies one of the key weaknesses in the efforts of the Central American Republics to develop a workable peace mechanism. If one president was toppled from office by a revolution or coup, the new one did not necessarily feel himself bound to an agreement made by a predecessor. Or alternatively, any of the presidents could either interpret the treaty as he pleased or take it lightly. Consequently, despite the solemn promises and commitments, by June 1, 1906, Guatemala and El Salvador each had 12,000 troops on the border facing one another, and war threatened daily. The issue arose from the invasion of Guatemala from El Salvador by a group of revolutionaries seeking to oust President Manuel Estrada Cabrera. Shortly thereafter Honduras joined the conflict on the side of El Salvador.

The circumstances regarding the treaties of Corinto, 1902, and the subsequent pact in 1903, have been explored in some detail because of their significance as initial steps for the creation of a Central American peace mechanism. These two early moves, ineffective though they were, nevertheless, helped set the stage for further developments in the same general direction. It is noteworthy that the United States did not participate in these two conferences. It did, however, follow events closely and as can be gathered from Minister Merry's dispatch relative to the Corinto pact, the latter elicited an optimistic augury for the future. There is some evidence that the United States encouraged the participating states, at least with respect to the Corinto effort. But it is unclear whether such urging reflected initiatives of the local U.S. diplomatic representatives or instructions from the Department of State. On balance, it appears that the Central American States made the initial moves, but encouraged by the U.S. Legations in the various capitals, particularly since it was official U.S. policy to support the unification of the Central American republics.

As stated earlier, by June 1, 1906, the situation had acquired grave characteristics, and the prospect of a generalized war was very real. The situation provoked rather intensive U.S. diplomatic activity to ward off the conflict. One aspect of the U.S. effort was to secure the assistance of President Porfirio Diaz of Mexico to cooperate with the United States in the peace initiatives. The net result was a conference on board the USS *Marblehead* as a neutral place for the warring factions to meet in mid-July.

THE MARBLEHEAD TREATY, 1906

The gravity of the situation as seen from Washington was reflected in a message from President Roosevelt to the Presidents of El Salvador and Guatemala:

> I earnestly appeal to Salvador to take immediate steps toward settling questions pending with Guatemala, either by agreement to arbitration or by direct negotiation for a definitive agreement between the two countries. Disturbance of the peace of Central America inflicts grievous

injury upon the affected States and causes the gravest concern to the United States, whose sole desire is to see its neighbors at peace. The recent deplorable renewal of hostilities should not be allowed to be the precursor of a protracted and disastrous struggle, perhaps involving other States and leading to results of which the scope cannot be foreseen. In the interest of humanity and the indispensable peace of Central America it becomes my duty to urge a settlement before it may be too late. I offer the deck of the American ship of war Marblehead, now on the way to the coast of Salvador, as a neutral place where representatives of Guatemala and Salvador may meet to consider terms of agreement, and armistice between the contestants being meanwhile effected. I am telegraphing in the same sense to the President of Guatemala. My action has the full concurrence of the President of Mexico.[15]

The meeting on board the USS *Marblehead* included representatives of the governments of El Salvador, Guatemala, and Honduras and observers from Costa Rica and Nicaragua referred to in the convention as special delegates. U.S. Ministers William Lawrence Merry and Leslie Combs, the latter accredited to Honduras and Guatemala, together with Federico Gamboa, Minister Plenipotentiary of Mexico in the region, served as honorary presidents of the conference. On July 20, 1906, Combs and Merry reported to the Secretary of State as follows:

Peace conference a success. Guatemala, Salvador, and Honduras have agreed to the following articles: First, peace established, withdrawal of armies within three days, disarmament in eight days. Second, the exchange of prisoners, the release of political prisoners, general amnesty recommended. Third, vigilance of emigrados in order to prevent abuse of asylum. Fourth, to negotiate treaty of friendship, commerce within two months. Fifth, any difficulties over treaty and all future concrete complaints between the three countries shall be submitted to the President of the United States and the President of Mexico. Sixth, this treaty made with the moral sanction of mediating nations and others assisting at conference, namely, Costa Rica and Nicaragua.[16]

In a communication dated August 18, 1906, from the U.S. Legation at San Jose, Costa Rica, Minister William Lawrence Merry informed the Secretary of State that "the Government of Costa Rica, having in view the fourth article in the Marblehead treaty of peace which provides for the meeting of Commissioners from the Republics of Guatemala, Salvador, and Honduras to celebrate a Treaty of Peace, Amity, and Commerce, within two months from July 20th, 1906, at this capital, has invited the delegates from the said Republics to meet at this city on Saturday, September 15th, the anniversary of Central American Independence."[17]

Costa Rica, Guatemala, El Salvador, and Honduras through their representatives at the San Jose meeting developed, between September 15th and September 25th, 1906, as a follow-up to the Marblehead Treaty, a broader pact of peace, amity, and commerce, negotiated an agreement consisting of 38 articles, a convention for the establishment of a Central American International Bureau (for the purpose of developing reports of commercial interest), and an agreement to establish a Central American Pedagogical Institute. The Treaty of Peace, Amity, and Commerce was broad in scope. It provided for arbitration, laid the basis for favorable foreign trade treatment among the signatories, extradition, agreement to keep troublesome emigrees away from the frontiers of their countries of origin and from serving in the armies of the signatories. One important purpose of the Pedagogical Institute was to work toward a common educational system.

In short, the new Treaty represented a broad amplification of the Corinto Pact of 1902, the one of 1903, and the Marblehead Treaty. Recognition of the need to start the coordination of regional economic efforts was farsighted indeed, as well as the advantage of sharing common information, and a uniform educational system. These concepts were eventually to flower in the structuring of the Central American Common Market and in other regional organizations over a half century later.[18]

Ominously, after initially accepting the invitation to participate in the San Jose meeting, Nicaragua withdrew, her President (José Santos Zelaya) alleging that as he had not been one of the belligerents, he had no connection with the treaty. It was stressed by the participants that there was no necessity for either Costa Rica or Nicaragua to join in the new treaty, and that all parties meeting to celebrate the anniversary festivities would have an opportunity to become better acquainted with each, and thus the occasion would strengthen the prospects for peace. Nicaragua did not respond and no representative arrived.

The sequence of events following the meeting at San Jose, which Nicaragua declined to attend alleging a flimsy pretext for its negative position, was most bewildering. A probable reason for Nicaragua's refusal to participate in the San Jose conference concerned disappointment with an arbitral decision made by King Alfonso XIII of Spain in favor of Honduras in a Nicaraguan-Honduran borderline dispute.[19] President José Santos Zelaya of Nicaragua wanted to retain freedom of action to resolve the border issue to his satisfaction by resorting to force against Honduras. Attendance at the San Jose session would have placed him in an awkward situation in view of his plans. He also resented bitterly the prospect of increased U.S. interference in Central American affairs.

However, more seriously the perennial issue of unification over-shadowed relations between the various Central American States. As had occurred in the previous century, much of the juggling by one caudillo or another of the various republics was related to how quickly or in what manner unification could be achieved. While the interminable military conflicts in the region threw in high relief the names of army chieftains, there were also deeply involved many well-educated civilians drawn from the liberal professions and business. Undoubtedly, venality and personal ambition attended the activities of these politicians, but there was also a measure of idealism both with respect to prospects for democracy per their lights and the desire to see a unified Central America. In fact, more frequently than supposed in each of the republics at one time or another there were periods of considerable stability and material progress, both as to infrastructure and foreign investment. José Santos Zelaya's actions must be viewed against these considerations if the situation in the region is to be understood.

The subsequent emergence of the Washington treaties in 1907 was no more the product of instant U.S. diplomatic success than the dream child come true of one of the Central American politicians. It was the logical development of efforts by the Central Americans to stabilize conditions, and based on innumerable precedents within the region. What happened was that U.S. policy concerning the canal prospects was evolving at the same time that the Cental Americans realized matters were about to get disastrously out of hand. This was a coincidence of events. To Secretary of State Elihu Root, a noted lawyer in his own right, the concept of treaties as a means of resolving differences among nations was very appealing. Hence, the United States supported treaty diplomacy.

To return to General Zelaya's policies, U.S. and Central American historians all concur in the thesis that Zelaya aspired to achieve at a minimum personal control over Central America, perhaps even unification of the region. The differences among the experts concern Zelaya's motives, methods, and the circumstance of heading a dictatorial regime in Nicaragua.

All of the Central American leaders implicitly seemed to be aware of one reality: that no one country was wealthy enough to support a military establishment which could impose unification by conquest. Thus, repeated attempts called for federation or unification through voluntary constitutional means. This approach might have worked if there had been a common perception of an external threat to their territorial integrity. But no such fear existed. The Central American leaders in the last third of the past century and in the heyday of U.S. Caribbean imperialism never felt that the Marine landings would lead to permanent U.S. occupation. On one hand the Monroe Doctrine was considered as a shield against

European adventures. On the other, the issue was how to keep U.S. meddling in their affairs at a minimum while enticing the flow of private investment and bank financing.

Zelaya's technique was based on setting up as presidents of the neighboring countries puppet chief executives who owed their positions to his military support. If the idea had unfolded to its logical conclusion, in time a network of "quislings" would perhaps facilitate the overall objective of de facto unification centered in Nicaragua as the fulcrum. Key to this rationale was control of Honduras. A close examination of the Central American geographical realities shows that if Nicaragua and Honduras had achieved "oneness" the pressure on El Salvador to succumb to such an axis would have been impossible to resist. Hence, a Nicaraguan-Honduras-Salvadoran combination under Zelaya would be in a position to take on militarily Guatemala with prospects of success. Costa Rica was too small and isolated to affect the military formula and would have fallen like a ripe apple into the basket. Against this rationale, it is possible to explain the moves that occurred between the San Jose conference of 1906 and the Washington Peace Conference of 1907, since El Salvador and Guatemala intuitively realized the danger of their independence.

The president of Honduras in 1906 was General F. Manuel Bonilla, who was not sympathetic to the designs of Zelaya with respect to Honduras. In El Salvador, General Fernando Figueroa had been elected president and assumed power on March 1, 1907. General Bonilla, not to be confused with General Policarpo Bonilla who, with the aid of Zelaya, had served as president in the 1890s, assumed power in 1903 and held the office until thrown out by Zelaya. Miguel Davila (1907–11), less objectionable to Zelaya than Bonilla, emerged out of the Tegucigalpa chaos as provisional president.

General Figueroa of El Salvador was partial to General Manuel Bonilla, hence an opponent to Zelaya. The latter's immediate objective was to eliminate Bonilla and replace him with someone more friendly to Nicaragua. Davila, while not a threat to Zelaya, nevertheless stood strongly for a neutral Honduras.

Once it was clear to Zelaya that General Figueroa was in the picture because of his election, he did not wait for the latter's official taking of office, but with some 3,000 Nicaraguans ordered the invasion of Honduras early in 1907. The invasion route was through San Marcos de Colon.[20] His troops defeated Honduran General Salomon Ordonez. El Salvador responded by supporting Bonilla and sending about 2,000 troops into Honduras under Generals José Dolores Preza and Alejandro Gomez.[21] On March 17, 1907, at Manasigue in Honduras, near Choluteca, the Salvadorans and Nicaraguans clashed with the Salvadorans routed. General Sotero Barahona, Honduran Minister of War met his opponents at

Yuscaran, and in the battle of "La Marcita" died in action, an event which contributed further to the weakening of General Bonilla's capabilities to resist the Nicaraguan push. Bonilla's last hope lay with forces in Tegucigalpa and in reinforcements from El Salvador. But Salvadoran President Figueroa was concerned about a suspected conspiracy against his government and ordered his troops to focus on this possibility, leaving General Bonilla in an abandoned situation.[22] The latter fled to Amapala, Honduran port in the Gulf of Fonseca, where he surrendered to the Nicaraguans through arrangements effected by the U.S. Charge d'Affaires Philip M. Brown.[23] In a situation which had drifted into anarchy, Davila emerged as provisional president.

Although Nicaragua had declared war on El Salvador, the latter had not replied in kind in hope of leaving open the possibility of a peace settlement. The stage was set for a peace attempt. The matter was urgent because Guatemala, alarmed by events, had placed troop reinforcements on its frontier with Nicaragua. The possibility of a joint Salvadoran-Guatemalan attack against Nicaragua could not be discarded. In fact subsequently a message from the Mexican Consul General in Tegucigalpa appeared to confirm this threat.

To digress briefly from the manner in which the peace process developed after Bonilla's departure from the immediate scene, an explanation is in order regarding why attention has been centered on what really were internal matters. One reason is that they led to U.S. mediation efforts and eventually to deep involvement in Nicaraguan affairs.

The other is because some of the considerations that affected the actions of the various Central American countries stemmed from geographic considerations applicable to some extent in the present Central American imbroglio. Note that the expansionist push originated in Nicaragua. Currently, expressions by Marxist-Leninist leaders in Managua point to the hope that their revolutionary efforts will one day touch the borders of the U.S. southwest. Clearly such as a long-range and ambitious prospect could not happen without absorption of Honduras. Hence, it is no accident that the present Honduran government, whose members are thoroughly familiar with the region's history, has concentrated troops on the Nicaraguan frontier and assigned facilities for U.S. training of Salvadoran and Honduran troops in counter-guerrilla techniques. Fear of reawakened Nicaraguan regional imperialism is at the bottom of Honduran acquiescence to stepped up U.S. military assistance and presence.

El Salvador, aware of the historical antecedents involving Nicaragua, and subjected to intense guerrilla pressure supported from Nicaragua with Soviet supplies obtained through Cuba, looked to linkage with Honduras as an offset. That social and economic conditions in the countries involved are conducive to internal disorder, and that major political and social reforms are crying for attention is as valid now, as they were in 1907. The difference is that the present urgency is that much greater and subject to exploitation by Marxist-Leninist cadres.

Gautemala, as it did in 1907, is watching the situation closely, while beefing up its military capability to deal with the consequences of a Nicaraguan-Honduran blowup, if one should occur, or to participate in the conflict as an ally of Honduras. At some point, however, Nicaraguans may realize as they did in 1907, that the military might and economic base for a hard push into the region, even through clandestine or guerrilla supporting efforts propped up by Cuba, is inadequate for the task that their ardent Marxist-Leninist adherents would like to see them undertake. The United States' interest in halting the Marxist-Leninist threat, and if possible turning it back in Nicaragua, coincides with the objectives of Honduras, Guatemala, El Salvador, and Cost Rica of preserving their independence, whether the menace comes from a wily dictator like Zelaya in the early 1900s or violence from a militant Marxist-Leninist state in the region. That steps must be taken by the region's states to remedy the grave social, political, and economic problems which plague the area is an absolute necessity, but that is a separate issue from the security aspect discussed within a historical context.

AMAPALA MEETING, 1907

On April 4, 1907, the U.S. Legation at La Union in Salvador reported that the President of Guatemala through the President of El Salvador sent a request to U.S. Charge d'Affaires Philip Brown for his mediation, stressing that a peace conference was necessary to clear the situation. President Figueroa of El Salvador sent President Roosevelt a telegram on April 8, 1907, expressing his appreciation for the President's "complaisance" respecting the continuation of Charge Brown's peace efforts. On April 11, Brown reported that "peace is assured" and "that the Government of Salvador accepts propositions made through him by the President of Nicaragua for a peace conference in the port of Amapala between the two presidents in person immediately upon the surrender of that port, which he expects will be effected within twenty-four hours." The availability of U.S. war vessels was considered as helpful for the process, presumably as in the case of the USS *Marblehead* as neutral ground.[24]

Acting Secretary of State Robert Bacon acknowledged Brown's message, and on April 13th replied that President Roosevelt was offering a warship as requested in a message to the presidents of Nicaragua and El Salvador. Roosevelt offered to cooperate with Mexico in calming down the situation on the frontiers of El Salvador and Guatemala in the sense of withdrawal of forces. Similar assurance was to be given Nicaragua by Presidents Diaz (Mexico) and Roosevelt. The USS *Chicago* was ordered to Amapala.[25]

Because of alleged ill health President Zelaya of Nicaragua did not attend the meeting at Amapala. Instead the foreign ministers of both Nicaragua and El Salvador met and signed on April 23, 1907 a treaty of peace and amity similar to the Marblehead treaty. It included provisions for a Central American Peace Conference in Nicaragua, a special commercial treaty between the two Republics, and acceptance as binding arbitration by the Presidents of Mexico and the United States. If the latter could not agree, they would select a Third Party, whose ruling would be binding. Brown explained that the meeting was held on land at Amapala and not on board the USS *Chicago*, at the request of Nicaragua.[26]

WASHINGTON PEACE CONFERENCE, 1907

By the end of August 1907, events had advanced to the point where a site for the holding of the peace conference became an issue. Nicaragua proposed Mexico City. Others preferred Washington. Eventually, the Minister in Washington of Costa Rica suggested that the five ministers resident in Washington

> under authorization of their respective governments, to conclude a provisional protocol providing for a formal conference to assemble upon the concurrent invitation of the Presidents of Mexico and the United States; for the friendly assistance of representatives of the Presidents of Mexico and the United States at such conference; for the unanimous choice of its place and date of meeting; and for a solemn engagement on the part of the five Central American Republics to mainain a mutually pacific attitude pending such conference. This proposal has been most fortunately carried out by the signature of the projected protocol on the 17th instant (September), in the presence of the Chargé d'Affaires of Mexico and the Acting Secretary of State of the United States of America.[27]

The above quote is from a message to the President of Mexico, dated September 17, 1907, from President Roosevelt.

Agreement was finally reached for the Conference to be held in Washington, to start on November 14, 1907, at 2:30 p.m. The conference facilities were made available in the offices of the Bureau of American Republics, located at 2 Jackson Place, near the White House.

Prior to the conference, Presidents Zelaya (Nicaragua), Figueroa (El Salvador), and Davila (Honduras) met at Amapala on November 6, 1907 "for the purpose of effecting a full settlement of the difficulties pending between Nicaragua and Salvador, which might, if still existing, hinder in some way the success of the conference that will be held in this city (Washington) under the auspices of your excellency's Government, et cet." The communication from the Nicaraguan Minister in Washington to the Secretary of State, dated November 13th, also added "I further have the honor to confirm the intelligence, already made public, of the signing at that meeting of an agreement in which the above-named Presidents Zelaya, Figueroa, and Davila have come to a perfect understanding, and express provisions are made for the adjustment of all differences between the countries governed by them and the calling of a Central America Congress, following the Washington conference, if so agreed to through the adhesion of Guatemala and Costa Rica to the above-mentioned in so far as it relates to said call."[28]

The Amapala session was probably a facesaving device for President Zelaya since the Amapala treaty signed under the shadow of the USS *Chicago* called for a Central American conference in Nicaragua. The agreement under reference left open that possibility after the Washington meeting.

At the start of the conference two important developments occurred. One concerned the proposal for unification submitted by Honduras. Nicaragua favored the Honduran initiative. The Salvadoran representation inclined toward unification in principle but voted against the Honduran proposal. What the Salvadoran stand meant was that they were leery of unification under the circumstances for fear they would be gobbled up by a Honduran-Nicaraguan *Anschluss*. Guatemala, as could also be expected, opposed the project. Costa Rica maintained that "the project was entirely out of order under the terms convening the conference." The vote against inclusion of the unification issue was three to two. The rules adopted for the Washington conference were based on those applied to the Third Pan-American Conference in Rio de Janeiro, 1906. Thus, the majority vote was binding, but recommendations of the minority would be accepted for inclusion in the record.

The other important factor was the motion introduced by Guatemala that "the conference should proceed to draw up the bases for a general treaty of peace, taking the San Jose treaty of September 25, 1906, as a guide." It is thus readily apparent that the end product in the Washington peace effort was the outgrowth or expansion of the earlier peace treaties concluded mainly as the result of local regional initiatives. The influence of the United States was largely in technical and procedural areas, as well as in smoothing ruffled feathers when the conference's atmosphere heated up over sensitive issues. Possibly, U.S. substantive contribution may have been in the arbitration aspects, an approach dear to Secretary Root's heart.

The work of the conference was intensive and wide ranging. In retrospect it would appear that the eight treaties and conventions produced represented rather wistfully the aspirations of all the participants including those of Mexico and the United States, rather than accords designed to deal with the hard facts of reality. Nevertheless, the goals and mechanisms developed were highly admirable and certainly provided additional bases for keeping alive conceptually the idea of Central America as a unique area. For the United States, the effort was an education for the nation's top policymakers in the complexities of the Central American picture. In time, the U.S. experience in Central America would help prepare the United States for the more difficult problem of developing policy or policies for the whole of Latin America.

Specifically, the Washington conference, which lasted from November 13th through December 20th, 1907, produced the following:[29]

1. A general treaty of peace and amity.
2. A convention in addition to the general treaty of peace and amity.
3. A convention for the establishment of a Central American court of justice.
4. A protocol in addition to the convention for the establishment of a Central American court of justice.
5. An extradition convention.
6. A convention for the establishment of an International Central American Bureau.
7. A convention for the establishment of a Central American pedagogical institute.
8. A convention concerning future Central American conferences.
9. A convention* concerning railway communications.

Of special interest to U.S. policy toward Central America, because of hope for bringing stability to the region, were the following features, as summarized by William I. Buchanan of the American Delegation:

1. Its absolutely obligatory character for a period of ten years (Articles I and XIX).
2. The declaration (Article II) that any disposition or measure tending to alter the constitutional organization of either of the Republics shall be deemed a menace to the peace of all.

---

*Actually "Notes" (Authors' Comment).

3. The excellent and in many ways the treaty's most important clause (Article III), making the territory of Honduras neutral in conflicts that arise between the other four Republics, so long as Honduras remains neutral. It will be seen by a reference to a map of Central America that the position occupied by Honduras is such that if this neutrality of Honduran territory is carried out, war between the signatory Republics is practically made impossible.

4. Article VI, by the terms of which all Central Americans are mutually recognized as citizens, a principle embodied in several of their constitutions.

5. The recognition of the right of asylum on ships and the prohibition against taking anyone from such asylum except by due legal process and on order from a competent judge.

6. The provisions of Articles XVI and XVII, by which political refugees and disturbers are not to be allowed to reside near the frontier of either of the five Republics.

7. The unusual obligations assumed in Articles I and II of the convention additional to the treaty, by which each Republic binds itself not to recognize in another a Government resulting from a coup d'etat nor to intervene in favor of or against the existing government of another Republic in cases of disorders therein.

8. The stipulation in Article III of the convention additional to the treaty, by which they agreed to use their efforts to secure constitutional reforms that will prohibit the election of a president for a second term.[30]

From a U.S. viewpoint the most significant aspect of the treaty was the principle embodied in Articles I and II regarding the nonrecognition of the governments coming to power by other than constitutional means. This doctrine is consistent with the principle expressed by Dr. Carlos R. Tobar, an Ecuadorian diplomat and former foreign minister, in 1907 and which had wide repercussions. While Mexico and the United States were not signatories to the pact, they were morally bound to abide by its terms. U.S. recognition doctrine generally was, and still is, based on effective control of its national territory by a government coming into power whether constitutionally or otherwise, and formally acknowledging its nation's international obligations. Because of the Tobar doctrine contained in the pact, the United States altered its recognition doctrine for Central America in order to comply with the treaty's requirement. The practice remained in effect until the convulsions of the 1930s dictated abandonment.[31]

The net effect of the new recognition doctrine was to perpetuate in power regimes wily enough to circumvent in substance, but not in form the constitutional requirement. This may have contributed to stability in the region, but it also hampered the possibility of further internal political maturation.

With respect to the Central American Court of Justice, it is ironic that it was the United States, in an issue subsequently concerning U.S. interest in a canal through Nicaragua, which disregarded the court.

THE TAFT ADMINISTRATION (1909–13)

As stated earlier in this study, U.S. policy announcements are generally lofty and one can say sincerely intended. The problem arises from strategies and tactics, that is implementing measures to reach overall objectives. It is in these phases of U.S. foreign policy that disappointments and frustrations develop, at times with grave consequences. Part of the problem lies in the periodic turnover of power characteristic of the Republic's political system. Successful policies are the result of long periods of maturation, whereas U.S. policymakers hold short-term assignments. Replacements come into power with different ideas reflecting their own experiences and domestic political evolution. U.S. policy in Central America, and for that matter in the Caribbean in general, should be examined against this reality, particularly during the administrations of Presidents Roosevelt, Taft, and Wilson. It was precisely in those years that decisions of principle and practice were taken which affect profoundly current dilemmas for U.S. policy in the Caribbean Basin.

The philosophy of the years prior to the return of the Republican Party to power after Wilson must also be seriously considered. It was an era when nations felt that under international law they could intervene militarily, if need be, to protect their nationals and their investments in foreign countries in times of strife. In the United States the doctrine of economic laissez faire was in general acceptance. U.S. political and economic success was viewed largely as the result of the nation's working democracy made effective through the mechanism of free elections, hard work, and massive investment of capital. Washington's political establishment saw no reasons why the turbulent small republics in the isthmus should not copy the U.S. model and thus reach the nirvana of economic, political, and social blessings.

The fact that these nations originated from distinctive, different roots was not understood as a key factor and impediment to the emulation of their Northern Neighbor. A few U.S. businessmen long familiar with the region knew the score but they were not influential nor were they policymakers. After the absorption of Puerto Rico, a growing number of educated nationals from that island emigrated to New York City. Bilingual, many were drawn naturally into the export trade either as independent merchants, or in the employment of major foreign trade firms. They helped open Latin American markets for U.S. products and were also intimately acquainted with conditions south of the border. But they were not in the political mainstream of U.S. life, and their influence on Department of State thinking was nil.

After achieving independence from Spain, the Latin Americans immediately experienced the beginning of a struggle between those who wished to maintain a social and economic status quo, and those committed to political and economic development. In this sense the characteristics of the conflict paralleled similar developments in Spain, the Mother Country. The contests soon involved the military figures who had fought against Spain and now wanted power as their due. The landed aristocracy and the Catholic Church adopted conservative stances. Intellectuals and businessmen would move in a liberal direction. Military leaders would side at times with the one and on occasion with the other. Violence became the order of the day in Central America in particular, a situation persisting well into the beginning of the present century. A key issue was the belief by the liberals and progressives that economic well-being was possible only through substantial influx of foreign capital and investment. In the last quarter of the past century Central Americans had seen the example of Porfirio Diaz's Mexico, as evidence that prosperity and stability were possible in a Latin American country. Massive U.S. investment and presence seemed to be the answer. Not taken into account was that only a small number of individuals at the top of the social and economic scale benefitted from the progressive push. With 90 percent of the mass of population living in misery, it was only a question of time before Mexico blew its lid.

Alternatively, Central Americans were not adverse to European sources for investment and borrowings. The fact that they might become European colonies if irresponsible governmental behavior resulted in nonpayment of foreign debts was not seen as a probability. Some awkwardness might ensue but they felt somehow matters would work out. Washington on the other hand took a more somber view of European actions. After the decision to build the Panama Canal was taken, U.S. meddling in Central America and the Caribbean became inevitable, if only for security considerations.

The change of administration from Roosevelt to William H. Taft, and from Elihu Root as Secretary of State to Philander C. Knox, in the elections of 1908, signaled a shift, not in basic policy toward Central America but in strategy and tactics. Taft had served as Secretary of War under Roosevelt in 1904–08, and as Governor of the Philippines in 1901. He was thus truly sensitive to the security aspects of the Panama Canal under construction. Knox was a lawyer, as was Root. But he did not appear to have the understanding that Root had acquired about realities in Central America. It is doubtful that Root would ever had countenanced military intervention in any of the Central American Republics except in case of extreme emergency. The evidence seems to point to his belief that in time, with patience on the part of the United States, the Central American countries would mature to the level of expectations established in the Washington treaties of 1907.

Before becoming Secretary of State, Knox had served as counsel to the United States-Nicaragua Concession, "a mining property owned by a Pittsburgh corporation which represented the principal American private capital in the Isthmian republic."[32] While it does not appear that previous connection per se might have influenced Secretary Knox's decisions regarding Nicaragua, it is conceivable that familiarity with the difficulties encountered by the corporation and other foreign firms in dealings with President José Santos Zelaya, President of Nicaragua, may have colored his view of this personality and the environment. Particularly galling must have been Zelaya's wish to cancel the concession given to the U.S. mining corporation to seek a better arrangement. Knox had reviewed the contract agreement while still in private practice.

Regardless of his prior relationship with the mining interest, Knox did not have the patience nor coolness of temperament essential to successfully deal with complex foreign situations. Furthermore, he was of an arbitrary disposition in matters related to diplomacy and lacked completely a background important to foreign policy matters. That he had no sympathy for Latin Americans was well known.[33] This negative attitude comes through in the instructions issued to the U.S. delegation attending the Fourth International Conference of American States in 1910 at Buenos Aires. He not only did not go to the conference, but confined the instructions to purely mechanical approaches. If anything he wound up the instructions with an unusually acerbic reference to the troubles in Central America and Zelaya's role.

Knox's immediate aide for Central American matters was Huntington Wilson, Assistant Secretary of State. Wilson reportedly was considered an able career diplomat. But he had never been south of the border and "like his chief he lacked the tolerant spirit and the genuine liking for Latin Americans that had marked Root's dealings with them."[34]

Zelaya was a thoroughgoing scoundrel. He had come into the Presidency of Nicaragua as a member of the opposing Liberal Party in 1893, following a split among the Conservatives who had governed Nicaragua with moderate stability during the previous 30 years. Zelaya developed a brutal dictatorship corrupt to the hilt. In line with Liberal philosophy of the time he helped develop some improvements in transportation, increased public schools, encouraged the production of coffee, but also handed out concessions and monopolies to friends and foreigners alike with disregard for the welfare of Nicaragua. He was xenophobic, detested foreigners, particularly people from the United States, since he saw the United States as an obstacle to his ambitions for the control of all Central America. As a dictator he probably was no better nor worse than predecessors in the general area of the same ilk. His brutality certainly was matched by his neighbor, President Manuel Estrada Cabrera of Guatemala. In borrowing money from foreign sources he was reckless, a circumstance which eventually contributed to his permanent exit from the Nicaraguan scene.

The point to be made is that while more able than his fellow dictators, his approach represented a philosophy more or less followed by many of his contemporaries not only in Central America but in the southern continent as well. Knox and Wilson in their passionate dislike for Zelaya, who they regarded as the Achilles' heel of the 1907 Washington pacts, considered Zelaya's rule as a unique political system. They did not see "Zelayism" within the context of the general behavior of those Latin American dictators who appeared on the scene with enough ability to stay in power for prolonged periods. This myopia led to U.S. strategy and tactics in Nicaragua which like a Greek tragedy resulted in events that over the years ultimately culminated in the very grave situation in Nicaragua at present.

Knox shared with Roosevelt and Root concern over the security of the canal under construction, and was equally sensitive to the danger of European intervention. He also reflected the Roosevelt-Root worry about the lack of stability in Central America and the Caribbean in general. So much for commonly accepted basic foreign policy considerations in the two administrations. The fundamental difference was in the strategies and tactics followed by both. The Root philosophy of patience and tolerance, with emphasis on the eventual rule of law as determinative in the relations among the Central American States, allowed the incoming Taft administration no such luxury. They left U.S. strategies and tactics locked in a pattern difficult to modify, and in the case of Nicaragua, conducive to potentially disastrous consequences for the United States more than a half century later.

The facts are that while Roosevelt did wield a "big stick" and "soft talk" with respect to the Panama issue, elsewhere in Central America and the Caribbean he merely brandished a light rod and spoke candidly and lucidly. In contrast Knox used a spiked mace in Nicaragua and a mandarin approach. The result was U.S. armed intervention which lasted from 1912 to 1933 (excepting a short interval in 1925); U.S. banks owning majority stock in the country's National Railway; control of the National Bank of Nicaragua; the Customs Collector General post in the hands of U.S. officer

(Colonel Clifford D. Ham, formerly of the Philippines Custom Service); U.S. control of the nation's finances which assured payment of the foreign debt and the meeting of governmental operating expenditures. Little was left for anything else, and public school teachers were frequently unpaid. Successive governments were imposed on Nicaragua representing minority interests, making it impossible for the give and take of politics to even germinate slightly.

If security of the canal was the primary objective, there is no doubt that the Roosevelt–Taft–Wilson behavior succeeded in this objective. But the achievement of internal stability was reached only at the point of a U.S. gun in Nicaragua and fear of gunboats in the neighboring states. Knox believed that a heavy infusion of loans from U.S. bankers would provide the sinews for internal stabilization. This approach proved a failure and even the bankers were pleased to back away from too excessive an involvement. Under the guarantee of Knox's attitude toward the desirability of U.S. investment in the Central American countries, however, there was some increase in this direction to the modest benefit of both the local economies and the U.S. investors.

Knox's decisions weakened greatly the achievements of Secretary Root in connection with the interregional peace framework developed in the Treaties of 1907. Although the United States was not legally bound to the treaties, it recognized a moral obligation toward their implementation. Through U.S. direct action in sponsoring or supporting one side in the Nicaraguan revolution after the ouster of Zelaya, and recognizing a regime that was the obvious result of a nonconstitutional process in defiance of the Nicaraguan majority's sentiments, U.S. insistence with the other Central American States that they abide by the treaties relative to recognition and nonintervention in one another's affairs sounded hollow and hypocritical.

One point must be stressed in connection with the shift in approach from Roosevelt to Taft. It was not subtle nor inevitable. Their strategies and tactics were dramatically different as were the attitudes of Root and Knox. That Taft and Knox were sincere in the belief that stability could be brought about through the infusion of sufficient loans into the area is unquestioned. That they did not have particular sympathy for the banking community on which they drew for implementation of their ideas is equally certain. The use of the dollar loans was viewed by Taft and Knox as means to support U.S. foreign policy and not as a windfall to the lenders. Professor Bemis quite aptly stated 40 years ago: "While not losing sight for one moment of the mistakes of foreign policy in the hands of the blundering Knox and Taft and it is fortunate that the United States did not have to confront under their leadership any major crisis of diplomacy during the years 1909–1913—it is only fair to say that dollar diplomacy was more an easily misusable journalistic alliteration, . . . that easily lent itself to hateful propaganda and exaggerated Yankeephobia, than it was a truthful characterization of the protective foreign policy of the United States."[35] But as Bemis recognizes, Taft and Knox in foreign policy implementation were inept, and one should add unimaginative. It is this kind of zigzag in policy implementation that has been damaging to U.S. national interests.

The details of the evolution of U.S. actions in Nicaragua in the era of "dollar diplomacy" have been examined amply by numerous scholars, congressional hearings, and participants. There is no need to repeat extensively the wearisome facts of the period. What may be helpful is to highlight the phase at which in the authors' belief, the crucial turning point from Root's approach to that of Knox occurred.

Zelaya's excesses eventually caught up with him and what appears to have been a genuinely internally inspired revolution broke out. Zelaya's position was further complicated by the firing squad killing of two U.S. citizens who had furnished dynamiting assistance to the forces in rebellion in the Bluefields area, and who had accepted officer status in the revolutionary group. This event, following vexing and complicated confrontations between the U.S. government and Zelaya concerning private U.S. interests in Nicaragua, was the straw which broke the camel's back. The U.S. government broke diplomatic relations with Zelaya's establishment. The dictator saw the inevitable consequence and took off for Mexico and permanent exile. Power was vested in a member of his own party, Dr. José Madriz, "a distinguished citizen of Leon, who personally was worthy of American recognition and support."[36]

Had Knox been an expert in the ins-and-outs of Central American politics, and had the U.S. diplomatic personnel in Nicaragua been able to rise above their biases, a circumstance which resulted in reports of questionable accuracy, temporary recognition of the Madriz government pending action by a constitutional assembly should have been the U.S. government's reaction. But Knox's obsession with Zelaya as the evil spirit in the region extended to all who had been associated with him. In effect this meant equating "Zelayism" with the Liberal party, and U.S. support at all costs for strategies and tactics designed to avoid a resurgence of the "system" which Zelaya stood for. The fact that Guatemala's Estrada Cabrera was no better appeared to be irrelevant as far as Knox was concerned. The eventual consequences of Knox's attitude have been mentioned. What might have happened if Madriz had been recognized and developments allowed to go their own way without U.S. intervention is of course anybody's guess. In all probability there would not have been a long U.S. military intervention and the country would have evolved more or less in the manner of its neighbors.

WOODROW WILSON PERIOD (1913-21)

In the President Woodrow Wilson era, despite reiteration of his nonintervention policy, the Marines remained in Nicaragua and landed elsewhere in the Caribbean Islands. Wilson intervened directly in Mexican affairs for the purpose of ousting General Victoriano Huerta who had come into power via the revolutionary route, with the U.S. navy in 1914 bombing and occupying Vera Cruz in the process. The occupation was brief. In 1916 he ordered General John J. Pershing to invade Mexico with 5,000 cavalrymen for the purpose of tracking down Mexican revolutionary General Francisco (Pancho) Villa, who had committed depredations on the U.S. side of the border. The memory of President Wilson's interventions in Mexico is still a shadow over the relations between the two nations.

Although consideration of Mexican-U.S. relations are outside the scope of this study, a brief mention must be made of the effect of President Wilson's Mexican policy on the Central American Republics. It aroused old fears of U.S. ambition leading to annexation of Mexico and the republics in the isthmus. For a time all Washington had to do to discourage a potential revolutionist would be to send a warship to the affected area. One other result was to freeze in power regimes that had arrived at the presidencies through questionable means. In short any possible forward movement in terms of democratic evolution was impossible in view of Wilson's perceived proneness to resort to military force.

One development during the Wilsonian period that disturbed the atmosphere of the region was the treaty negotiated in 1916 by Secretary of State William Jennings Bryan and Nicaraguan General Emiliano Chamorro for a U.S. option on the canal route through Nicaragua via Lake Nicaragua and the San Juan River. El Salvador and Costa Rica maintained that Nicaragua could not concede exclusive rights to the San Juan River nor permit the establishment of a U.S. base in the Gulf of Fonseca on which all three abutted. The matter was taken to the Central American Court of Justice, which favored the position taken by El Salvador and Costa Rica, but cautioned that the Court had no jurisdiction over the United States and therefore could not enforce its judgment. The United States ignored the Court's findings and thereby helped destroy an institution which Root had hoped would lead to the rule of reason and law.

4

EVOLUTION OF U.S.-CENTRAL AMERICAN RELATIONS, FROM HARDING TO REAGAN, 1921–84

> Counsel is the sure buttress
> of determination; wars must
> ever be won by statecraft.
>
> Proverbs 20: 18–19

With the end of the Wilson era, the peak was reached for U.S. military intervention in the Central American region, and for that matter the Caribbean. With the return of the Republicans to power and a feeling throughout the nation that danger to the Panama Canal was remote indeed, the Warren Harding administration (1921–23) through Secretary of State Charles E. Hughes initiated the task of trying to find a way to extricate the nation from the various military occupations. The situation in the Caribbean and Central America was roughly as follows.

CUBA

Upon conclusion of the Spanish-American War, the United States military occupied Cuba from 1898 to 1902. The fact that it was the U.S. flag which replaced the hauled down Spanish emblem rankled Cubans who had battled in the jungles against overwhelming Spanish forces. Many had fought in the long ten years war against Spain from 1868 to 1878. They thought U.S. entry into the war meant independence for Cuba, not switching masters. Eventually, as the price for independence, Cuba had to accept the Platt Amendment as a permanent part of the Cuban constitution. It in effect gave the United States veto power over certain aspects of future Cuban foreign relations, foreign loan possibilities, and provided the United States with the right to intervene in the internal affairs of the island to protect life and property, as well as the independence of the new Republic. The Amendment thus established a U.S. protectorate in Cuba. In 1906 internal conflict developed and the President of Cuba, Don Tomas Estrada Palma, asked the United States to intervene.

This led to a military occupation for the period 1906–09. Later in 1917 for a brief period when internal commotion again flared up, President Wilson landed the Marines. Thus, when Secretary of State Hughes began his appraisal of the Caribbean region there was no military occupation in Cuba to be eliminated.

DOMINICAN REPUBLIC AND HAITI

This history of the Dominican Republic has been truly one of tragedy.

Occupied by Haiti from 1822 to 1844 it suffered terrible brutalities. Free in 1844 it underwent long periods of distressing dictatorships. In between it once again became a Spanish colony from 1861–65 and continued to be exposed to misgovernment.

By 1899 the country was indebted heavily to French, Belgian, German, Italian, British, Spanish, and U.S. interests. In default on these foreign debts the danger of European occupation was serious. In 1904 President Roosevelt appointed a customs collector in Puerto Plata and in 1905 a collector for all customs revenues. Under the arrangement, 55 percent went to creditors and 45 percent to the Republic's Treasury. All went fairly well as long as Don Ramon Caceres was president (1908–11), but after his death in 1911 chaos again visited the nation. By 1916 affairs had reached such a state that President Wilson ordered the landing of the Marines. They remained until 1924. The new Republican administration struggled with the problem of how to remove the military presence without Dominican affairs falling apart.

In Haiti anarchy reigned from 1908 to 1915 when President Wilson ordered the Marines to the island. They remained until 1934. One important consideration for the occupation was fear that Germany through merchants of that nationality married to Haitian wives might acquire naval facilities.

Haiti presented a serious problem for the Harding administration's objective of troop removal because by 1915 U.S. private interests controlled Haiti's banking system and railroads. It was feared that too quick a departure would plunge the country again into chaos with heavy U.S. financial loss.

CENTRAL AMERICA

In Central America the Marines were in Nicaragua. There was also the problem left by Wilson of assuaging Costa Rica, still smarting over the Bryan-Chamorro Treaty.

Another problem that arose concerned the possibility in 1922 of

Nicaragua, El Salvador, and Honduras having a go at each other. Faced with the immediate problem of a possible war in Central America involving these three countries, Secretary of State Hughes reverted to Elihu Root's diplomacy. In a move closely resembling that taken by Root when he dispatched the USS *Marblehead* in 1906 to the region to serve as a neutral meeting place for representatives of Guatemala, Honduras, and El Salvador, the Harding administration dispatched the USS *Tacoma* to serve for the same purpose. On August 20, 1922, with the USS *Tacoma* anchored in the Gulf of Fonseca, the presidents of Honduras, El Salvador, and Nicaragua met in the presence of the U.S. ministers accredited to the three countries. The potential conflict stemmed from meddling by the three nations in each other's internal affairs. The conference dissipated the crisis. Several very important consequences resulted from the meeting and an accord the three presidents signed.

They recognized the validity of the 1907 peace treaties, the fabric of which had been severely strained under the impact of local perennially shaky relations and the not too helpful strategies and tactics of Knox in Nicaragua. They settled again on the principle of arbitrating their differences. Nicaragua and El Salvador agreed "to endeavor to secure from their respective governments the granting of free trade in the natural products of their respective States and also in goods therein manufactured from their own raw materials. Whatever may be accomplished on this point shall be by way of experiment and an effort will be made to establish the system of free trade on January 1st of the coming year 1923 for a period of one year."[1]

Again in a repeat performance similar to that which led to the 1907 Washington Peace Conference, in November 1922, the five Central American Republics invited the United States to "designate" delegates to a Conference on Central American Affairs to be held in Washington. Harding appointed Secretary Hughes and Sumner Welles (U.S. Commissioner to the Dominican Republic) as delegates. The emergence of Welles was to have over the years far-reaching consequences for U.S. policy toward Latin America in general. Welles was fluent in Spanish and an expert on the area.

Hughes either as the result of Welles' advice, or as a consequence of his own perceptions, reached the conclusion that a revitalized 1907 Peace Treaty was the most logical approach to the deteriorating situation in Central America. Hence, as in the case of Root he favored strongly the holding of the requested conference for the purpose of focusing on respect for international law and agreements, as the way to peace in the region. Committed personally to disarmament ideals and peace as a concomitant objective through international treaties, he saw the possibility of persuading the Central Americans to develop an arms limitation agreement for themselves during such a conference.

In his speech of welcome Hughes set the tone of the conference by stating:

> You will find here the most friendly atmosphere, the helpful spirit of cooperation, and an intense desire to aid you in the furtherance of your own wishes for an abiding peace and a constantly increasing prosperity. The Government of the United States has no ambition to gratify at your expense, no policy which runs counter to your national aspirations, and no purpose save to promote the interests of peace and to assist you, in such manner as you may welcome, to solve your problems to your own proper advantage. The interest of the United States is found in the peace of this hemisphere and in the conservation of your interests.[2]

He further proposed that the following subjects should be discussed:

1. The negotiation of a treaty or treaties to make effective those provisions of the treaties signed at Washington on December 20, 1907, which experience has shown to be effective in maintaining friendly relations and cooperation among the Central American States.
2. Measures whereby, in view of the achievements accomplished with regard to the limitation of armaments by the Powers participating in the Conference at Washington in 1921, the Central American States may carry on this endeavor and set an example to the world and above all to the powers of this hemisphere, by adopting effective measures for the limitation of armaments in Central America.
3. The working out of a plan for setting up Tribunals of Inquiry whenever any disputes or questions regarding the proposed treaty or treaties, which can not be settled by diplomatic means, shall unfortunately arise between any two or more countries.
4. Any other questions which the countries represented at the conference unanimously desire to consider.[3]

It will be recalled that the flurry arising from the Bryan-Chamorro Treaty with respect to Costa Rica and El Salvador led to United States' disregard for the opinion of the Central American Court of Justice, a circumstance that just about dealt the court's usefulness a coup de grace. The Central American delegates to the new Washington conference were a bit skittish about how to deal with the subject in view of the previous U.S.

position on the matter. Not a man to hide behind subterfuge, and well aware that some such organism was essential to any broad ranging peace treaty as a complementary measure, he introduced the sensitive subject itself:

> With your permission, I desire to emphasize the fact, as the separate treaty establishing the Central American Court of Justice was terminated in 1917, it is most important that adequate provision now be made for appropriate arbitral disposition of controversies and that suitable methods be devised for carrying out the fundamental purpose of existing treaties in securing a basis for a lasting and just accord.[4]

The Conference met between December 4, 1922 and February 7, 1923. It refined the accords of 1907, strengthened the role of the International Central American Tribunal and its responsibilities relative to arbitration, and laid the basis for later agreements which included the United States and all of the Latin American nations. Professor Bemis put it very well:

> These Central American treaties of 1923 were another miniature experiment in inter-American peace and solidarity worked out in a Washington laboratory, this time under the general superintendence of Dr. Hughes, with Mr. Sumner Welles as the trained technician. The new pacts fashioned a regional precedent for the greater continental solidarity that expresses the Latin American policy of the United States today.[5]

Professor Bemis' comment appeared in his book on Latin America and United States policy published in 1943, but his conclusion is as generally valid for 1985, as it was when stated 40 years earlier. The importance of the approach developed in these treaties, the outgrowth of the San Jose treaties of 1906 and the Washington accords of 1907, cannot be overestimated because they offer a formula for the future. Although the peace mechanisms developed in the 1930s engulfed also the Central American states, it may be advisable for the United States, and the Central American nations, to resurrect in principle the 1922–23 approach, as a major step toward calming down the grave situation currently afflicting the States of the isthmus. However, with a difference, the Organization of American States should be brought into the picture.

The Conference produced a General Treaty of Peace and Amity and 12 conventions dealing with the establishment of the International Central American Tribunal; limitation of armaments; the creation of a permanent commission in each State for matters related to finance and another to means of communication; extradition; preparation of projects of electoral legislation; protective laws for workmen and laborers; experimental stations for agriculture and animal industries; reciprocal exchange of Central American students; practice of the liberal professions in all five republics; convention between Guatemala, El Salvador, Honduras, and Nicaragua regarding free trade; and agreement between the United States and the five republics for the establishment of international commissions of inquiry.

With respect to the General Treaty, its most significant feature was retention of the Tobar Doctrine in a still tighter form. Not only should recognition of governments arriving at power be withheld, but relatives and certain persons connected with those in power were excluded from aspiring to the presidencies. The United States, while continuing to recognize *de facto* governments elsewhere, adhered to the Tobar principle with respect to Central America until the political explosions of the 1930s led to abandonment of the Tobar practice by all.[6]

To deflate the possibility that Costa Rica might take advantage of the facilities in the new arbitration arrangements and place the United States in an awkward position concerning its complaint about the Bryan-Chamorro Treaty, the United States in 1923 signed a protocol with Costa Rica disposing of the issue. In effect the United States agreed to negotiate with Costa Rica regarding its rights on the San Juan River, and other areas which might be affected, before building a new canal across Nicaragua.

With further reference to the General Treaty and the narrowed provisions of the Tobar Doctrine, Professor Lester D. Langely has perceptively pointed out that:

> In retrospect, the stipulations of the 1923 treaties appear unnecessarily severe. As imperfect as the 1907 arrangement had been, it had not served to exclude political aspirants trained with a revolutionary background. The 1923 accord, it could be argued, placed such severe restrictions on the political participation of former revolutionaries (and their kin) as to perpetuate regimes in power and to virtually eliminate a truly popular political figure denied power because the encumbent ran a fraudulent election. When the system came apart, as astute observers of the Central American scene knew it would, the United States became more willing to accept authoritarian, personal rule which provided continuity and political stability as the alternative to political disarray.[7]

That the General Treaty failed over the years to resolve the ever present problem of internal political instability in the region is unquestionable, but it did contribute to the prevention of out-and-out war among the nations of the region.

The 1923 accords were soon put to a test. In Honduras a grave internal conflict developed. Following a period of administrative chaos, a new National Party emerged designed to resolve the internal mess through a national unity effort. The candidate of the newly formed political organization in 1923 won a plurality in the presidential elections, but through parliamentary tactics in the Honduran congress the opposition was able to thwart his taking office and violence followed. In addition matters were complicated by an overwhelming debt owed British bondholders well beyond the capability of Honduras to meet.

For the U.S. government the event posed a series of dilemmas both juridical and practical. If not strictly to the letter of the law, at least in spirit and principle, the opponents of winner Tiburcio Carias Andino had provoked a grave Honduran constitutional crisis. On the other hand, while the United States was attempting to move away from the practice of military occupation as a means of insuring internal stability and debt paying mechanisms, the principle of intervention had not been abandoned.

As late as 1928 intervention was the key issue at the Sixth International Conference of American States held at Havana and attended for its opening by President Calvin Coolidge. The United States fought hard to defend this right. In this respect it is interesting to note that with regard to a proposed convention dealing with the "rights and duties of states in the event of civil strife" proposed at Havana, and included as Appendix 15, in the official Report of the U.S. delegation to Secretary of State Frank B. Kellogg, there was no reference to any reservations by the U.S. group. The gist of the convention called for a hands-off posture by all signatories in the event of civil war or strife in any of the states. The U.S. delegation finessed the issue in its Report to Kellogg by making no reference to the U.S. position, knowing that the Convention would not be binding on the United States until submitted to the U.S. constitutional process.[8] But everybody knew that in the committee sessions the arguments on this point had been sharp.

Fortunately, the United States was able to draw on the services of Sumner Welles who had emerged as the Department of State's able trouble-shooter. With the help of the USS *Milwaukee* as his headquarters in the port of Amapala and another ship cruising off the Caribbean side, by early spring in 1924 Welles had mediated successfully between the warring factions. The Marines were landed but only briefly. Not long after, an arrangement was made for the debt problem which scaled down dramatically the figure to one within Honduran capabilities.

The Honduran episode highlighted the contrast between strategies and tactics characteristic of the Taft and Wilson eras, which tended to trigger quick U.S. military intervention and occupation to insure stability and to solve debt collection problems, with those of the Coolidge years. The overall objective was the same, namely, stability in the region, and in regard to Honduras, preservation of its neutrality in the face of intraregional bickering.

However, there were other reasons for the difference in approach. As mentioned earlier, in the aftermath of World War I a threat to the Panama Canal seemed an extremely remote possibility. Likewise a terribly weakened Europe was in no position or mood to intervene in any country militarily solely for the purpose of collecting old debts. Hence, the Roosevelt Corollary was well on the way to obsolescence. U.S. public and official perceptions of Latin American policy were moving quickly to concern for all of South America, and not just the Caribbean and Central America. World War I had also widened enormously the horizons of many U.S. citizens who had served in the army abroad or in an official capacity. It was becoming more difficult for the nation's political leadership to take foreign policy decisions and actions without convincing the public about the wisdom of their acts.

It was also an era when U.S. people in unprecedented numbers were enjoying great prosperity and released tensions from the war period. There was a yearning for the "good old days" of isolationism. The reminder of U.S. troops in Nicaragua, Dominican Republic, and Haiti was distasteful.

Within the Harding–Coolidge administrations there was a general feeling of "let things well enough alone" unless it was the pursuit of international disarmament and general peace agreements. Thus, when the Honduran crisis emerged the attitude in the White House and Department of State appeared to be one of "get it over with" as quickly as possible and with minimum complications. The fact that an expert of Sumner Welles' caliber could be pressed into service and would be given a free hand to resolve the issue proved the decisive factor. In the Taft–Knox and Wilson–Bryan years formulation and implementation of foreign policy was actually in their hands. None had any previous direct experience either in diplomacy or in Central America, nor were they apparently willing or disposed to rely on someone with the background for the task of dealing with the issues south of the border.

The immediate problems after conclusion of the 1923 Central American Conference, other than the cited Honduran episode and the satisfying of Costa Rica's San Juan River concerns, was how to remove the U.S. troops from the Dominican Republic, Haiti, and Nicaragua. As the

United States gradually edged away from a Caribbean and Central American focused policy toward concerns for all of South America, the troop presences proved increasingly embarrassing. U.S. officials could not possibly continue announcing a U.S. noninterference dogma while maintaining protectorates in the Caribbean, Central America, and of course Panama.

By 1924 Welles had worked out a plan with the Dominican leaders whereby the U.S. military force departed, but a customs receivership in existence since Roosevelt's administration was left. This arrangement continued until 1941. It was hoped that the U.S. trained constabulary could maintain internal law and order.

With regard to Haiti, U.S. press reports referred to abuses by the U.S. military forces, and in 1920 a congressional investigation followed. The net result was a reform in the manner of the occupation, not evacuation. The U.S. forces remained but a High Commissioner from the Department of State was appointed with full authority. Although some material progress had been achieved and the country's debt considerably reduced, by the end of the Coolidge administration the troops were still there. Internally, attempts to develop political and economic maturation were a dismal failure. If anything, prospects were more dreary than they had looked in 1915 when Wilson ordered the troops to occupy the country. By 1929 the situation had become intolerable as the result of internal dissensions and tensions between the U.S. civilian and military, aggravated later by the effects of the Great Depression, complicated by the outbreak of public disorders.

President Herbert Hoover who had succeeded Coolidge in 1929 requested Cameron Forbes, at one time governor of the Philippines, to lead a commission to Haiti and examine the situation. The consequence of the Forbes mission was preparation for evacuation. But it was not until 1934 that the last Marine left Haiti, already in President Franklin Roosevelt's era. However, the decision to leave was made in Hoover's day and it was accidental that it could not be achieved until the Roosevelt administration assumed power. But, as Professor Langely states: "The financial protectorate lived on until the last bonds of indebtedness were retired after World War II."[9]

The military occupation of Haiti had kept foreign powers out, achieved some financial stability at the expense of internal growth and modest infrastructural improvement. But otherwise it was a disaster.

With respect to Nicaragua, the Coolidge administration believed that the small military presence in Nicaragua could be terminated. The nation's finances were in reasonably good shape and internal stability appeared to be at last a reality. In the elections of 1925 Carlos Solorzano of the

Conservatives, the party long favored by the United States, and political heir of Bartolome Martinez, president from 1923 to 1925 (who did not hold free elections), retained power. The Marines departed.

It was not long before revolution again was the order of the day, with the Mexicans involved in supplying arms to one of the warring factions. This disturbed Washington which feared a spread of Mexico's antiforeign revolution into Nicaragua with severe detriment to U.S. holdings in the country. Hence, mediation by the United States followed, and the Marines were back in 1926. This time they remained until January 1933. In the interim a national constabulary was organized and trained by the United States, the head of which, General Anastasio Somoza, eventually became president and founder of the Somoza dynasty which ruled Nicaragua directly or indirectly from 1936 to 1979.

The participation of General Augusto Cesar Sandino in Nicaragua's history came about in this fashion. During the 1926 revolution when the Marines returned, Sandino considered the agreement worked out at Tipitapa by Colonel Henry Stimson in May 1927 as unacceptable even though temporary. He had favored the Liberal cause and had received some arms from General José Maria Moncada of the Liberal group. When the call was made for the surrender by Moncada's troops of their rifles for $10 each, in line with the accord developed between General Moncada and Stimson so that a national constabulary could be formed, Sandino considered the act treacherous and took to the hills. Moncada's constabulary or national guard as it became known and the Marines literally chased the guerrilla leader and his band all over Nicaragua, without ever catching him.

After the U.S. forces had definitively departed, Sandino worried about a possible coup d'etat by General Anastasio Somoza, commander by this time of the national guard, against liberal President Sacasa, and returned to Managua to discuss this issue with the latter. Sacasa, the first Liberal to return to the presidency since Knox engineered their exclusion from power, had been elected in the Marine supervised elections of 1932. Sandino, who asserted that his only interest in maintaining alive his guerrilla movement was the elimination of the U.S. military presence, felt his job was done and wished to arrange for his group to lay down their arms. But, after dining with Sacasa and other prominent Nicaraguans, he was arrested by the national guard as he left the party, taken out to the Managua airstrip, and assassinated in cold blood.

Sandino's hold on the imagination of the Nicaraguan masses stems from the fact of never having been caught. He proved that a guerrilla movement could successfully defy a powerful modern military force, establishing a precedent of considerable importance for the future. Another factor stemmed from the ideals held by Sandino. He had worked for some time in Mexico during the period of revolutionary fervor in the 1920s when new concepts for social reform in that country accompanied by strident antiforeign actions and campaigns were at their peak. Impressed, Sandino brought these ideas with him to Nicaragua. Hence, in the uprising of 1926 against the Conservatives in favor of liberal Sacasa (supported diplomatically by Mexico including with arms shipments) in which Sandino also took part, he was not just another politico looking for personal advantage. He probably was the only idealist among the leaders in the revolutionary camp, a matter of worry to General Moncada who originally had furnished arms to Sandino. It was not surprising when later, after the U.S. organized and trained constabulary came into being with Moncada at its head, and the revolution was over, that he pursued Sandino who had refused to stop fighting. In short, he could not be bought, and his stand against the social order of the day was regarded by both the Nicaraguan governmental establishment and U.S. private and official interests as most undesirable and threatening.

One of the problems confronting the Coolidge administration as it edged away from a policy committed to military intervention was the matter of the Roosevelt Corollary. The Taft–Wilson actions had been based on the doctrine represented in the Corollary. It was awkward for the Coolidge administration to be pressing for peace pacts and support for nonintervention while it was generally accepted that U.S. policy in the Caribbean and Central America rested on the Corollary to the Monroe Doctrine.

In a brilliant move Kellogg charged Undersecretary of State J. Reuben Clark, Jr. to study the issue from the viewpoint of legitimacy of the Corollary as derivative of the Monroe Doctrine. On December 17, 1928, Reuben transmitted to Kellogg his *Memorandum on the Monroe Doctrine*. In an oft quoted extract from the Memorandum, Reuben stated that "it is not believed that this corollary is justified by the terms of the Monroe Doctrine, however much it may be justified by the doctrine of self-preservation." However, although rejecting the Corollary, the right of intervention was retained. Nevertheless, the interpretation moved the U.S. government one step further in the direction of renunciation of intervention as a basic policy instrument. The burying of the Corollary also made it more comfortable for Kellogg to press in 1929 for various inter-American treaties concerned with arbitration and peaceful resolution of differences.

Under President Herbert Hoover (1929–33) and his Secretary of State Henry L. Stimson, the basis for better relations with Latin America was expanded. The significance for the Caribbean and Central America of the broadened horizons for U.S. policy concerned the gradual elimination of regard for the region as something distinctly apart from overall Latin

American considerations. Hoover and Stimson must have suspected that it was only a matter of time before the Latin American desire for a promise of nonintervention by the United States in their affairs would be accepted. Hence, relations with the Caribbean Islands and the Central American States had somehow to be developed in a fashion that would permit U.S. policy to be applied to all alike. Hoover came close to achieving this objective, but it was left to the Roosevelt administration to provide the capstone.

What Hoover and Stimson had in mind was made very clear in a speech delivered by Secretary Stimson in New York City before the Council on Foreign Relations, February 6, 1931. Stimson stated:

> As a background for this discussion a brief review of the general policy of the United States towards the other republics of this hemisphere during the past century is pertinent. That policy, in its general conception, has been a noble one. From the beginning we have made the preservation of individual independence of these nations corres- pond with our own interest. This was announced in the Monroe Doctrine and has been maintained ever since. That doctrine, far from being an assertion of suzerainty over our sister republics, was an assertion of their individual rights as independent nations. It declared to the world that this independence was so vital to our own safety that we would be willing to fight for it against an aggressive Europe. The Monroe Doctrine was a declaration of the United States versus Europe . . . not of the United States versus Latin America.

The implication of Stimson's statement was a formal renunciation of the Roosevelt Corollary, or rather a reiteration of the renunciation. It left the Monroe Doctrine to stand on its own stripped of any amendment.

Hoover and Stimson furthermore understood the complexities in- volved in trying to help nations of a different cultural setting develop effective self-government. In this respect, in the same speech Stimson stated:

> The hundred years which have ensued since the announcement of our policy towards these republics [Latin American] have contained recurring evidence of how slow is the progress of mankind along that difficult highway which leads to national maturity and how difficult is the art of popular self-government. Years and decades of altercations between arbitrary power at one time and outbreaks of violence at another have pointed out time and again how different a matter it is in human affairs to have the vision and to achieve the reality.

While Hoover and Stimson groped toward setting the basis for what eventually became officially known as the "Good Neighbor" policy, a grave situation developed in Cuba putting to an acute test the evolving American policy of the United States. In view of the Platt Amendment the United States had the right to land military forces in the island and "set things to right." Certainly the situation in Cuba was degenerating into chaos, and there was no doubt of threat to U.S. lives and property. By 1931 the government of strongman President Gerardo Machada had become desperate and despotic. The Great Depression with its serious adverse impact on the price of sugar had plunged the island into economic catastrophe. A condition developed of the kind that the Platt Amendment had been formulated precisely to deal with. Consistent with the non-intervention thrust of Hoover's government, other than precautionary steps to provide for the evacuation of U.S. citizens if such should become necessary, Cubans were allowed to stew in their juice.

THE GOOD NEIGHBOR POLICY

Almost immediately after his inauguration, President Franklin D. Roosevelt (1933–45) found the extremely serious Cuban problem on his doorstep. With the collapse of sugar prices the island was in desperate economic straits. Since 1931 the University of Havana had been closed by President Machado, and all of the country's public secondary school students were on strike. Forty to fifty bombs exploded per night throughout Havana. With thousands of teenagers and university students idle and nurturing a profound hatred toward the regime, in addition to some 500 now unemployed faculty members, they meshed with professional politicians in various new political parties for the purpose of totally destroying the Machado government. Every night Machado's thugs, known as *la Porra*, would assassinate some militant leader of the opposition, usually a student. The latter would retaliate by killing someone in the establishment's security forces, or closely connected with the regime. The situation was terribly violent and aggravated by practically a standstill in the business world. The government was unable to meet payments due U.S. banks on loans made several years before for extensive public works developments, such as the national capital and the construction of a road from Havana, through the center of Cuba, to Santiago in Oriente Province at the other end of the island.

Some of the politicians were hopeful that there would be U.S. military intervention which would result in the ouster of Machado and the rebuilding of the political system, each desiring that opponents would be ruined in the process. Matters had gone beyond the capability of U.S. Ambassador Harry F. Guggenheim to understand and offer decisive advice to a hesitant Department of State. U.S. investments in Cuba were very considerable, in fact the largest in Latin America.

With the change of administrations from Hoover to Roosevelt, Guggenheim departed. Roosevelt turned to his old friend from Groton days, the able and experienced diplomat Sumner Welles. Welles was assigned to Havana as ambassador amid a great deal of anxious speculation in the island about who Guggenheim's successor would be. Also, would the Marines land again?

Roosevelt, however, had long been critical of military interventions in the Caribbean and he was determined moreover to develop a Latin American policy applicable to the entire area south of the Rio Grande. The Seventh International Conference of American States soon was forthcoming in Montevideo. The issue of nonintervention which Hughes had been able to finesse so skillfully at the Havana conference in 1928 would be high on the schedule. He was not about to jeopardize the basic new position he wished to develop for the United States in Latin America by a military landing in Cuba for the sole purpose of stopping the squabble in the political arena. Nor for that matter did he appear to harbor any intent to protect U.S. investments through the use of force. If U.S. citizens for their safety would have to be evacuated and Marines used to safeguard such an action, all well and good. In fact there was a time during the prolonged crisis when the U.S. Embassy advised local U.S. citizens about the possibility of evacuation. But there would be no landings for the purpose of political objectives.

As expert as Welles was in Latin American affairs and in dealing with South American and Caribbean statesmen and politicians, the Cuban mess escaped his grasp and understanding. He was able eventually to provoke the departure of Machado. But he was wholly unprepared for the bewildering sequence of events which included three presidents and a "pentarchy" between August 1933 and January 16, 1934, with one lasting only 24 hours, another with a sharply radical twist but frightfully inefficient, and an army mutiny staged by sergeants which ousted all of the commissioned officers. The latter holed themselves up in the Hotel Nacional, the finest in Havana, only to have the army led by Sergeant Fulgencio Batista bomb them into surrender. In time Batista promoted himself to Colonel and his fellow sergeants to commissioned officers and emerged as the only power capable of stabilizing the situation. Out of the chaos, Batista settled on a respected veteran of the War of Independence of 1895 and experienced politician, Colonel Carlos Mendieta, as president. The United States recognized Mendieta's administration without worrying about constitutional requirements and Welles departed for Washington. Mendieta lasted only from January 17, 1934 to May 1936, when he was followed in rapid succession by two more presidents. Finally, Batista settled on a pliant personality, Federico Laredo Bru who served from December 24, 1936 until 1940, when Batista became president for the period 1940–44. The uselessness of the Platt Amendment became apparent under the emerging Doctrine of Nonintervention and was repealed in 1934, ending the U.S. protectorate over Cuba.

The damage done by the Machado government to Cuba and its future was incalculable. By having closed the university for several years, and with the secondary schools also out of operation because of the students' strikes, an entire generation of Cubans was politicized and imbued with deep questioning of the general order of society. Many who served considerable time in prison became highly radicalized, some emerging many years later as officials in Fidel Castro's Marxist government. But regardless of the cynicism which most acquired from the excitement and ordeal of the Machado period, they also emerged with highly nationalistic sentiments, a fact never fully grasped by the Department of State until Castro capitalized on the events of a quarter of a century earlier.

In Central America serious changes were also taking place, partly as the result of the effects of the Great Depression and partly from purely internal political causes. An era of "strongmen" had begun, with Maximiliano Hernández Martínez in El Salvador (1931–44), Tiburcio Carias Andino in Honduras (1933–49), Anastasio Somoza Garcia (1937–56) in Nicaragua, and Jorge Ubico in Guatemala (1931–44). Costa Rica matured rapidly politically within the framework of a genuine democracy which reflected stability. With "strongmen" Batista and Trujillo in control respectively in Cuba and the Dominican Republic, and Haiti left to its own devices, Roosevelt could move quickly toward the development of his hemispheric policy and approach. The problem of acute instability in Central America and the Caribbean had eased markedly from Washington's viewpoint.

Of considerable importance for the future policy of the United States in Central America was withdrawal from the General Treaty of Peace and Amity of 1923 by El Salvador and Costa Rica in 1934. This development released the United States from the moral obligation of nonrecognition in cases where a government came into being through revolution, and in violation of constitutional process. Thus, the policy in effect for Central America since the treaty of 1907, and applied by Wilson in his effort to unseat Huerta in Mexico, lapsed into oblivion and with it the Tobar Doctrine. From that point on the United States would be free to recognize any government should it desire to do so regardless of origin. Abandonment of the special policy for Central America permitted a uniform approach to the recognition issues throughout the world. With the nonrenewal of the 1923 General Treaty of Peace and Amity, for all practical intent, the special situation of the United States and Central

America ended. U.S. attitudes in the future would be conditioned by hemispheric considerations. Furthermore, by 1936 the United States also had ended its de jure protectorate status in Panama, reinforcing commitment to the Doctrine of Noninterference. And in the crisis with Mexico over the expropriation of U.S. oil company properties in 1938, Roosevelt supported Sumner Welles' advocacy for nonintervention and acceptance of the principle (in that situation) of Mexico's right to such an action provided fair compensation was given the affected parties. The oil companies were unhappy with the solution but the storm blew over.

In the Seventh International Conference of American States, 1933, held in Montevideo and attended by Secretary of State Cordell Hull, the issue of nonintervention loomed high on the agenda, as a carryover from the Conference at Havana in 1928.

It was also at Montevideo where Hull launched his concept of the reciprocity trade agreements program, softening the excessively high Smoot-Mawley tariff of 1930, which had warmed Latin American trade with the United States.

The nonintervention matter came up as Article 8 of the proposed Convention of Rights and Duties of States which stated that "No state has the right to intervene in the internal or external affairs of another." Hull accepted the measure but quite correctly with some reservation because of the need to clarify the precise scope of the commitment.

In the reservation attached to the Convention as part of Article 8 reflecting the U.S. position, Hull included this reasoning: "I feel safe in undertaking to say that under our support of the general principle of nonintervention as has been suggested, no government need fear any intervention on the part of the United States under the Roosevelt Administration. I think it unfortunate that during the brief period of this Conference there is apparently not time within which to prepare interpretations and definitions of those fundamental terms that are embraced in the report. Such definitions and interpretations would enable every government to proceed in a uniform way without any difference of opinion or of interpretations." The Senate approved the U.S. commitment to the Convention with the Hull reservation.

With the nonintervention matter out of the way Roosevelt could press forward for tighter hemispheric solidarity. In his long advocacy for nonintervention Roosevelt also believed, with true quid pro quo reasoning, that when law and order broke down in an individual country and created a situation affecting others the matter then became the concern of the whole continent.[10] It was this kind of thinking that influenced subsequent U.S. efforts, both during World War II and afterward, in pursuing cooperation within the Organization of American States or with Latin American States as a group, often in dealing with developments affecting U.S. opinion and hemispheric security.

The issue of nonintervention requires further comment. Secretary Hull interposed reservations to the U.S. acquiescence to Article 8. In contrast the Latin American delegates approved the Article without reservations amidst considerable enthusiasm. The problem was that noninterference from Roosevelt's viewpoint appeared to refer only to military operations. If accepted without qualifications, those desiring to embarrass the United States in future unforeseen situations, could claim that recognition or nonrecognition of a revolutionary state signified interference in the internal affairs of an independent nation. In fact there are indications at times by Latin American jurists that such action by the United States constituted indirect intervention. Aid programs, shipment of military supplies either on a grant basis or sold for cash, cultural exchanges, visits by military or economic missions, presidential visits, official and private loans conceivably could all be interpreted as interventionist issues.

Subsequently, at the Ninth International Conference of American States held at Bogota, Colombia, March 30–May 2, 1948, the Organization of American States was established. The issue of nonintervention arose again and is covered in the Organization of American States (OAS) Charter. Of special interest in this regard are the comments included in the *Report of the Delegation of the United States of America With Related Documents*, Department of State, Publication 3263, released in November 1948. The Report explained in reference to Chapter III, *Fundamental Rights and Duties of States*, concerning which there was considerable discussion in the drafting committee in the sections dealing with nonintervention, that:

> It was recognized that the principle of nonintervention must not be permitted to prevent the international community from discharging its functions of maintaining international peace. Of the two methods of assuring this—one of rephrasing the principle of nonintervention and the other of excepting from its operation action by the international community—the Conference chose the latter. Indeed, in including the principle of nonintervention in Article 15, the drafters apparently made a more sweeping statement than previously. It reads:

> No state or group of states has the right to intervene, directly or indirectly, for any reason whatever, in the internal or external affairs of any other state. The foregoing principle prohibits not only armed force but also any other form of interference or attempted threat against the personality of the state or against its political, economic and cultural elements.

> This differs in two respects from previous statements: 1. it refers to action by a 'group of states' as well as by one state; and 2. it includes the

additional sentence referring to interference or threats against the state. This addition it was pointed out by its proponents had a universal significance and was a reaction to fear of types of indirect aggression such as those to which certain Eastern European countries have been subjected. Although the statement of principle is broad, the exception is also broad. It reads:

> Measures adopted for the maintenance of peace and security in accordance with existing treaties do not constitute a violation of the principles set forth in articles 17 and 18 (Article 19).

> Article 17 relates to the inviolability of the territory of a state, and the phrase, 'existing treaties,' appearing in Article 18, has particular reference to the United Nations Charter and the inter-American treaty of reciprocal assistance. (Latter developed at Rio de Janeiro in 1947)*[11]

As is apparent from the text of the Articles quoted and the discussion in the report, the matter of close definition of what actually constitutes intervention is still a matter of subjective judgment. International jurists are yet in quest of a definition or definitions capable of earning the support of all states. The matter is complicated further by virtue of the fact that the United Nations is also concerned with the general issue.

Essentially, Article 15, because of its lack of specifics other than an undefined reference to the use of force, is a declaration or commitment to a principle, which taken in conjunction with the cited exception does not necessarily preclude an American state or group of states, or the Organization of American States itself, from taking whatever actions are necessary if national or group security becomes a crucial issue. The example of the Dominican Republic giving itself away to Spain in 1861–65 is a reminder that given a peculiar set of circumstances a weak and driven American republic could do so again to another extracontinental power, raising a serious security threat for the hemisphere, a group of nations, or even only one.

From the discussions at Bogota, it was clear that the concerns of the Latin American nations and those of the United States differed greatly with regard to the role of the newly created Organization of American States (OAS). The primary interest of the United States was continental security, particularly with respect to communist threats and aggression, internal or external. Of considerably lower priority were economic assistance and trade matters. With respect to the Latin Americans, their views were the exact reverse with the added factor of seeing in the OAS an instrument which would inhibit, they hoped, U.S. unilateral intervention in their internal affairs.

---

*(Authors' clarification).

Early adoption by the Franklin D. Roosevelt administration of the nonintervention doctrine was in effect a switch from the Monroe Doctrine of unilateral defense, to one of collective security. Adoption by the United States of the OAS Charter buried the Monroe Doctrine, seemingly. But the spirit of the latter refused to be exorcised. Thus, when a situation arises in which the United States perceives a potential or actual communist threat to itself or continental security, it has taken unilateral action and at some point endeavored to bring the OAS into the picture (i.e., Dominican Republic, 1965). However, an example of prompt OAS-U.S. coordination concerned the January 1955 incident involving an attempt by Nicaragua's Somoza to unseat President José Figueres of Costa Rica, considered an enemy by the Caribbean area dictators of the day. Figueres appealed to the OAS, and the latter energetically responded with the United States selling immediately some fighting planes to Costa Rica. The U.S. action signaled to Somoza that the United States would not support his effort and the issue finished quickly.

Although the OAS is a matter of continental importance and not specifically related to a subregional grouping such as the Central American States, it can be very helpful to U.S. diplomacy in connection with perennial intraregional squalls in the Caribbean Basin. Particularly in Central America with the region's penchant for truce and treaty diplomacy, the OAS, if drawn into problems early and with skill, can be the means of averting the escalation of crises. This reasoning lies behind our detailed discussion of truce and treaty diplomacy in Central America and the emergence of the OAS, rather than a study of the historical aspects of events in this area per se. However, it should be recognized that when situations occur in which the state of the continent reflects grave internal political schisms, the efficacy of the OAS might be called in question. It might not be possible to obtain the degree of consensus essential for effective action.

It is beyond the scope of this book to review the multitude of issues which have arisen in the post-World War II period in the Caribbean Basin, and their possible nexus with the many general inter-American Special Conferences held during those years, as well as the periodic meetings of foreign ministers, and the Regular General Assembly Sessions of the OAS. But, underlying all of these meetings are the fundamental differences already mentioned regarding the respective priorities of the United States and the Latin American nations. These divergent stances are not likely to change in the foreseeable future based on the record of the past 35 years or so. In this respect, it is difficult to see what role the OAS could have played, for example, either in persuading President Fulgencio Batista of Cuba in the latter part of his regime to restore democracy, or later to stop Dr. Fidel Castro in the early stage of his regime.

After weathering the political upheavals of the 1930s, U.S. policy in the Caribbean and Central America settled generally into one dominated by normal trade relations, and traditional diplomatic and consular functions. With the entry of the United States into World War II, the islands in the Caribbean and the nations of Central America followed suit. They subscribed to the various inter-American defense pacts. They also cooperated with the United States in intelligence coordination, mainly with officers of the FBI assigned to Embassies throughout Latin America as Legal Attaches. U.S. military missions were in frequent contact with their counterparts in the Basin as concern for the safety of the Panama Canal heightened. Airport facilities in some of the countries were improved. Near Havana an important airbase was constructed, which later, after the war, was turned entirely over to the Cuban government. Business activity increased considerably as the United States became the source of goods, materials, equipment, and essentials that could no longer be supplied from Europe. U.S. purchases of the area's exports also augmented sharply in order to meet the demands of the U.S. wartime economy.

By the war's end the region's economies were closely tied to the United States'. Their financial position in general was healthy. Unable to buy in the United States to the extent that favorable trade balances permitted, all the countries in the Basin underwent inflation but with substantial dollar reserves on hand. However, as Professor Langely has pointed out, purchasing power did not actually increase.[12] One other important consequence of the war, in the region, was the close contact established with Jamaica and other British possessions as the result of the presence of U.S. military personnel manning bases acquired in the 1940 destroyer deal with Great Britain. At times there would be tension between the U.S. military and island nationals, the easing of which depended upon the quality of the commanding officers and their understanding of a foreign culture. But these were not usually grave. The local economies as a whole benefitted from the official U.S. government expenditures, and from those of U.S. soldiers assigned to a particular base. Contact between the two cultures, however, influenced local levels of postwar aspirations both materially and politically.

Through President Harry F. Truman's administration there was little U.S. government interest in Central America and the island republics, nor for that matter in the British colonies which obviously were headed for independence. Europe and its revitalization through the Marshall Plan, the Cold War, the incipient problems in the Middle East, the problem of China, Korea, and the redirection of the U.S. economy were the key concerns at the time. The Caribbean Basin nations, in common with the other Latin American states, were deeply disturbed that the United States had no plans for their economic health and prospects. They resented that vast sums were being poured elsewhere leaving them out of the mainstream.

They had reasons to worry because of the great international trade dislocation which followed World War II, and the effects on terms of trade. Particularly concerned were the Central American nations and the Caribbean islands because of their dependence on one, two, or three export crops for their foreign exchange earnings. Small price declines for these commodities like sugar and coffee had serious adverse effects on the domestic economies as income would also decrease reducing resources necessary to cover much needed imports.

In the late 1930s, the war years, and in the immediate postwar period, industry and commerce had gradually expanded throughout the Caribbean giving rise to a greatly increased urban middle class, growth in the numbers of professionals, development of sophisticated labor unions which included able communist leaders (especially in Guatemala and Cuba), large numbers of increasingly radicalized university youths for whom there were no jobs in the offing, and army officers acquiring better education and a sense of social concerns. The lack of foresight by the U.S. government in planning to work with the Caribbean Basin governments to cope with the consequences of these developments left the issues entirely in local hands. But, the Caribbean economies had become so tightly dependent on the U.S. market, that it was impossible for the governments of the region to solve the growing problems by themselves. A cushion of some kind was necessary so that these nations could stabilize their economies when export commodity prices dropped. In fact throughout the years there has been a relationship between political upheavals and the movement of export prices when these showed substantial declines, more about which will be said in Chapter 5.

Despite his recognition of the fact that not enough attention had been devoted to Latin America, the reason for which Dr. Milton Eisenhower was requested to survey the situation first hand, President Dwight D. Eisenhower's years from 1952 to 1957 reflected little interest in events south of the border. An exception was the dislodgment in Guatemala of the Jacabo Arbenz Guzman government which had become quite permeated with able communists.

The background of the Guatemalan episode can be recounted briefly. In the elections in Guatemala, in the summer of 1950, Jacobo Arbenz Guzman, Defense Minister in the left leaning government of Juan José Arevalo whose term was up in 1951 after governing since 1945, won a substantial majority over his nearest opponent. There was no question about the legitimacy of the election even if life was made more difficult for Arbenz's opponent Miguel Ydigoras Fuentes, who had to go into hiding as the result of an arrest order by Arevalo's government. So, that while the election's validity was never an issue, it was by no means a free expression of the popular will. Nevertheless, observers believe Arbenz would have won handily in any event over conservative Miguel Ydigoras Fuentes.

Once in power Arbenz moved quickly in the direction of close relations with the Soviet Union and the bloc. His government became infiltrated by communists, at the expense of moderates and other noncommunists. Conservatives were greatly harrassed, imprisoned, and tortured. Additionally, they were a prime target for expropriating properties owned by the United Fruit Company. The labor unions had already become completely communist controlled in the previous Arevalo administration.

The arrival of a shipload of arms from Czechoslovakia greatly disturbed Washington and the latter reacted. Some 300 to 500 rebels operating from Honduras and Nicaragua under General Carlos Castillo Armas invaded Guatemala on June 18, 1954. The Guatemalan army, 6,000 strong, interposed no opposition, which leads one to believe that the rebels and the regular army leaders must have been in an agreement of some sort. It was widely known that the army was unhappy with the way Arbenz handled matters, particularly regarding communist infiltration. It simply is inconceivable that the Guatemalan army could not have wiped out the invaders if it had so chosen. The operation was successful. General Castillo assumed power, Arbenz went off into exile, and the communist infiltration was squeezed out.

The U.S. role was mainly in flying military equipment to the rebels and providing instruction in their use, all assembled in Honduras and Nicaragua with the cooperation of these two nations.

Earlier at the Tenth Inter-American Conference, in Caracas, Venezuela, held March 1–March 28, 1954, the United States, reflecting Secretary John Foster Dulles' concern with developments in Guatemala, had proposed that an item be included on the agenda dealing with the "Intervention of International Communism in the American Republics." Dulles managed to get approved a resolution expressing concern with the problem, but rather weakened by recognition that the resolution did not infringe on the right of any country to have any kind of government desired. Nevertheless, Argentina, Mexico, and Guatemala voted against the resolution, while the other states went along, with the exception of Costa Rica which was absent from the Conference.

The repercussions appeared to be more acute within the United States than in Latin America. Circles opposed to the Eisenhower administration were quite strident in their criticism of the U.S. role, perhaps touted more by the administration than it really had been. Supporters applauded. It seemed, however, that the large majority of voters reflected only a mild interest in the matter.

In Latin America there was some concern that the United States might be moving in the direction of neo-imperialism. But at the same time there was a good understanding of the problem developing in Guatemala and its possible consequences. U.S. diplomacy acted to assure the Latin Americans that acceptance of the Doctrine of Nonintervention had not been repudiated by the United States.

Probably the most serious significance of the U.S. action in the Guatemalan episode, as Ambassador Woodward indicated to the authors, was "the most drastic departure, up to that time, from the nonintervention policy that had become the keystone of U.S. political relations with the other American Republics. Moreover, since the action was taken in that instance without any consultation with the other American Republics or any use of the Organization of American States (until the last moment when an abortive 'investigating committee' was sent by the OAS and, as I recall, stopped in Mexico City), tended to undermine the practice and policy of working through the OAS."[13] Thus, the Eisenhower Administration's effort to assuage Latin American fears that the United States was still committed to the Nonintervention Doctrine had little effect on the credibility of U.S. policies in Latin America.

Subsequently, the U.S.-supported Bay of Pigs attempt at unseating Castro at the start of the Kennedy era, President Johnson's actions in the Dominican Republic, the U.S. role in the Allende matter, and more recently U.S. unilateral involvement in the Central American imbroglio have heightened Latin American concern about the role of the OAS as an instrument of continental solidarity and defense.

When Fidel Castro took over the Cuban reins of government, he very quickly disintegrated the regular Cuban army and consolidated his own revolutionary forces. This decision prevented any counteractions by remnants of Batista's government forces. In Nicaragua the Sandinistas, also remembering Arbenz's experience and Castro's actions, did away with the regular army (national guard) almost immediately after winning the revolution.

The possibility of an elected government actually turning sympathetically toward a philosophy and new international relations with elements wanting the destruction of the capitalist system in Western Europe and the United States, and possibly becoming an advanced military, social, and economic base for the purpose, was no longer only a theoretical matter.

Unfortunately, neither Dulles nor his advisors in the upper echelons of the Department of State, and certainly not Secretary of the Treasury George Humphrey (whose judgment counted heavily), profited from the Guatemalan scare. They had no inclination to examine in depth the reasons for the surfacing of an Arevalo-Arbenz regime, nor a realization of the profound social changes taking place in the Caribbean Basin. Had they dug deeply into the causes of these changes and evolved U.S. policies, strategies, and tactics designed to cope with them, there might not have been a Castro phenomenon. The threat of communism to the Basin had replaced the earlier danger of a European threat to the Panama Canal, as perceived before World Wars I and II. Their reaction was instinctively the indirect use of force, without the accompanying social, political, diplomatic, and economic measures called for by the circumstances in Guatemala itself, but also needed throughout the Basin.

Admittedly, the task of convincing the U.S. public and Congress to go along with an approach of this magnitude would have been formidable. Given the enormous trust which the average U.S. citizen had in President Eisenhower, he might well have put across such an approach, if Dulles had come up with something solid and convincing.

Instead there was an increase in aid for the Castillo administration in Guatemala and a return to major reliance on private capital investment as the means to achieve progress. These were accompanied by preachments from George Humphrey that if the countries concerned would get their houses in order, then the atmosphere would be propitious for U.S. capital to flow and do the job. The result in 1959 was Castro's Cuba. Not even Dr. Milton Eisenhower's modest but important recommendations saw reality.

Despite the channeling of modest aid and loans to Latin America in general, and Central America in particular, since the time when Mr. Truman succeeded to the Presidency, their magnitude was insufficient to offset the very deep resentment which had been developing against the United States. This "yankeephobia" was further heightened by the award of the United States Legion of Merit to Dictator Marcos Perez Jimenez of Venezuela by the Eisenhower administration. Perez Jimenez's ruthlessness in stamping out opposition plus the corruption of his regime made a mockery of United States' reiterated admonitions about the need for honest self-government and respect for democracy!

In April 1958 Vice President and Mrs. Richard Nixon traveled to Latin America on a goodwill tour. The pent-up resentment against the United States resulted in disagreeable anti-U.S. incidents in Lima, Peru, but reached dangerous proportions in Caracas where the partiality shown to Perez Jimenez had been a bitter pill. The dictator had since been toppled and at about the time of the Nixon visit, he had been given permission to reside in the United States (a circumstance which contributed to the demonstration). The crowds got out of hand and for a while Nixon was literally in grave danger. In fact President Eisenhower ordered a U.S. paratrooper command on standby for action in Caracas if Nixon's jeopardy deepened to a critical point. Fortunately, matters did not come to that stage, but the entire southern continent was convulsed with anxiety over the issue. Nixon made it safely back to Washington, but one cannot help but wonder if his experience in Caracas was a factor in the later "benign neglect" of Latin America during his presidency.

It was readily apparent to President Eisenhower that something had to be done about affairs in Latin America. Fortunately for the nation with respect to the southern neighbors, in 1957 there had been two important high level changes in the government. Secretary of the Treasury George Humphrey had resigned and was replaced by Robert B. Anderson who proved considerably more pliable and understanding of the need for broad assistance to South America. Thus, the rigidity of the Export-Import Bank gave way to more flexible policies. But most importantly, C. Douglas Dillon, a most distinguished internationalist, member of one of Wall Street's leading firms, ambassador to France (1953–57), well traveled, and enjoying the respect of both major political parties accepted the appointment of Undersecretary of State for Economic Affairs (1957–59), later the position of Undersecretary of State (1959–61), and eventually under the Democratic administrations of Presidents Kennedy and Johnson held the post of Secretary of Treasury (1961–65).

Dillon brought to the Department of State, and the Eisenhower administration in general, vigor, imagination, and a grasp of the fundamental issues at stake. Accustomed to dealing with large sums at an international level, Dillon was not awed by the magnitude of the amount which obviously stood before the United States. He played a major role in the reshaping of U.S. policy and strategies toward Latin America in the latter part of the Eisenhower era, and in connection with the development of the Alliance for Progress program.

At the time of the meeting of the Organization of American States in Bogotá in 1948 (Ninth Inter-American Conference), it was proposed that an Economic Conference for the American states be held in Buenos Aires in the last quarter of 1948. The main concern of the Latin American nations was the problem of commodity price fluctuations and the perceived need for the creation of an Inter-American Development Bank. Although the member states met several times over the next few years to discuss economic matters, the actual Conference agreed upon at the Bogotá Conference did not take place until 1957. The Latin Americans were eager to hold the meeting, but the United States kept shying away, committed as it was to the principle of most favored treatment in foreign trade and private capital for development. The Truman and Eisenhower administrations knew that the Latin Americans were interested in a commodity agreement and in public capital for basic projects.

As anticipated the Latin Americans raised the points concerning which the United States had policy objections. However, Dillon attended the Conference and grasped quickly what the key issues were. Following the Nixon incident in Caracas and the Eisenhower administration resolve to focus on Latin American relations as a high priority item, Dillon understood the responsibility for redirecting the approach to the southern nations.

The atmosphere of change was detectable. President Juscelino Kubitschek, in tune with the situation proposed to President Eisenhower that a high-level meeting be held to seize the issue of development, and submitted his Operation Pan-America proposal. Following a conference of foreign ministers in Washington in early fall 1958, a "Committee of 21" consisting of representatives of the presidents of the countries concerned was created for the purpose of studying the Kubitschek proposals. Out of the study group came the recommendation that a development bank be established to handle projects not ordinarily dealt with by private banks. They would be concerned in part with social improvement proposals. At another meeting in 1960 the Committee of 21 in the Act of Bogotá agreed that in addition to economic development, there needed to be funds invested in housing, education, land settlement, water supplies, and other social needs.

The U.S. response to these initiatives was positive and under Dillon's dynamism a momentum developed which called for the entire arsenal of weaponry used in economic assistance to be brought into play. Increased contributions to the World Bank and to the International Monetary Fund, enhanced capability for the Export-Import Bank, issuance of food surpluses, broadened technical assistance, a vastly increased foreign aid bill, support for the creation of an Inter-American Bank which would administer a Social Trust Fund to which the United States would contribute $500 million—all were proposed.

As former U.S. Ambassador John Bartlow Martin (Dominican Republic) succinctly stated in his book, U.S. Policy in the Caribbean, Dillon "was convinced that the most important economic issue of the time was what economic system would be adopted by the poor countries of the world."[14] The comment is still valid!

The shift from the years of complacency regarding Latin American affairs to overnight intensified attention as reflected in Dillon's efforts, to frenzied concern under President John F. Kennedy's Alliance for Progress, to a lowering of interest under President Lyndon B. Johnson, and back to "benign neglect" in the Nixon era illustrates dramatically the bewildering and frustrating zigzags in U.S. foreign policy. The connection between these changes and the advent of new presidential administrations is undeniable. And nowhere have these variations been more obvious and damaging than in relation to Latin America, specifically with respect to the Caribbean Basin and Central America. Unfortunately, such will probably continue to be the case, until a crisis situation develops in the region of so grave a magnitude that broad public understanding will emerge to the extent required for long-term stability in U.S. policy toward at least the Basin. It took the Cold War to remove the "zig" out of the "zag" in U.S. policy toward Europe, four wars and billions of dollars in expenditures to do the same for U.S. dealings in the Middle East, and the Korean and Viet Nam conflicts to inject common sense in policies relative to the Asian continent.[15]

Nevertheless, in each policy spurt toward Latin America there always remains a residual of knowledge which contributes to the next meaningful episode in U.S.-Latin American relations. Particularly affected, for better or worse, is always the Caribbean Basin because of geography. Thus, when the measured dynamism of Dillon became overwhelmed by the vortex of Kennedy's Alliance for Progress, it was in Central America that forward movement was most noticeable and durable, albeit at a markedly reduced level once the Alliance for Progress ran out of steam. But enough has remained from the Alliance push for Central America to build on, once the present crisis in the region is resolved. Hence, a closer look at the Alliance is warranted.

The genesis of the Alliance in technical terms appears to lie in Dillon's programs of response to long-standing Latin American desires combined with the thrust of Kubitschek's Operation Pan-America. President Kennedy supplied the idealistic component within the framework of provoking social change and achieving justice, based on free political democratic structures.

President Kennedy first unveiled his ideas at a gathering of Latin American diplomats at the White House on March 18, 1961. In August of the same year at the Punta del Este Conference in Uruguay the formal character of the Alliance took shape. A charter was developed calling for accelerated economic development and broader social justice within the concept of political liberty. In essence the United States would supply the financial sinews and technical assistance over a decade in response to programs developed and implemented by the Latin Americans themselves. The achievement of broader social justice within the framework of democracy was the responsibility of the Latin Americans. Actually, the latter phase of the Alliance program really called for peaceful revolution. Therein was the reason why the Alliance ran into difficulties from the start. Latin American leaders realized how delicate the balance was in most of their countries between violence and peace. To alter the social and political balance in nations where democracy had but the scantiest of roots, and genuine democratic leadership was few and far between, at the speed which Kennedy's "young men" and activist ambassadors wanted, might have plunged the entire continent into chaos. The prospect of peaceful revolution within a brief time represented an illusive ideal. Leaders of

Latin America did not respond to Kennedy's desires to move rapidly in the direction of social change, causing deep disappointment to the Kennedy administration.

Another problem consisted of the fact that Kennedy's team talked about political democracy and its emergence in South America as a counter movement and alternative to communism. Unfortunately, Kennedy's advisors had not studied in depth how democracy could evolve in the miscellaneous Hispanic-based cultures to the south, nor was there agreement among the leaders of the Program regarding how economic development actually occurs. The result was a buckshot approach without tied-in relationships between cause and expected effects. Even before President Kennedy's death, it was apparent that there were grave problems with the Alliance.

In 1958 the five Central American countries met and planned the creation of a Central American Common Market. Two years later they signed a treaty that gave substance to the concept. It called for a customs union, one which would gradually eliminate import duties applicable to products of the member countries, establish common external tariffs, encourage the development of "integration" industries, and establish what would eventually become the Central American Bank for Economic Integration. Help from the United States was both bilateral and multilateral through assistance to the Inter-American Development Bank and the new Central American Bank. The Central American effort was eminently successful from the start, a trend interrupted in 1969 by the "soccer war" between Honduras and El Salvador and some structural problems stemming from the very success of growth. During the 1960s trade among the five countries increased hugely, yet U.S. trade with the region was little affected despite growth.[14]

While the Central American Common Market entered a stage of little activity after the "soccer war," it proved that as an economic unit the whole of Central America possessed great potential vitality. A by-product of the experiment consisted of accelerated foreign investment, particularly from the United States.

With respect to developments among the islands in the Caribbean, Jamaica became independent in 1962, Barbados in 1966, and eventually Grenada acquired independence in 1974 and Trinidad-Tobago in 1976. U.S. policy toward these new states is still in a process of development as future relations will have to be conditioned by overall U.S. considerations regarding the Caribbean Basin as a whole.

In 1965 the Dominican Republic again engaged the attention of Washington. Following the elimination of the Trujillo regime resulting from the dictator's assassination, Juan D. Bosch, a scholarly gentleman in his mid-fifties who had battled Trujillo's regime for a major part of his life and paid the price of exile for his efforts, had been elected president. Perhaps his many years away from the Dominican Republic made it difficult for him to grasp the reins of government firmly. In any event a coup d'etat deposed him in September 1963. A triumvirate took power dominated by the Dominican military responsible for the overthrow. In the spring of 1965, a group of midlevel army officers staged their own revolt in an effort to pave the way for Bosch's return. Supported by miscellaneous left wing and radical groups who were given arms, it was not long before chaos struck the island's capital.

Attempts by Washington to get the OAS into the picture proved fruitless. The ambassadors of some of the Latin American countries in Santo Domingo asked for U.S. military protection, as U.S. warships had been dispatched for the possibility of evacuating U.S. nationals from the island. The representatives in Washington of the very countries whose ambassadors were seeking help from the U.S. Embassy for their personal safety dilly dallied on the possibility of OAS intervention. Finally, the Embassy itself came under fire while Ambassador W. Tapley Bennett was on the phone to President Johnson. Marines and airborne troops landed. Once again the U.S. military was on Dominican soil.

With U.S. troops now on the island, the OAS bestirred itself and called for a cease fire between the opposing parties, while U.S. troops interposed themselves between the Dominican warriors. Under OAS sponsorship, a peace-keeping force commanded by a Brazilian officer consisting of 1,300 troops from Brazil, with additions from Honduras, Costa Rica, Nicaragua, and Paraguay in token numbers arrived on the island. The U.S. troops still made up the bulk of the force. After complex mediations and negotiations, arrangements were made for new elections. The contest was between Joaquin Balaguer and Juan Bosch. Balaguer won handily. The troops departed soon after.

The Dominican episode highlighted a grave flaw in the OAS Doctrine of Nonintervention. It did not take into account that a terribly weak state might not be able to protect itself either from serious internal chaotic developments endangering the lives of foreigners, while making itself vulnerable at the same time to takeover by well organized communist cadres. The latter circumstance could pose a major threat to the hemisphere in general, and the United States in particular, because of the inevitable linkage to the Soviet Union that would follow, or to Cuba as the latter's surrogate. Any nation's highest moral obligation is to its national security, and it would be absurd to suppose that in such danger a nation would refrain from resorting to force.

The United States on a number of occasions has raised with the OAS the advisability of creating an inter-American peace force to stabilize dangerous situations, without success in furthering the concept. Hence, when confronted with a Dominican type crisis the United States can be expected to act reluctantly as it did, until such time as the OAS nations recognize the flaw in the Nonintervention Doctrine. Legally, given the very broad exceptions in the section in the Charter which deals with nonintervention, the United States could elaborate a defense for its action in the Dominican Republic. It is quite possible that a pattern may have been established in the Dominican case of following up a U.S. military action with an OAS peace-keeping force, thus assuring U.S. withdrawal in similar situations. For all one knows a policy along these lines may be in the making, ready to emerge should U.S. forces find themselves exploring the Central American jungle once again, resulting from the present crisis.

The Nixon–Ford years under the impact of the Viet Nam conflict and its aftermath, coupled with Watergate, have aptly been described as a period of benign neglect for Latin America. Nevertheless, substantial aid continued to flow southward, albeit without specific purpose or philosophy.

Throughout President Jimmy Carter's administration (1977–81) Central America and the Caribbean islands continued to be covered by the same policy umbrella as the rest of Latin America. The usual rhetoric about support and encouragement of democratic governments abounded in Washington policy statements, with one important difference. President Carter anchored his foreign policy heavily on human rights performance and attempted to hinge strategies and tactics accordingly. This approach insinuated "rewards" and "punishments." But the net result was little difference from the "benign neglect" approach of the previous administration. As it was difficult to connect directly U.S. national interest considerations with the Carter human rights approach, as a fundamental tenet in U.S. international relations, the aid programs merely became further disjointed. The Carter administration also continued, as had its predecessors, some military assistance and sales in Central America, but with checkered consequences due to the application of human rights criteria.

The region, already in the throes of deep social unrest, with revolution in Nicaragua, increasing violence in El Salvador, sporadic fighting in Guatemala, and unsettled conditions in Honduras merely suffered further from the uncertainties introduced by Carter's "fits and starts" military assistance policy. In the absence of a broad comprehensive program backed by a generous Congress to attack the profound ills of the region, the Carter preachments served little positive purpose.

In Nicaragua the long festering sore of the Somoza regime finally came to an end in July 1979, with a resounding Sandinista victory. Although the regime's collapse probably was inevitable, the withholding of arms sales by the United States probably helped its demise. There is no quibble with that decision. But it was well known that the Sandinista movement in a broad sense included elements from all segments of the political rainbow. It was also common knowledge that Castro had rendered assistance in the training of guerrillas and furnished arms. Hence, it was highly predictable that after the ouster of the Somoza regime, in a country devoid of democratic institutions and suffering serious economic troubles derived from the long civil war, there would be a determined push by the well organized and ideologically motivated Marxist-Leninists to assume control of the government. A plan to maintain the National Guard intact as an institution after Somoza's departure collapsed when the interim President Urauyo failed to live up to the terms of the agreement to stay in office for only 48 hours. His failure provoked cries of trickery from the Sandinistas who broke the truce and began rounding up deserting National Guardsmen. The breakdown of the agreement left the Carter Administration with little choice but to try to co-opt the Sandinistas and force them to live up to the pledges of their San José declaration. The Carter Administration pushed through Congress a special supplemental aid package of over $100 million to assist the new Sandinista government rebuild. Much of the aid was conditional on keeping lines of credit open to the private business sector and the agricultural sector. The Sandinistas, however, gradually moved to eliminate the private sector and, taking advice from Castro, moved to create a large military establishment designed to "protect the revolution" and aid other revolutionaries in neighboring countries. The Sandinista policies resulted in the gradual internationalization of the conflicts in Central America.

Tensions with skittish, isolationist Guatemala heightened when the government of that country refused to accept Carter's human rights conditions for the acquisition of arms.

In El Salvador the social fabric was being torn apart with extreme right and left factions committing atrocities. A rightist military government was ousted in October 1979 by a group of military officers who instituted basic agrarian and banking reforms, wrestling control of the economic and political systems from the old ruling oligarchy. The left, seeing its cause adopted by the military, stepped up its efforts to seize control. The Carter Administration increased its assistance (both economic and military) to the moderate Christian Democratic junta that was installed to promulgate the wide-reaching reforms. But the level of violence increased as both the extreme left and right sought to block the reforms. By the time Carter's responsibilities were passed on to President Ronald Reagan, Cuban interference through the furnishing of arms via Nicaragua to Salvadoran guerrillas had reached massive levels. This reality conditioned immediately Reagan's policy in the region not only to step up support for the government of El Salvador, but also to cut aid to Nicaragua. The issue of American Central American policy, as a result, was destined to engage national attention and consequently became the subject of acrimonious debate in Congress.

In February 1971 in the Department of State's issue concerning El Salvador in the Background Notes series, one finds a clear statement of a basic condition against which these complicated political developments were taking place:

> The basic economic and social problems of the underdeveloped Salvadoran economy include a heavy population pressure on the land, a very high population growth rate, an economy excessively dependent on coffee, limited unused arable land and mineral resources, a high illiteracy rate, high seasonal unemployment, and a very uneven distribution of income. The industrial sector, mostly related to the processing or production of light consumer goods, has been developing well in the recent favorable investment climate. The economic infra- structure, such as roads, electric power, and banking facilities, also is fairly well developed.

Some ten years later when the present violence gathered momentum, the 1971 description still applied but now considerably aggravated by continued rapid population increase. Thus, the appearance of a newish and restless but still small urban middle class, combined with the critical employment situation and uncertainties in the countryside, provided the ingredients for the current strife in that unhappy nation. The fact is that a long-range solution to El Salvador's social, political, and economic problems is impossible without an important slowing down of population growth. Even so, the small size of the nation may already preclude future economic success without evolution within the Central American Com- mon Market context.

A positive achievement during the Carter period was settlement of difficulties with Panama arising from the question of sovereignty over the canal. Two treaties were signed in Washington in 1977. The one transferred the canal to Panama. The other guaranteed the neutrality of the canal. The United States, however, retained the right to employ military force should the use of the canal be impeded at any time. What this signified was that if Panama should be unable to keep the canal clear of foreign military action, the United States would enter the picture with force.

Shortly after the Carter Administration assumed office, an effort was made to develop better relations with Cuba. A U.S. Interest Section headed by a U.S. diplomat was opened in Havana under the auspices of the Swiss Embassy. In Washington, Cuba established an Interest Section under the umbrella of the Czechoslovakian Embassy. A provisional fisheries agreement was signed. Trade and travel bans were somewhat relaxed. However, the momentum was interrupted by Carter pique at intensive Cuban meddling in Angola and Ethiopia.

It was during the Carter period that the Mariel boat exodus of well over 114,000 new exiles reached Miami. Also intensified was the flight from Haiti of thousands of "boat people" in desperate bids to escape atrocious economic misery. The Carter Administration recognized the problems arising from this migration and sought congressional action to deal with the problem within the United States. However, long range solutions designed to avoid a repeat of the Mariel episode will depend on future Cuban-U.S. relations. Regarding the very difficult problems in Haiti, until somehow economic and social conditions in that country can be sharply improved, Haitian "boat people" dramas could be repeated, although migrants are currently interdicted by U.S. Coast Guard patrols and are returned to Haiti.

In retrospect, the Carter Administration closed one aspect of U.S. policy toward the Caribbean Basin. It should be the last time for years to come when the United States would apply the same yardstick to Central America and the Caribbean islands, as it would to Mexico and mainland South America. In the early 1900s the United States developed a Caribbean Basin policy because of concern for the Panamanian canal project and fear of European encroachment, mainly from Great Britain or Germany. Gradually after World War I U.S. policy envisaged the Basin within a frame of thinking applicable to all Latin America. This philosophy flowered dramatically under President Franklin D. Roosevelt, and flashed brilliantly for a brief period in Kennedy's Alliance for Progress days. But once again because of security considerations, the Caribbean Basin will warrant special U.S. attention. The threat of the Soviet Union encroaching through a surrogate Cuba and possible Nicaraguan foothold has forced the United States to develop a policy for the Basin independent of that for the rest of South America.

The formal manifestation of the new approach was House Bill 2769 of April 27, 1983, entitled the *Caribbean Basin Economic Recovery Act*. This bill called for authority to be given the President of the United States to grant import duty-free treatment at his discretion to specific nations in the Basin, subject to certain qualifications designed to protect U.S. industry and agriculture, as well as Puerto Rico and the Virgin Islands, from unfair competition. All of the islands in the Basin are named as were also the Central American Republics and Panama. Excluded from the list because of the strength of their economies and acknowledgment of their advanced stage of development are Mexico, Colombia, and Venezuela.

The bill was the outgrowth of the new approach to the Caribbean Basin announced by President Reagan quite early in his administration. It represented a recognition that the countries in the region needed easier access to the vast U.S. market to survive. While the effort is an essential move, it must be regarded as only the first step.

Public concern over Central America worried the White House in late 1983 leading President Reagan to appoint a panel headed by former Secretary of State Henry A. Kissinger, to make recommendations on the area. Their report, completed in late January 1984, suggested first, that the area be considered vital to U.S. interests. Second, it made economic recommendations ranging from local economic development to increasing by $5 billion U.S. aid between 1985 and 1990 and immediate infusion of dollars. Third, the Kissinger Commission urged the White House to support counter-insurgency against Soviet and Cuban backed fighters in the region, particularly directing these efforts against Nicaragua. It urged immediate aid to El Salvador.

The White House felt that in addition to the commission's thoughts on economic and military issues, that its insistence that human rights violations be reduced would help sell the President's policies to the U.S. public. It did not. The Congress did not increase foreign aid to $400 million in 1984 as recommended and U.S. military aid and covert participation increased sharply by mid-1984 at the expense of other, long-term solutions. Finally, the U.S. public remained worried and confused about the region. While the Kissinger Commission cannot be blamed for these turns of events, clearly its vague and nonspecific, let alone lack of original ideas, did not improve U.S. thinking. Social and economic problems call for additional imaginative and understanding approaches by the nations of the Basin and by the United States.

5

POLICIES AND OPPORTUNITIES IN CENTRAL AMERICA AND THE CARIBBEAN

> The states in the isthmus of Panama,
> as far as Guatemala, will form perhaps
> an association. This magnificent
> position between the two oceans may
> become in time the world's emporium;
> its canals shall shorten the earth's
> distances, tighten the commercial ties
> of Europe, America and Asia, there
> will be brought to so fortunate a
> region tributes from the
> four corners of the globe.
>
> Extract from Simon Bolivar document, 1815

In its *GIST* publication dated February 1982 entitled *The Caribbean Basin Initiative*, the Department of State described the background of this policy move as follows:

> The Caribbean Basin includes some two dozen small developing countries in Central America, the Caribbean, and northern South America. They have been seriously affected by the escalating cost of imported oil and declining prices for their major exports such as sugar, coffee and bauxite. This has exacerbated the region's deeply rooted structural problems and caused serious inflation, high unemployment, declining economic growth, enormous balance-of-payment deficits, and a pressing liquidity problem.

The document states further with respect to our national security interests:

> The Caribbean Basin forms the third border of the U.S., contains vital sea lanes through which 75% of our oil imports must flow, is an important market for US exports, and is the second largest source of illegal immigration to the US. We have a basic interest in preventing the political and economic collapse of this region. The economic crisis threatens political and social stability throughout the region and creates

conditions which Cuba and others seek to exploit through terrorism and subversion. If the economic problems are not resolved, a vast increase in illegal immigration to the US would be inevitable. It is not in our interest that a major border of the world's richest nation consist largely of hostile states, among which are some of the world's poorest countries.[1]

In an address by President Ronald Reagan on February 24, 1982 before the Organization of American States, the fact of considerable differences between the countries in the "Caribbean Basin" was recognized in the following comment:

We all seek to insure that the peoples of this area have the right to preserve their own national identities, to improve their economic lot, and to develop their political institutions to suit their own unique social and historical needs. The Central American and Caribbean countries differ widely in culture, personality and needs. Like America itself, the Caribbean Basin is an extraordinary mosaic of Hispanics, Africans, Asians, and Europeans, as well as native Americans.[2]

It is readily apparent that although some broad general policy principles can be established for dealing with the region, the diversity of the countries concerned requires carefully tailored strategies and tactics to fit rather specific situations. Hence, the Central American nations with their deep sense of a common destiny, and geographic proximities, call for considerations different from those essential to the island republics. Even among the latter, various approaches are indicated because of individual differences stemming from size, population, natural resources, and historical development.

What is proposed in this chapter is to examine the broad specifics of the Central American countries, and of selected island republics, regarding what the general thrust of U.S. policies should be.

CENTRAL AMERICA

In common with the island republics in the Caribbean, it is extremely difficult for a U.S. foreign policy to evolve relevant to Central America reflecting consistency from one U.S. presidency to another. What such a policy should be is not particularly difficult to determine. There is no shortage of experts in the Washington career bureaucracy, business, academe, and think tanks with the capability of developing policies, strategies, and tactics toward Central America and the Caribbean islands, beneficial to our national interest, as well as to the countries concerned.

The problem lies rather in the nature of U.S. domestic politics, complicated by parochialism and superficial understanding at Congressional and Senior Executive Branch levels of the character and situations endemic to the areas. Additional complexities relate to fuzzy U.S. public opinion stemming from poor, haphazard, and frequently faulty or biased media reporting and editorial comment. Matters are further confused by the injection of moral versus practical considerations emanating from the nation's intellectual and ecclesiastical circles, at times intertwined with actual or potential domestic political clout reflecting internal situations frequently at odds with the logic of U.S. foreign policy requirements.

Important for a further understanding of why the Central American Republics cherish a vague ideal of unity despite the existence of the five countries as independent entities since 1842, is awareness of the origin of their independence from Spain. The latter governed the general area now known as Central America through the *Audiencia de Guatemala* (highest court of appeal), technically under the Viceroyalty of New Spain centered in Mexico, and presided over by a president who functioned as a chief justice, who also held appointment from the Crown as governor and captain general, and was thus both de facto and de jure the King of Spain's personal representative. From 1570 to 1821 the region informally referred to as the Kingdom of Guatemala was subjected to personal and often despotic rule by governors who were natives of Spain and alien to the province over which they held sway. Appeal to a governor's decision could only be made in Spain, a complex and costly procedure. The absence of a democratic political base was total.

The last Spanish governor was the aged Lieutenant General Carlos Urrutia y Montoya, appointed by King Fernando VII on March 3, 1817. During Urrutia's term a new constitution was proclaimed in Spain reflecting liberal overtones. According to the new national charter, there was provision for the creation of a provincial junta in Guatemala to be formed by elected members. Initially the junta favored loyalty to the Crown, but amidst bitterly divided sentiments because of the independence movement in Mexico. The ailing Urrutia was urged by the junta to step down and appoint to his responsibilities Brigadier General Gabino Gainza, a native of Guipuzcoa, Spain. Urrutia followed the Junta's direction and resigned March 10, 1821. Gainza had recently arrived to discharge the post of subinspector of Spanish military forces in Guatemala. Gainza, a veteran of the Spanish efforts to retain their possessions on the west coast of South America, initially supported the Junta's pro-Spanish Crown's position. But as Mexican General Agustin Iturbide's power grew and important factions in the region favored association with Mexico, Gainza, in the fall of 1821, switched to support for independence with himself as head of a new government.

During the period 1821–23 considerable uncertainty prevailed regarding the old Audiencía de Guatemala's future. However, upon Iturbide's abdication in 1823 the Central American leaders opted for the holding of a National Constituent Assembly from June 24, 1823 to January 23, 1825. A direct consequence of the Assembly's deliberations was the declaration of independence on July 1, 1823 for the *Provincias Unidas del Centro de America* (United Provinces of the Center of America). As Gainza had departed for Mexico, the new state came into being without having to fight either Mexico or Spain for its independence.

The National Assembly completed the writing of a constitution on November 22, 1824.

Beset by intense internal conflict and violence the new nation fell apart in 1842, and the independence of its five component provinces as separate republics gradually emerged. Central Americans have repeatedly attempted to achieve unity once again, but inability to agree on key factors essential to the success of such a development has always thwarted what remains still a wistful desire, one which did find some hope in the creation of the Central American Common Market in the 1960s. The collapse of the Alliance for Progress endeavor and its support for the Common Market in effect doomed the latest attempt to achieve at least a common economic policy.

Special Characteristics

There are two Central American behavioral traits inherited from Spain and common also to the indigenous cultures which combined with other social and economic factors contribute to dissension in the region.

One concerns the absence of "compromise" as a general means for settling differences. The concept does exist in Spanish culture and can be translated as *transigir*. But to give in is also interpreted as involving loss of face even if the quid pro quo is in balance. To compromise as a voluntary action free from pressure can be viewed as an act of magnanimity. But to do so in the face of "do it or else" even by force of circumstances raises a challenge to one's machismo, or manhood. One consequence, if not death itself, would be profound and enduring hate for the cause of embarrassment.

Related to the compromise issue is the intense individualism felt by both men and women in Central American society, perhaps more so than in Spain itself. The result is a very high degree of personal sensitivity. Probably one of the most serious difficulties in the way of the achievement of a peaceful settlement in the Salvadoran problem concerns the two traits mentioned. The consequences override philosophical considerations. U.S.

policymakers not trained to deal in such an environment can hardly hope to achieve success through diplomatic means. Historically, their failures and frustrations wind up with the landing of U.S. forces somewhere in the area.

Last, before discussion of the economics of the region, care should be exercised in not equating culture and race in Central America. As stated earlier, a pure blooded Indian may be thoroughly Spanish in language and outlook, as much so as the child born in Central America of parents immigrated from Spain. The same would apply to someone of mixed Spanish-Indian parentage but the large majority of Indians are not assimilated into the Spanish culture.

Economic Factors

The *Statistical Bulletin of the OAS* published annually by the General Secretariat of the Organization of American States, Washington, D. C. contains a wealth of data concerning its members. The International Bank for Reconstruction and Development, the Inter-American Bank, the Central American Bank for Economic Integration and other international financial institutions, the U.S. Department of Commerce and other domestic and foreign government agencies make available considerable information regarding the Central American nations and those in the Caribbean. However, this chapter does not purport to analyze in detail the economics of the countries of immediate interest. But reference to some basic figures is essential for highlighting the nature of the problem confronting the United States and to give a direction for U.S. policy.

All five Republics have basically agricultural economies exporting coffee, cotton, shrimp, sugar in the case of El Salvador; coffee, cotton, sugar, bananas, beef, essential oils, timber, and shrimp from Guatemala; bananas, coffee, wood, and meat from Honduras; Costa Rica ships coffee, bananas, meat, and sugar; and Nicaragua ships cotton, coffee, meat, and cottonseed. All in varying degrees export a few manufactures either to each other or elsewhere except in times of intense intraregional tensions.

A review of the data in Table 5.1 reveals serious declines in real Gross Domestic Product (GDP) rates in 1980 and 1981 compared to averages for the 1970–80 decade for Guatemala, Honduras, Costa Rica, and El Salvador with the exception of Nicaragua. Correlative figures are shown in Table 5.2 for real GD per capita rates for the same years for these five countries. From Table 5.1 a reverse phenomenon is noted for Nicaragua which averaged only 1.9 percent growth in real GDP for 1970–80, but increased by a dramatic 10.4 percent in 1980 followed by a decline to 7.8 percent in 1981. The high point of 10.4 percent reflected immediate reaction in terms

TABLE 5.1. Real GDP Growth Rates in Central America[a] (%)

	1960–70[b]	1970–80[b]	1980	1981[c]
Nicaragua	6.9	1.9	10.4	7.8
Guatemala	5.5	5.6	3.5	1.0
Honduras	5.2	4.3	2.5	0.5
Costa Rica	5.9	5.7	1.2	−2.0
El Salvador	5.6	3.1	−9.6	−9.5

[a]Gross domestic product.
[b]Averages.
[c]Preliminary estimate.
Source: Statistical Bulletin of the OAS, Vol. 4, page 5.

of recovery efforts after conclusion of the civil war in 1979, a trend not since sustained.

Table 5.3 reflects rather dramatically root causes of the GDP decline for the region. In general, they relate to major adverse merchandise trade balances in the years 1978–81 for Guatemala, Honduras, Costa Rica, El Salvador, and similarly for Nicaragua in 1980 and 1981.

A similar trend can be found in international balance of payments data for the same period as reflected in Table 5.4. Thus, current account statistics for 1978, 1979, and 1980 show a consistent pattern of deficits for Guatemala, Honduras, and Costa Rica. El Salvador had deficits in 1978 and 1980, but a surplus in 1979. Data available show a deficit for Nicaragua in 1978, surplus in 1979, and no statistics for 1980. Positive substantial balances for Nicaragua and El Salvador in 1979 resulted from unusually substantial exports of cotton from the former and coffee from the latter. By 1981, all five countries reported deficit foreign trade balances, a trend reportedly still in effect.

TABLE 5.2. Real Per Capita GDP Rates in Central America[a] (%)

	1960–70[b]	1970–80[b]	1980	1981[c]
Nicaragua	4.2	−2.0	6.5	4.5
Guatemala	2.2	2.3	0.5	−2.2
Honduras	1.5	0.8	−1.1	−2.9
Costa Rica	2.5	3.0	−1.0	−4.6
El Salvador	2.1	−0.3	−12.4	−12.4

[a]Gross domestic product.
[b]Averages.
[c]Preliminary estimate.
Source: Statistical Bulletin of the OAS, Vol. 4, page 6.

TABLE 5.3. Merchandise Balance of Trade, 1978–81 in Central America
(In Millions of U.S. $)

	Exports of Goods [Free on Board (FOB)]				Imports of Goods (FOB)			
	1978	1979	1980	1981[a]	1978	1979	1980	1981[a]
Nicaragua	646.0	615.9	450.4	506.0	553.3	388.9	802.9	840.9
Guatemala	1092.4	1221.4	1519.9	1348.8	1284.0	1401.7	1471.0	1571.7
Honduras	626.1	750.1	834.5	817.9	654.4	783.4	956.0	906.1
Costa Rica	863.9	942.0	1017.2	1031.2	1049.4	1257.2	1375.7	1204.8
El Salvador	848.9	1224.2	967.0	740.0	951.0	938.5	971.0	904.0

[a]Preliminary estimate.
Source: *Statistical Bulletin of the OAS,* Vol. 4, page 27.

The total population of the five Central American republics at the end of 1981 was 21,240,000 divided as follows: Nicaragua, 2,650,000; Guatemala, 7,500,000; Honduras, 3,820,000; Costa Rica, 2,300,000; and El Salvador with 4,970,000. For the period 1970–80, the average annual population growth rate was 3.50 percent for Nicaragua; 3.26 percent for Guatemala; 3.41 percent for Honduras; 2.62 percent for Costa Rica; and 3.41 percent for El Salvador.[2] It is readily apparent from these rates that population pressure has been running ahead of the five countries' economic growth record during the comparable decade (See Table 5.2). Combined with increasing foreign trade deficits and no other source for instant wealth, or prospects of one, these factors put together spell continued social, political, economic, and military unrest; in short, revolution. One other set of figures which should be taken in conjunction with the data discussed is the region's international balance of payments position, as reflected in Table 5.4. The significance of the statistics outlined

TABLE 5.4. Balance of Payments, Current Accounts in Central America
(In Millions of U.S. $)

	1978	1979	1980
Nicaragua	−24.9	160.9	—
Guatemala	−270.5	−205.6	−163.3
Honduras	−157.0	−198.5	−319.7
Costa Rica	−363.2	−558.2	−653.3
El Salvador	−238.5	129.5	−85.7

Source: *Statistic Bulletin of the OAS,* Vol. 4, *passim.*

is that the pie has been for at least a decade too small for the number of consumers.

The five countries concerned have been trying to halt the decline in their respective standards of living by expanding internal deficits, piling up external loans, and securing grants. In the case of Nicaragua, initially after the revolution ended in 1979, loans reportedly were obtained from Sweden, The Netherlands, France, Federal Republic of Germany, Hungary, Libya, Iraq, Cuba, Mexico, and Venezuela. These helped cover import requirements, but as the character of the Nicaraguan government unveils, these sources may well moderate their financial aid, except for the radical nations such as Cuba or Libya. But, the capacity of the latter to pull Nicaragua through a prolonged crisis is very limited save for arms, of which the Soviet Union can be an indirect supplier without limit.

The internal violence ripping apart El Salvador during the recent past probably has resulted in a decline in the industrial sector of as much as 25 percent because of destruction by the guerrilla forces of physical infrastructures. In addition, agricultural output for both export and domestic use sustained serious bruising.

To the two areas undergoing violence, Nicaragua and El Salvador, must be added the potential for explosion in the other three countries. Capital flight and jittery nerves among leaders in the latter are factors leading to a situation that cannot be resolved by simply stepping up military aid, and the channeling of miscellaneous kinds of economic aid, whether by the Soviet Union and its friends to Nicaragua, or the United States to the other Republics still free of direct Soviet-Cuban influence. Possibly one of the questions that may restrain greater Soviet financial entanglement in Nicaragua through Cuba, probably relates to how far Nicaragua can drift into the Soviet circle before private U.S. banking sources become irrevocably closed to that nation. The Soviet Union may not be willing to carry a burden in another Latin American country as heavy as that of Cuba. The Kremlin's leaders know that Cuba's island condition permits a certain isolation, a feature of interest to both the United States and the Soviet Union given present circumstances. But in Central America the possibility of guerrilla infiltration from a neighboring state would be an ever present reality; a "quarantine" situation applicable to an island condition is impossible on the mainland.

Without a resumption of energetic activities on behalf of the economic unification of the Central American Republics, prospects for current and long-term political, social, and economic stability are truly nil. From a U.S. viewpoint, it should be axiomatic from one presidential administration to another and from Congress to Congress that strong U.S. support for the Central American Common Market be the essential cornerstone of our policy toward the area.

One figure of importance, particularly for those in Congress and academe who wish to see an instant democracy emerge in the region, especially in El Salvador, and preferably as a carbon copy of our system, relates to literacy. In Nicaragua the literacy rate is 49 percent; Honduras 50 percent; Guatemala 30/40 percent; El Salvador 50 percent; and Costa Rica 85 percent. These data must be considered with per capita income which roughly is as follows: Nicaragua—$980.00; Honduras—$490.00; Guatemala—$1,020.00; El Salvador—$610.00; and Costa Rica—$1,370.00.

Leaving aside for the moment the case of Costa Rica, it will be noticed that the other four countries have a literacy rate roughly 50 percent or less and per capita incomes ranging between $490.00 and $1,020.00. The basic stagnation of the region is apparent.

Costa Rica, because of an accident of history, was the last to be colonized if it indeed ever was since the indigenous population was very sparse. There was little miscegenation. Land was plentiful for the small stream of Spanish immigrants, groups with farming and commercial backgrounds instead of military aspirations. The area that became Costa Rica is composed largely of independent landowners and until now it has been spared overpopulation.

But, as already noted, the demographic pressure is on in the entire region, and there is an important movement of rural people to the urban centers. If Costa Rica's industrial and commercial base does not expand, and as exports have little prospect of marked increase, the horizon for this fine country is indeed clouded. Let us not forget that it was not so long ago that Uruguay was the most democratic country in the southern hemisphere. Its agricultural economy could not provide the earnings necessary to meet the social program demands of an expanding population, and consequently the nation's democratic system collapsed. In brief, it should not be taken for granted that Costa Rica will always be an oasis of peace in Central America, if the Common Market does not develop substantially, a prospect which cannot occur without long-term U.S. support.

All five countries are endeavoring with varying success to develop domestic manufacturing activities with a view toward satisfying national and regional markets. The latter factor is crucial because in general none of the Central American Republics *per se* has a large enough population to provide a substantial national market, one which would enable local industry to produce products that can compete with imports except behind excessively high tariff barriers. Yet, without considerable industrial and commercial expansion, the future is certain disaster. When civil strife develops in any one or more of the region's countries, such as the present situation in El Salvador and in Nicaragua, the area's delicate balance is unsettled with extremely negative consequences for all concerned.

A prime example of this disequilibrium relates to the 1960s, when with considerable encouragement from the United States, important strides were made in advancing the region's common market concept. But the "soccer war" in the summer of 1969 between Honduras and El Salvador, the root of which was population overcrowding in El Salvador, with some 300,000 emigrants spilling into Honduras, tossed the proverbial monkey wrench into the regional efforts. That situation, coupled with a lessening of U.S. enthusiasm for the Alliance for Progress after the assassination of President Kennedy and consequent decline in aid funds, caused an interruption in the common market movement from which the region has never recovered.

A word or two is in order to speculate what might happen in the area if the United States were to step out of the picture entirely and leave the five countries to their fate. Probably the extreme Marxist-Leninist Left in El Salvador, Honduras, Guatemala, and Nicaragua would view the abandonment as an opportunity to impose its will militarily on the region. But the extreme Right Wing in these four countries might also see the situation as playing into its hands. Free from restraints imposed by military and civilian moderates desirous of continued U.S. aid and committed to political democracy, the Right Wing probably would embark on a no quarters policy toward any opponents who might get in their way. In the process, Costa Rica would find its peace and quiet gone and prospects for democracy, remote as they now are for the region as a whole, nil.

Regardless of who the winner might be, a situation would emerge in which the vast majority of the people would be squeezed to an extent intolerable to U.S. public opinion. The result could easily be rash U.S. actions with disastrous international political consequences. The United States might find it necessary under the circumstances to embark in a neo-colonialist military course from which there would be no retreat. The Soviet Union would then feel free to levy its heavy hand on the Middle Eastern and Asian border countries. The possibility of direct military confrontation between the two superpowers would be immensely enhanced.

The half-hearted current economic and military assistance to four of the countries in region, for the primary purpose of preventing a possible takeover by the Soviet-Cuban guerrillas, is inadequate in conception and magnitude. The consequence of present U.S. policy will be to prolong the agony of the region indefinitely.

What is required is a ringing and stirring declaration by the United States of its commitment for at least a decade, or perhaps two, to underwrite support for the revitalization of the Central American Common Market. Essential ingredients in the proposal would be the structuring of an initial ten-year Plan by the Central American experts themselves. Their role in the Common Market effort in the heyday of the Alliance for Progress showed they have the capacity to do the job if helped by the United States.

U.S. support would be in the form of direct budgetary grant support, special tariff preferences, and/or free duty consideration for agricultural products, which combined with long-term loans from both private and official multilateral banking institutions, plus earnings from exports, should be of sufficient magnitude to cover the international balance of payments deficits. In time the expansion and strength of the Central American region will more than compensate in trade with the United States, and stability, for a prolonged U.S. support effort. Moreover, the region has the expertise to develop such a plan.

The Marxist-Leninist elements in the various antiestablishment movements in the region can be expected to oppose such an approach in the same manner in which the Soviet Union militated against the Marshall Plan. Much of this leftist opposition will remain violent, particularly in El Salvador and Guatemala. Thus, for some time U.S. military assistance will have to be rendered to protect the initial forward movement of the new concept. However, this aid preferably should not involve U.S. military advisors in the region. Training should take place out of the region, preferably in the United States. The care of internal security in Central America must be solely a responsibility for the region's nations; otherwise "political" generals will rely on the United States to eventually pull their chestnuts "militarily" out of the fire.

Probably no action taken by the United States could contribute to the ending of armed hostilities in Central America more than the dramatic announcement of a massive and dramatic area policy. But all political groups in the region must be persuaded of steady U.S. resolve to truly get behind the much desired regional economic integration. While each of the five countries wishes to preserve its own political independence, they all desire somehow to pull their weight in the boat together. Such a prospect, if genuinely believed, would provide the necessary incentive to government troops in El Salvador in particular to battle for an ideal, and for those in rebellion to consider seriously collaborating in the new direction. In fact, it is difficult to see how any lasting mediation efforts by the United States or any other country can succeed in Central America without an announcement of the kind suggested.

Nonetheless, the hardcore Sandinistas will not find themselves impotent. They will be around for a long time, serving as a negative factor in the future of the region. Still, no amount of Marxist efforts in the region could halt the surge of hope engendered by such a U.S. move with its internal domestic political repercussions. The Soviet Union and Cuba would face a competitive situation beyond their capabilities to match. At present in the Salvadorian issue, the rank and file in the armed forces, the ones who are called upon to fight the highly motivated guerrilla groups, lack an ideal to fight for one, readily understood, and which would touch their lives directly.

With respect to the mechanics of strategy and tactics, the Marshall Plan approach should be paralleled as closely as feasible.

A quid pro quo requirement by the United States as crucial for its ten-year commitment should be insistence on the development of plans having the ultimate objective of creating substantial literate and pros-perous *rural and urban* middle classes. Without the emergence of a strong middle class in Central America, the establishment of democracies strong enough to withstand by themselves assaults from the violent radical Left and equally violent Right would be impossible. If encouraged by the United States, experts in the region are fully capable of developing approaches leading in this direction. They know their countries and cultures well and have the skill to cope with the problem.

However, the evolution of democracy based on middle class sectors and implicit support for liberal capitalism is no easy prospect. To begin with the Catholic Church with its enormous following in the area is and has always been opposed to liberal capitalism, an economic way of life crucial to the emergence of broadly based middle clases. At the Third Conference of the Latin American Bishops in Puebla, Mexico, in 1979, the results of which were endorsed by Pope John Paul II, among the Resolutions there were three ideologies specifically cited as unacceptable approaches to politics and liberation: Marxism, liberal capitalism, and the national security doctrine.[3] How the Church would resolve in a practical fashion, given the frailties of mankind, the maldistribution of wealth and power is fuzzy, but it certainly would not be along the lines of the U.S. success story. In all probability it would favor some kind of approach based on a form of corporatism, a concept long viewed favorably by the Catholic Church, and compatible with the "dependency" psychology inherent in the region's culture. Because of its position in Catholic thought, further comment is required about corporatism.

In *The New Corporatism*, edited by Fredrick B. Pike and Thomas Stritch, and which contains a number of penetrating essays on the subject, Howard J. Wiarda in a paper on "Corporatism and Development in the Iberic-Latin World," states the following in order to clarify what is meant by the term:

> It should be made clear at the outset that when we use the term corporatism, we are using it in two distinct, but often interrelated, senses. The first refers to the manifestly corporist experiments and regimes of the 1930s and 1940s and may be defined as a system of

authority and interest representation, derived chiefly (though not exclusively) from Catholic social thought, stressing functional representation, the integration of labor and capital into a vast web of hierarchically ordered "harmonious" monopolistic, and functionally determined units (or corporations), and guided by the state ("This definition derives from Schmitter, *Portugalization of Brazil?*, page 3, and Elbow *Corporative Theory*, page 11–12"). The second sense in which we use the term corporatism is broader, encompassing a far longer cultural-historic tradition stretching back to the origins of the Iberic-Latin systems and embodying a dominant form of sociopolitical organization that is similarly hierarchical, elitist, authoritarian, bureaucratic, Catholic, patrimonialist and corporatist to its core.[4]

In an article concerned with "Authoritarianism, Corporatism and Mobilization in Peru," by James M. Malloy, also included in the book edited by Pike and Stritch, there are further perceptive comments regarding corporatism:

> Corporatism assumes that a harmonious process of development and modernization can be achieved if society is correctly organized and based upon an adequate notion of distributive but not necessarily egalitarian justice.

> The state is charged with overseeing the process by maintaining correct organization and regulating intergroup relations: the state intervenes in the society and economy but does not absorb them; thus the state is regulative but limited.

> Corporatism rejects liberal individualism and Marxist class analysis in that both proceed from the belief that conflict is inevitable and to a certain extent legitimate. In corporatism conflict is not seen as inevitable and is therefore illegitimate. Corporatism seeks to eliminate conflict by basing social integration around functional and vocation groupings seen to be the "natural" basis of society.

> Corporatism rejects the liberal politics of citizen constituencies, political parties and votes for representation in a legislative assembly based on territorial divisions.

> Corporatism is antisecular and stresses moral dimensions of social life which it equates with natural groups and the organic social whole opposed to "classes for themselves" or utility-maximizing individuals.[5]

While no program advocated by the Catholic hierarchy in Central America has surfaced specifically identifiable as a reflection of corporative thinking and its antiliberal bias, neither has the Church come down firmly on the side of social and political doctrines which enhance individual initiative and movement toward democracy within the framework of liberal capitalism. The Church calls for respect for human rights, the end of violence, and the end of poverty but it does not state how to reach these goals.

On the other hand, a substantial number of the clergy committed to the doctrine of liberation theology openly express their animosity and contempt for the capitalist system. To quote from the previously mentioned study by Richard C. Brown, he states the following regarding the basic philosophy in liberation theology:

> The chief theologian and intellectual author of liberation theology, however, is Gustavo Gutierrez, a Peruvian priest whose extensive works on the subject have been circulated widely in Latin America and elsewhere. In his writings, he relies heavily on Marxian analysis and terminology:
>
>> Liberation expresses the aspiration of oppressed peoples and social classes, emphasizing the conflictual aspects of the economic, social and political process which puts them at odds with wealthy nations and oppressive classes (Carlos Gutierrez, *A Theology of Liberation*, Maryknoll, N.Y., Orbis Books, 1973, page 36).
>>
>> Christ is presented (in the Bible) as the one who brings us liberation. Christ the Savior liberates man from sin, which is the ultimate root of all disruption of friendship and of all injustice and oppression (Carlos Gutierrez, *ibid*, page 37).
>>
>> The class struggle is a fact and neutrality in this question is not possible (Carlos Gutierrez, *ibid*, page 37).
>>
>> Today we must identify with oppressed classes of this Continent . . . which is marked by injustice and spoilation on the other hand and hope-filled yearning for liberation on the other.
>>
>> Efforts to project a new society in Latin America are moving toward socialism.
>>
>> Private ownership of the means of production will be eliminated.[6]

Given the very great influence of the Catholic Church in Central America, evident by the visit of Pope John Paul II to the region early in 1983, the views of the clergy are important relative to the emergence of democracies based on the principles of liberal capitalism and its emphasis on private ownership and individual self-reliance.

The following extract from Brown's paper sheds a startling light on the position of the Catholic hierarchy and rank-and-file clergy regarding liberationism:

Starting with a few adherents in the late 1950s and early 1960s, the growth of liberationism in Latin America has been steady and impressive. Although no statistics are available to determine the precise size of the movement, an estimated 20 to 30 percent of the bishops (including archbishops and cardinals) are probably dedicated proponents of liberationism. A larger percentage of the hierarchy (possibly over 60 percent) are sympathetic to much of the philosophy behind liberation theology but are not disposed to activate their parishioners toward revolutionary rearrangement, favoring violence if necessary, of economic and political structures that the more radical proponents require. These moderates would favor a more evolutionary change and eschew violence from any quarter. The remaining 10 to 20 percent of the hierarchy fall into the conservative, traditional category, favoring a secondary role for the Church in the social activism area, but emphasizing ministry to society's spiritual needs.

A different picture exists among the rank-and-file clergy. Possibly as many as 40 to 50 percent could be classified as enthusiastic advocates of liberationism, with some 30 to 40 percent in the moderate category and a relatively small percentage siding with the conservative position. In Guatemala, about 80 percent of the five hundred priests working in rural areas are considered to be supporters of the liberationist cause, although only two to five priests are actually fighting alongside the insurgents. (One of the guerrilla priests is Irishman Don McKenna, who is convinced that violence and Marxism are necessary elements to achieve true revolutionary change.)

In El Salvador, Archbishop Rivera y Damas has estimated that twelve to fifteen priests have joined the ranks of the armed guerrillas in the countryside. A large number lend support to the left by providing safe houses, monies, and contacts with the international press.

In neighboring Honduras, Spanish Jesuits and Passionists, as well as several French and a few American priests are actively aiding Salvadoran insurgents with food, funds, and propaganda support through various solidarity and refugee relief committees. There are reports of collaboration between certain priests and the Honduras Communist party to assist the Salvadoran guerrillas jointly.

In the case of Nicaragua a number of priests fought by the side of the Sandinistas against Somoza, and at least twenty now occupy key positions in the government. Maryknoll priest Miguel D'Escoto is foreign minister, and Jesuit Ernesto Cardenal heads the Ministry of Culture. Both are avid liberationists and travel widely internationally promoting their cause. A significant number of parish priests (most of whom are foreign) in Nicaragua also actively support the Sandinista government. Some sixty priests and nuns reaffirmed the depth of their liberationist convictions by signing a document circulated in Managua in March 1981:

Not to support the Sandinistas in Nicaragua today is equivalent to supporting a political model that does not radically change the

> society of exploitation and domination we have inherited. We do
> not just want a change of names in power or simply an end to
> traditional corruption. We want firm and solid moves on a
> noncapitalist basis toward a new society. This is our choice,
> justifiable as Christians.[7]

It should be noted further that historically the Church in Latin
America has never been sympathetic generally either to the United States
as a nation or to the liberal capitalism characteristic of our nation. In this
anti-U.S. aspect there has been little fundamental change in the shift from
an ultraconservative posture to its present radicalization. In brief, the
Catholic Church in Central America, while championing the under-
privileged and rightfully protesting abuses of human rights in the area,
nevertheless is a formidable obstacle for the development of democracy in
the region as visualized by congress and successive U.S. administrations.

Another serious problem affecting the evolution of democracy in the
area, with the possible exception of Costa Rica, concerns the "dependency" complex inherent in the region's psyche, particularly in the rural
sectors. The combination of age long poverty with a cultural inheritance
from both Indian and Spanish backgrounds has perpetuated a perceived
need for peasant reliance on a leading wealthy or political personality or
the government, as the case may be, for basic family well-being. The idea
of high economic personal risk taking is not an attractive prospective if
there is an alternative assuring at least survival. The price of failure means
total disaster.

Translated into political and practical terms such as those concerned
with large scale land reform, while wanting to own a bit of land the
beneficiary will nevertheless seek support within a grouping offering
financial help and technical guidance, as well as moral support. This
anchor could be independent cooperatives if adequate private leadership
emerges, government-run organizations, or politically influenced associations. In any event the emphasis will be less on how the individual small
landowner wants to deal with his affairs than how he is told to do so by
whoever is in control of the grouping. Under those circumstances it is easy
to understand why votes cast in any election will be apt to reflect the
desires of the groupings' leadership with questionable regard for the
members' possible true sentiments.

To some extent the situation would not be too different from that
existing in our country when political machines have held tight control
over the politics of a state or city. But our nation is too large and complex
for a local condition to affect the destiny of the total national body politic.
In any of the small Central American countries (Costa Rica excepted) the
practice of cacique politics influences national events, making a mockery of

elections as a key to representative democracy. Until such time as illiteracy is wiped out in the countryside, independent landownership a fact, and technically competent proprietors emerge having ready personal access to financial resources (banks, credit unions, etc.), as well as establishment of industries in the countryside, the possibility of genuine democracy in rural Guatemala, El Salvador, Honduras, and Nicaragua is illusory.

In the urban centers where a middle class is already emerging with higher levels of education and financial prospects, the "dependency" issue is of greatly lessened importance and reduced largely to extended family interrelationships. Thus we see the nucleus for a true manifestation of democracy in the city of San Salvador thanks to the development of considerable industry, commerce, and service trades in the past 20 years or so. But this core is terribly fragile. Continued violence and sabotage from the Left and squeeze from the Right would result in the destruction of the nascent Salvadoran middle class and with it hopes for democracy.

In Costa Rica there has long been a rural and urban middle class, hence a working democracy. In the capitals of Guatemala, Nicaragua, and Honduras the rural sectors are practically devoid of a middle class and are marked by a high "dependency" characteristic. Small middle class sectors have been emerging in the urban centers of these three republics but they have a long way to go before being in a position to exert meaningful influence, as a bloc, over the armed forces and other governmental institutions.

Economic conditions prevailing in Central America are no doubt both a collection of problems and an opportunity for reform. There is one consideration, although complex, that must also be appreciated: demographics. Periodically in this chapter and elsewhere we have made reference to related demographic factors such as poverty, illiteracy, and conditions of health among others. Yet cultural factors are also important and affect economics and politics. Nowhere is this more obvious than with the Central American Indian. In addition to a Spanish culture there are Indian cultures to be concerned with. As a general statement of averages, 10 percent of Central America's population is Indian and therefore distinctly not Spanish. At one extreme is Guatemala, in which the Indian population makes up 60 percent while at the other end is Costa Rica with only a 3 percent Indian community. In El Salvador and Honduras, 90 percent of the population is *mestizo*. In Costa Rica *mestizos* account for some 47 percent of the population while nearly 50 percent claim to be pure white.

Central American Indians have their own cultures as rich and varied as any found in the New World. They resist public education for fear that they will lose their own identities and languages by learning that of the Spaniard. Indians leave school at an earlier age than others to go to work and usually in poor paying jobs (often they are called *ladinos*). It is not uncommon to find six-year-old Indians working. Young working Indians barely speak Spanish and like most others are often exploited by the Spanish societies that govern the area. Yet even with these depressing facts, Indian portions of the population are not immune to the processes of change and modernization. For example, in 1983, according to Guatemalan government sources, half of all Guatemalan Indian children had access to elementary school and 1 percent of school age Indians went to high school. Nonetheless, using Guatemala again as an example, it has 22 distinct and separate Indian languages to contend with which serve as real barriers to communications. Thus hand-in-glove with the process of modernization is the spread by most government agencies in the use of Spanish as the common language.

Demographic issues, particularly as they affect Indians, may be considerably altered as concerns by the current fighting in Central America. Between January 1982 and the summer of 1983, some 10,000 Indians had reportedly been killed by Guatemalan troops fighting leftist rebels. No statistics are available to suggest what is happening elsewhere with Indian deaths. We know that over 1 million have been uprooted from their homes and that some 30,000 have fled into southern Mexico. A similar tale could be told about Nicaragua. In neither can one realistically foresee an end to this uprooting of Indian life within the near future. Thus a combination of circumstances—war, government attempts at education, the necessity to use the Spanish language—are all contributing either to a smaller population that is less prone to accept the regional language and culture of the Spanish or which is being drawn into that European culture more sharply if for no other reason than physical survival. As a consequence, one might expect over many decades that the population of Central America as a whole would become culturally more homogeneous and therefore lend itself even further to the shared values essential to an economically stable and perhaps politically democratic society.

To return to the concept of a U.S. "Marshall Plan" for long-term support for the Central American Common Market, recognition is essential of the probability that once the Marxist-Leninist threat to the area either closes or is severely curtailed, Congress will lose immediate interest in the plan. We must recall that some 20 years ago enthusiasm for the Alliance for Progress, a concept which envisaged support for the Central American Common Market, sharply waned both at home and in Latin America after President Kennedy's death. Not only did Congress balk at prolonged underwriting prospects, as did also the administration of President Lyndon Johnson, but there was widespread resentment in Latin America about many aspects of the Alliance's approach. In Professor

Fredrick B. Pike's *Spanish America 1900–1970* he refers to the Alliance in the following terms:

> An important factor alienating the Spanish American upper classes and wounding their pride was the much advertised demand for internal reform imposed by the architects of the Alliance for Progress. The Alliance, launched by President John F. Kennedy at the outset of his presidential term in 1961, aimed at the improvement of conditions in Latin America through a ten-year allotment of 10 billion United States dollars, both public and private, to the republics to the south. Assignment of funds was to be dependent upon acceptance by Latin American leaders of social and economic reforms designed largely in Washington. Profoundly insensitive to deep-seated cultural differences, the United States experts who shaped Alliance policies assumed that socioeconomic measures judged appropriate to their own country would provide a panacea for problems south of the border. The Alliance was noted chiefly for arousing hopes in Latin America that could not be fulfilled and for alienating directing classes through demands for reform that were viewed, understandably, as a new type of United States intervention in internal affairs.[8]

One merely has to substitute the words "rulers" for "upper" in the first sentence of the aforesaid and the caution is as valid for today as it was when written by Professor Pike. It would be hoped that in the event of a revival of interest in the Central American Common Market (as revived in August 1984 when economic ministers from five Central American governments met to reactivate the institution), such U.S. insensitivity would be avoided through the expediency of asking the Central Americans to come up with their Plan.

The main thrust of the "Plan" would be to consider a region of some 22 million people as a total area to be coordinated economically and socially. A systematic drive toward remedying the illiteracy problem, expanding health care facilities, developing adequate school facilities and sharing faculty resources, creating new industries and commercial opportunities, pooling foreign exchange resources and intensive encouragement of tourism would establish goals to which people could move with hope and enthusiasm. Militarily the armed forces would coordinate their efforts for the purpose of protecting the region from both Left and Right extremists. In time, the growth of middle-class-based democracy would serve as a brake on military aspirations.

The key problem is how to keep successive congresses and presidential administrations committed to sustained support for the Central American Common Market. Political life being what it is in the United States, the only solution lies in the intensified lobbying efforts of nonprofit foundations concerned exclusively with Latin America, and particularly with Central America and the Caribbean Basin.

One should add that a "stitch in time saves nine." Funds judiciously spent in direct budgetary support in the underpinning of a major economic plan for Central America will represent far less expenditure than the eventual alternative cost of massive troop involvement, let alone the world-wide repercussions affecting U.S. interests everywhere.

An important step which the Department of State could take to help make a Central American policy consistent throughout succeeding administrations is inclusion of greater detail in the contents of its *GIST* publications. These are a "quick reference aid on U. S. foreign relations." Because of their wide distribution *GIST* is a ready-made instrument through which U.S. support can be developed strongly from within the nation, if aspects dealing with strategies and tactics, traditional weaknesses in U.S. foreign policy implementation, are sufficiently explained. Combined with an expanded *GIST*, special efforts should be made by expert personnel in the Executive Branch to make sure that the senior staff aides of Representatives and Senators in Congress understand fully what may be happening. Congressmen because of their enormous workloads must depend on these aides for guidance, and enlistment of their support is fundamental for the continuation of any foreign policy in areas where geopolitical considerations are paramount. In short, preparation of the *GIST* series warrants the most serious attention within the Department of State. At present, they are too succinct and spotty in quality.

THE ISLAND REPUBLICS

In both the *GIST* issue of February 1982 entitled "Caribbean Basin Initiative," and in President Reagan's address on February 24, 1982 before the Organization of American States as reported in the Department of State's publication, *Current Policy No. 370*, also dubbed in the same fashion, Central America and the island republics in the general Caribbean area and Gulf of Mexico are grouped together for purpose of foreign policy objectives. According to the cited statements it appears that the measures contemplated would be common to the total grouping.

The problem with this approach is that fundamental differences between the Central American countries as a group and the island republics call for basically varied strategies and tactics. The idea of substantial and prolonged support by the United States for a revitalized Central American Common Market concept based on a Marshall Plan approach is not applicable strategically and tactically to the island republics. U.S. approaches to these nations must rest on bilateral considerations without concern for an island republics' common market. Some interisland trade can be developed but does not appear as a viable or fundamental concept. Their economies are not sufficiently complementary to each other. However, as agricultural products are important for the nations in the area, duty-free entry into the U.S. market as permitted by the Caribbean Basin Economic Recovery Act, should be helpful, but only the passage of time will show results. The question of trading terms and actual application of the act may point the way to further measures.

Generally speaking, Jamaica and a number of the other island countries require easier access to the U.S. market, intensified encouragement for capital formation in their private sectors both for light industry and the service trades, greater facilities in the availability of public and private capital for the aforementioned purposes, and assistance in land programs designed to create or strengthen a rural middle class. While there has been U.S. interest in developing healthy relationships with the islands, these have been limited mainly as a matter of policy in depending on private U.S. investment and modest official aid. We believe both efforts must be greatly broadened to have any significant impact.

Tourism as a source of revenue is crucial for the well-being of the islands. The closest cooperation should be urged between U.S. and island official and private agencies concerned with travel. The promotion of tourist travel is a complex proposition involving not just the construction of facilities, but equally important the cultivation of attitudes conducive to the development of massive repeat clienteles. Responsibilities for the development of such attitudes lie with the authorities of the island republics to a very great extent, since treatment of visitors frequently reflects internal political biases regarding foreigners, particularly U.S. citizens.

Underlying general U.S. policy toward the Caribbean Islands in the sense of *quid pro quo* relationships, should be a clear understanding of commitment by the island republics to the strengthening of the middle classes in their countries, as essential to the evolution and survival of democratic institutions, and to free elections as the basis for governmental selection. From the U.S. viewpoint, resulting political stability in the Caribbean and economic prosperity rebounding in profitable foreign trade and other business activity with the region, will more than justify adoption of impressive economic assistance programs for the new republics. Strategies and tactics should be tailored accordingly.

Not all prospects for the immediate future, even under the most optimistic forecasts, offer certain hopes of success for this recommended approach. Haiti's problems are almost unsurmountable. But Trinidad–Tobago, Jamaica, the Dominican Republic, Barbados, possibly Surinam, and even Grenada are ripe for important development. Success in our

dealings with these islands will affect eventually the course of developments in Cuba, particularly as population growth in that nation, European
resistance to continued bankrolling of the Cuban government, and
probable Soviet reluctance to pick up the difference creates internal
pressures of a serious dimension. With respect to Haiti, in time it may be
possible for various of the island nations to assist in the problems of that
country.

For purpose of discussion, attention will be centered on the islands
mentioned rather than on all of the newly independent countries in the
area. The variety of contrasts in the selected group is sufficient to project a
view of the general panorama. One important point to highlight is that
those islands long under British sovereignty have inherited political and
governmental infrastructures based on the principles of liberal democracy.
Additionally, the use of English as *lingua franca* combined with the
mentioned inheritance from Great Britain favors healthy bilateral relations
with the United States in view of a common basic governmental heritage.
These observations apply particularly to Jamaica, Trinidad–Tobago, and
Barbados. Because of the Spanish background in the Dominican Republic
and the Franco-African heritage in Haiti, the gap between instinctive U.S.
approaches to economic, social, and political issues affecting our individual
bilateral relationships complicates these to a greater extent, than with
Jamaica, Barbados, and Trinidad–Tobago. Thus, it is axiomatic that greater
U.S. expertise is required in dealing with the Island Republics which do
not share with us the commonality of language and political philosophy.

A brief overview of the resources of the selected Republics relative to
population and the latter's rate of growth would be helpful in drawing a
basic picture of their respective situations. Trinidad near the coast of
Venezuela, and part of the Commonwealth of Nations (former members of
the British Empire), has important oil refining facilites and an inexhaustible supply of pitch (asphalt). Hence, petroleum products constitute a major export component. It also exports ammonia and fertilizer.

In the agricultural sector there are produced sugar cane, cocoa, coffee,
rice, and bananas. It nevertheless imports foodstuffs, as well as crude
petroleum and miscellaneous machinery and industrial equipment.
Because of its petroleum industry it enjoys the highest per capita annual
income of the countries selected, in excess of $4,350. Literacy rate is 95
percent. The Republic's population for 1981 was estimated at 1,115,000
with an average annual growth rate for the years of 1970–80 of 0.98
percent.[9]

Tobago, adjoining Trinidad and the other part of the Republic is
practically devoid of industry, but is a tourist paradise. While the
industrial, commercial, and services sectors are moving along, the
agricultural sector because of low export prices is relatively stagnant. Any

policy of the United States affecting relations with Trinidad-Tobago should help with the problem of the island's agricultural exports. The preferential tariff approach may be one solution.

Jamaica's population in 1981 was estimated at 2.220 million with an average annual growth rate of 1.59 percent for the years 1970–80.[10] It has an impressively large middle class in the urban centers, considerable skill in top management, weak at middle management levels, and roughly an estimated 20 percent of rural land ownership in the hands of small proprietors, a fact crucial to the Jamaican political stability. But in common with other nations in the Caribbean Basin relying heavily on agricultural exports for foreign exchange earnings, the U.S. market must remain consistently attractive for their products. Thus the new U.S. policy calling for selected free import duty treatment is an important and perhaps determinative consideration.

In broad terms Jamaica produces sugar cane, citrus fruits, bananas, pimentos, coconuts, coffee, and cocoa. Of these sugar, bananas, citrus fruits, and cocoa are leading exports. The nation also produces bauxite, a key item in the island's economy and major export. Rum is another by-product of the sugar industry with a market in the United States. Internally, there is a fairly wide range in light industry, including textile manufactures and the processing of food products. Imports include fuels, an important and costly necessity, machinery, transport, and electrical equipment, food, and fertilizers. Literacy rate is reported variously at between 40 and 60 percent.

Essentially, the nature of the island's economy and its political stability points to U.S. *quid pro quo* approach based mainly on normal private commercial and banking interrelationships, with U.S. official backing for such assistance as may be required from the international private and official financial institutions, and supportive of U.S. and island private endeavors. However, steps to help stabilize the agricultural sector may depend on the new tariff established under the new U.S.-Caribbean Basin measures.

An important development in recent years is an intensive and enlightened effort by Jamaica to attract large-scale tourism to the island. Combined with appropriate advertising activities is an internal campaign designed to encourage attitudes within the island conducive to making tourists feel comfortable and at ease.

Jamaica offers intriguing possibilities for the future and one suspects that it has the potential for emerging eventually as a force for progress in the Caribbean, a position from which it may render technical and perhaps even limited financial aid to some of the other developing island economies. Of striking importance is the transition it made in 1980 through democratic means, despite some violence, from the Marxist-oriented government of Michael Manley to the capitalist philosophy of Edward P. Seaga's Labor Party. The fact that this change was made despite high unemployment demonstrated the maturity of Jamaica's political system. Nevertheless, the future is rife with pitfalls as the island must struggle with the key problem of overpopulation relative to the existing economic base. Failure of Seaga's efforts could lead to a return to Marxist dogma and destruction of Jamaica's democratic system. Hence, it is very much in the interest of the United States to work closely with Jamaica in order to assure the country's future prosperity.

The quid pro quo basis for Jamaican-U.S. relations should rest largely on traditional private sector commercial ties, tempered by free import duty tariff treatment for certain Jamaican products.

The Dominican Republic's economy is largely agricultural with more than 70 percent of the labor force in this sector and under 10 percent in industry. Its main exports are sugar, coffee, cocoa, tobacco, and some mineral products such as nickel and bauxite. In addition to the last two minerals there is limited silver and gold mining. Imports are foodstuffs, petroleum, industrial raw materials, and machinery. Literacy rate is about 65 to 70 percent. Population in 1981 totaled about 5.090 million and average annual population growth rate for the 1970–80 period was 2.95 percent.[11]

Although long an independent nation, nevertheless democracy is thinly rooted. There is only a very small middle class in the island, and with so large a proportion of nonproperty owning labor in agriculture there is a dilemma about how to create such a class in the countryside. Overcrowding in the capital city of Santo Domingo (1.250 million) and limited employment possibilities has further complicated the task of consolidating gains in political democracy. The per capita income of about $1,200 veils the widespread low standards of living. The island's history is sadly marked by upheavals caused from abroad, interference on repeated occasions by U.S. military forces, internal violence, and until the early 1960s an ironfisted dictatorship which lasted 31 years. In common with other nations in Latin America no democratic institutions were inherited from the Spanish colonial eras. On the other hand, the Dominicans are very much a peace-loving people, wish to be masters of their destiny, preserve their Spanish heritage and language, and move forward to a securer and more promising economic and political future.

The task to achieve both Dominican aspirations, and those of the United States in terms of long-term stability, is too complex for the United States alone. It is not just a matter of dollars spent in the proper amount and at the right time. It involves dealing with the Hispanic psyche of the Dominicans, a chore most elusive for U.S. officials concerned with policy problems both in Congress and in the Executive Branch, as well as the practical problem of land reforms without igniting internal disorder.

Assistance from Venezuela with respect to the Dominican Republic's fuel requirements long into the future is needed. Help in connection with land reform from exports in the multilateral banking institutions is probably essential. U.S.-free import duty treatment for sugar and other agricultural products may help. Until now reliance on U.S. private investment, some loans, and modest official U.S. aid have proven inadequate for marked progress. A ten-year plan developed cooperatively by Dominicans, Americans, and Latin American experts for the expansion of light industry and the service trades, in cooperation with U.S. and Dominican private interests aimed at alleviating unemployment and underemployment, and developing at least an expanded urban middle class, should be developed. Apart from the extension of credits from official and private international banks, the possibility of direct budgetary assistance by the United States to help cover foreign exchange deficits should be weighed carefully as a desirable strategy. This would free scarce Dominican resources for attention to internal social service needs, which if not requited might easily render alternative radical and explosive possibilities attractive, a development highly inimical to U.S. security interests.

The quid pro quo essence of U.S.-Dominican relations would have to rest on a complex of normal commercial relations, common understanding of regional security problems, and mutual commitment to a certain degree of regional cooperation. Commendable efforts by the Dominican government on behalf of the tourist industry are well underway, and in time may reach very important proportions. U.S. official encouragement in this respect as well expert help as appropriate is most desirable.

Haiti, which shares with the Dominican Republic the island of Hispaniola, presents an almost intractable policy problem for the United States. With a population of about 5.090 million in 1981, an average annual population growth rate for the period 1970–80 of 1.68 percent,[12] with an annual per capita income of between $250 and $275, literacy rate of roughly 12 percent, a mountain-ridden topography severely limiting prospects for large-scale agricultural development and devoid of petroleum or fast rivers for power generation, the future is difficult indeed for this country. In addition the lack of minimal health facilities, and obviously schooling, creates a condition under which desperation drives large numbers of Haitians to flee the island under extremely hazardous circumstances in the attempt of illegal entry into the United States through the Florida coasts. Thus, for the United States not only is there a worrisome situation in this country, but its source as the point of departure for massive illegal immigration to our country and its attendant complications, requires careful attention to the Haitian issue.

The United States is at its best in developing aid programs for nations in an advanced stage of economic and social evolution. Our experts are conditioned by the very size of our nation to think in macro terms. Yet an economy such as that of Haiti, in addition to a social and political milieu so drastically different from that of the United States, renders the formation of policies, strategies, and tactics required to deal with Haiti on effective terms very difficult to develop. The main reason is the great difficulty of U.S. experts, the Congress, and officials in the Executive Branch to think "small."

Haiti's future political, social, and economic health calls for attention over the next several generations to its health facilities and educational requirements within a series of building blocks approaches. The Haitian situation is not too different from that of some of the former French possessions in Africa. Because of the experience of the French in that environment and the fact of a French dialect in Haiti, Washington might do well to work with France on aid for Haiti. A cadre of French teachers and medical technicians in association with carefully selected U.S. counterparts might be a proper approach.

Apart from agricultural products characteristic of its tropical environment, the country's other main natural resource is bauxite, also an item of export. Other products shipped abroad are coffee, sugar, essential oils, sisal, and handicrafts. Imports cover foodstuffs, petroleum, construction materials, machinery, and a wide range of consumer goods. Tourism is a source of income and this sector of the economy has the potential for important further development, but facilities are as yet quite limited for substantial expansion.

Clearly, the new U.S.-free import duty policy should help. U.S. aid in the past has been inadequate for the country's needs, and it may well be beyond the capability of the United States to cope with the problem. Perhaps direct U.S. budgetary support might also be desirable to help in the development of medical and educational facilities in response to plans developed by Haitian officials. A more extensive international effort is probably in order.

Barbados, with a population of some 250,000 in 1981, average annual growth rate of 0.53 percent for the years 1970–80[13], literacy rate of over 90 percent, close connections with the United Kingdom and Canada through continued membership in the (British) Commonwealth of Nations although independent since 1966, and a per capita annual income in excess of $3,000, is an oasis of political stability in the Caribbean.

Its main agricultural output consists of sugar cane and subsistence foods supplemented by light manufactures and a very lucrative and well-organized tourist trade drawing heavily on U.S. travel. Sugar is the main export. Imports are fuel, consumer goods, and foodstuffs. The new U.S.-Caribbean policy should prove helpful in this area.

Grenada, independent since 1974 but still a member of the (British) Commonwealth of Nations is a prime example of the failure of U.S. policy to deal with new mini-nations on a micro basis. Grenada has a population of only 110,000—1981 estimate—with an annual average growth rate of 1.3 percent for the ten years 1970–80.[14] It has a basically agricultural economy producing nutmeg, cocoa, bananas, and mace for export while importing foodstuffs, machinery, construction materials, and a wide range of essential consumer goods. Information about its literacy rate is not readily available. Its infrastructural capacity for developing an important tourist trade is sharply limited, hence an acute imbalance in its balance of trade. Average annual per capita income is under $700.

Wobbly economic conditions in the Island and unemployment at one point perhaps as high as 49 percent, combined with dismal prospects, rendered Grenada vulnerable to Soviet Union blandishments through Cuba, reflected in the construction of expanded airport facilities. Another consequence was the widespread presence of Cubans in various capacities in the Island, and the transfer of military equipment far exceeding Grenada's reasonable requirements. Captured documents obtained as a result of the U.S. military intervention in late October and November 1983 revealed secret agreements in this respect.

The U.S. action was effected in conjunction with forces from St. Vincent and the Grenadines, St. Lucia, Dominica, Antigua-Barbuda, all members of the Organization of Eastern Caribbean States (OECS) established on July 4, 1981 (which includes Grenada, Montserrat still a British Crown Colony, and newly independent St. Kitts-Nevis), with forces also from Jamaica and Barbados. It was precipitated by a violent situation, which developed following the overthrow and assassination of Grenadian Prime Minister Maurice Bishop, initiated by his deputy and Marxist extremists in the Grenadian military. These developments placed in jeopardy a considerable number of U.S. students studying in Grenada's St. Charles' Medical College.

Elimination of the Marxist regime and Grenada's close ties with Cuba and the Soviet Union would appear to offer the United States an excellent opportunity to restructure its policy toward the Island. The United States should develop a long-term plan based on direct budgetary assistance, general economic and technical assistance, and free U.S. tariff treatment for the Island's products as well as for the other members of the OECS. Because of its status as a British Crown Colony, Montserrat may well be the exception. Quid pro quo basis for broadened U.S. economic and financial help should be at the exclusion of any direct or indirect Soviet or

Cuban military aid, or presence not beyond token diplomatic representation at most.

A clearer picture of the economic situation in the islands examined can be obtained from gross domestic product data, foreign trade, and balance of payments figures.

From Tables 5.5 and 5.6, dealing respectively with real gross domestic product growth rates and per capita rates for this item, the basic economic health is evident of Trinidad–Tobago over the past 20 years or so, the effect mainly of the island's oil refining industry.

In contrast, Jamaica which enjoyed steady growth in the 1960–70 years showed a marked downward trend in the decade of the 1970s, as population increase and a relative stagnant agricultural sector, combined with the economic stifling policies of the socialist regime of the Manley government, failed to spur essential development in the industrial and commercial sectors. Furthermore, the tourist trade suffered in those years as the consequence of a less than friendly attitude toward foreign visitors, particularly U.S. citizens. Yet note that with the advent of the Seaga government and reversal of the Manley policies, and change in local attitudes to tourism and tourists, by 1981 the beginning of a positive trend in the economy was noticeable. This favorable observation is not intended to deny that Jamaica is still in a terrible economic fix. Massive foreign assistance and an increase in world bauxite prices would be required to bring it out of its doldrums.

The Dominican Republic showed steady growth in the 20 years between 1960–80. But lower international sugar prices, curtailed domestic spending as foreign exchange earnings from exports weakened plus increases in the rates of foreign currency borrowings, reflected a downward trend in the economy by 1981. The need for strengthening the

TABLE 5.5. Selected Caribbean Island Republics Real GDP Growth Rates, 1960–81

	1960–70[a]	1970–80[a]	1980	1981[b]
Trinidad and Tobago	4.0	4.4	3.5	4.0
Jamaica	5.4	−0.7	−3.5	1.5
Dominican Republic	5.1	6.9	5.4	3.5
Haiti	0.8	4.3	5.5	0.0
Barbados	8.1	1.8	5.4	−1.1
Grenada	—	—	−2.0	−2.0

[a]Average annual growth.
[b]Preliminary estimates.
Source: Statistical Bulletin of the OAS, Vol. 4, No. 1–2, page 5.

TABLE 5.6. Selected Caribbean Island Republics Real Per Capita GDP Growth Rates, 1960–81

	1960–70[a]	1970–80[a]	1980	1981[b]
Trinidad and Tobago	1.8	3.4	3.5	3.1
Jamaica	3.9	−2.2	−4.8	0.1
Dominican Republic	2.1	3.8	2.5	0.5
Haiti	−0.8	2.6	3.7	−1.3
Barbados	7.6	1.4	5.4	−1.1
Grenada	—	—	−2.0	−2.0

[a]Average annual growth rate.
[b]Preliminary estimates.
Source: *Statistical Bulletin of the OAS*, Vol. 4, No. 1–2, page 6.

market for its agricultural exports is essential if a healthy long haul economic trend is to be developed.

The erratic behavior of the Haitian economy and vulnerability to causes beyond its control is mirrored in the statistical pattern. Heavily dependent on coffee exports and the tourist trade, any wobbles affecting these have an immediate effect on the Island's well-being. From 1960–70 Haiti's economy was obviously stagnant, one reason for substantial Haitian migration to the United States. Some improvement was noted in the years 1970–80, but in late 1980 hurricane Allen severely damaged the agricultural sector, particularly the coffee crop. This disaster added to lower tourist travel to the Island, resulting in sharp declines in terms of real gross domestic growth rates and sparked renewed internal pressure for emigration.

Despite internal stability and a capable government, the fragility of Barbados' reliance of sugar exports and tourism is reflected in growth figures for the past 20 years or so. The acute decline in 1981 in the economy's behavior stemmed from a combination of adverse weather conditions affecting the production of sugar cane, labor problems in that industry, and weakened international prices. The recession in Western Europe and in the United States adversely affected the flow of tourists to Barbados in that year. The need for greater stability for the sugar sector is essential for long-term economic health.

Very little information is readily available about the economy of Grenada in the 1960–80 years. However, data for 1980 and 1981 dramatically show the island's economic weakness and predictable political problems as a result.

Table 5.7, concerned with the foreign trade picture of the Island Republics for the years 1978–81, highlights dramatically the extreme

TABLE 5.7. Selected Caribbean and Gulf of Mexico Island Republics Merchandise Balance of Trade, 1978–81 (In Millions of U.S. $)

	Exports of Goods (FOB)			
	1978	1979	1980	1981[a]
Trinidad and Tobago	1275.9	1649.1	2535.5	2738.3
Jamaica	794.5	814.7	964.6	1025.0
Dominican Republic	675.5	868.6	963.3	1000.0
Haiti	150.0	138.0	211.7	153.3
Barbados	111.1	131.4	188.5	177.7
Grenada	17.0	21.0	17.0	19.5
	Imports of Goods (FOB)			
	1978	1979	1980	1981[a]
Trinidad and Tobago	1044.8	1324.8	1752.4	2032.8
Jamaica	749.9	882.6	1039.1	1500.0
Dominican Republic	859.7	1093.9	1425.7	1326.0
Haiti	207.5	234.0	294.6	320.0
Barbados	287.6	379.1	479.5	585.2
Grenada	35.7	53.6	50.6	53.0
	Trade Balance			
	1978	1979	1980	1981[a]
Trinidad and Tobago	231.1	324.3	783.1	705.5
Jamaica	44.6	−67.9	−74.5	−475.0
Dominican Republic	−184.2	−225.3	−462.4	−326.0
Haiti	−57.5	−96.0	−82.9	−166.7
Barbados	−176.5	−247.7	−291.0	−407.5
Grenada	−18.7	−31.9	−33.0	−33.5

[a]Preliminary estimates.
Source: Statistical Bulletin of the OAS, Vol. 4, No. 1–2, page 27.

fragility of the economic position of the Islands dependent heavily on the exports of their agricultural output. With the exception of Trinidad–Tobago, which thanks to petroleum shipments and its pitch lake, shows consistent favorable merchandise trade balances, the others indicate an almost unbroken story of negative performance.

Interestingly, Trinidad–Tobago (See Table 5.8) (showing current account balance of payments positions for 1978–80) reflected a negative position at the end of 1979, a development covered from the Island's foreign exchange reserve holdings. However, the record for the other countries reviewed correlated with the negative balances reflected in the merchandise foreign trade movement. These differences had to be covered

TABLE 5.8. Selected Caribbean and Gulf of Mexico Island Republics Balance of Payments, Current Accounts (In Millions of U.S. $)

	1978	1979	1980
Trinidad and Tobago	38.1	−39.2	NA
Jamaica	−50.4	−139.6	−176.9
Dominican Republic	−311.9	−331.3	−669.8
Haiti	−44.9	−59.0	−77.6
Barbados	−31.1	−33.8	−26.8
Grenada	NA	NA	NA

NA = Not available.

Source: *Statistical Bulletin of the OAS*, Vol. 4, No. 1–2, pages 103–217.

by diminishing reserves and increased foreign borrowings at high rates of interest.

SUMMARY

Central America and the Caribbean area are obviously important to the United States geopolitically, militarily, and economically. Yet their economies are terribly fragile, the internal political structures of most inherently unstable and very limited in capacity to fend off overtures from elements desiring injury to the United States.

U.S. policy, strategies, and tactics toward the two regions have been inadequate as already discussed. Dependence on private U.S. investments is not enough. The net result has been the loss of Cuba as a close friend and ally, Soviet-Cuban involvement with Grenada, turmoil in Nicaragua, Guatemala, El Salvador, and Honduras with the threat of an intraregional war hanging over these countries. To continue along the same wobbly policy path will lead eventually to a situation involving the direct use of U.S. military forces on a large scale, once a clear Soviet threat through some surrogate or surrogates is unequivocally perceived by the U.S. public. Such a development with the resulting emigration to the United States of a million or so refugees would profoundly shock the U.S. body politic. The cost of military action in terms of treasure, lives, and damage to our national psyche, as well as tremendous world-wide reverberations would be enormous. We should all remember that the mediocrity and lack of vision of British, U.S., and French statesmen during the 1918–39 period was a major factor in bringing on the catastrophe of World War II. In fact there are those scholars who suggest in connection with events prior to World War I, that had Germany suspected the eventual entry of the United States into the conflict that ensued, that horror would not have necessarily been ignited.

The fact is that Central America and the Caribbean nations require special U.S. consideration. The general import tariff policy followed by the United States applicable to all Third World countries has been totally inadequate for these countries near our borders. The Caribbean Basin Economic Recovery Act is both a practical and psychological expression of intensified U.S. interest in the Basin.

Development of a policy and strategies for a Central American "Marshall Plan," one underwriting a vibrant Central American Common Market; free entry for certain agricultural products; encouragement of U.S. private capital investment for expanded light industry and the trade services sector; all based on relations stemming from mutual respect and consideration will go a long way to avoiding ultimately more costly and possibly catastrophic developments.

One important feature of what is proposed is that the eventual result would not be a conglomerate of mini-nations dependent on U.S. largesse forever in some sort of semicolonial status. Rather, the substantial expansion of the economies of these two dozen or so nations will add up to a very substantial two-way foreign trade and financial proposition. Our initial investments in the future of the regions discussed would prove profitable for all concerned beyond our present capability to forecast. Let us not forget that at one time European investors viewed our economic life and prospects with much skepticism, and at our internal political fluctuations with intense distrust.

One serious weakness consistently marking our approaches to Latin America in general, and the regions of immediate interest specifically, has been confusion related to the evolution of democracy. The outward symbols of democracy such as elections tend to be equated to democracy itself. While there is no question that free elections, in which an informed electorate participates without coercion, is fundamental to democratic evolvement, a thorough understanding by Congress and our policymakers is essential regarding what makes such a political phenomenon possible. Thus, without the creation of substantial middle classes in both rural and urban areas true democracy is impossible. Hence, it is imperative that as we develop jointly policies leading to the economic health of Central America and the Caribbean, we do so bearing in mind the issue of the middle class. Urban dwellers with healthy bank accounts and rural property owners will support democracy and not radical and violent revolution.

One puzzling aspect of U.S. relations with Latin America in general and Central America in particular, as well as the Caribbean region, is the weakness of U.S. business interests in the maintenance of an active and effective lobby on behalf of realistic policies and behavior toward these areas. The pattern of oil company lobbies regarding the Middle East could serve as a possible model. More than 200 U.S. firms have either substantial direct investments "south of the border" or important trading relationships.

If these or some new Latin-American foundation sharpened their focus on the specific nature of our dealings with the Latin countries and the Caribbean Islands, with concrete proposals for policies, strategies, and tactics, specially persistent lobbying activities with regard to Congress and the media, a greater element of consistency might be injected into U.S. official attitudes. There are similar organizations doing splendid work in connection with U.S. relations with Europe and the Middle East. Something like them should function toward Latin America. Leaving the field open to academe and religious organizations is not in the best interests of the United States.

Zigzags in U.S. policy toward Latin America in general, and the Caribbean Islands and Central America in particular, can be corrected to some extent through major efforts by corporations and private nonprofit foundations concerned with specific areas. Business interests frequently have taken the position with respect to official U.S. attitudes that commerce could be dealt with separately from U.S. internal and external political considerations. This view is untenable. Business and politics go together. They are the obverse and reverse of the same coin.

With respect to the Caribbean Basin, among a number of organizations, Caribbean Central American Action (C/CAA) is an increasingly dynamic nonprofit entity with main offices in Washington, D.C., and a branch in Miami, Florida. It is supported principally through contributions by U.S. business enterprises. Close to 100 firms underwrite the organization, including many of the nation's most important business concerns engaged in foreign trade or operations. To quote from a pamphlet prepared by this group, the "C/CAA works to raise public awareness of the Caribbean Basin as a place to do business; create a positive momentum for closer U.S./Caribbean relations; and educate Congress, U.S. agencies, and the media to Caribbean needs." It is to be hoped that a group such as the C/CAA will continue to grow in strength so that its efforts can be further intensified in the immediate years to come. David Rockefeller's Council of the Americas and the U.S. Chamber of Commerce's Latin American Association are also concerned with the Basin. Congress, unfortunately only responds to continuous pressure.

U.S. business is very conscious of the need to draw on *quid pro quo* tactics in dealing with foreign matters, and should be drawn closer into the policy process for countries to our south.

Finally, the Department of State in its *GIST* series has the means of helping mold Congressional and public opinion by presenting policy positions in a more thorough and extended fashion, particularly dwelling on strategies and tactics. The scope of recipients should be considerably broadened. One suspects that to some degree the series is now treated a bit within the Department with less attention than should be the case.

If to an expanded *GIST* program dealing more extensively with strategies and tactics, recipients are encouraged to submit comments to the Department of State, should these seem appropriate, two important aims would be achieved. On one hand a vehicle would be established whereby the academic community at large would be able to convey views direct to the policy implementors, and thus academe would be afforded a greater opportunity to participate in the policy process. On the other, business-men and newsmen not in the Washington, D. C. arena receiving the *GIST* issues could offer insights on specific problems of particular interest, which could prove helpful. Overall the approach would be very helpful with respect to an Administration's public image and relations.

While problems and possibilities augur well for future courses of action, the area in question must be understood within a broader geographical perspective. For that reason, and because of its unique importance, the role of U.S.-Cuban relations must be examined.

6

WHITHER CUBA?

> Our wine is bitter, but it is our wine.
>
> José Marti

Historians writing in depth about Cuba invariably have found it necessary to discuss the role of sugar in the island's history. Certainly since the late 1820s[1] Cuba's destiny has been, is, and will be for the foreseeable future linked to what happens to this commodity in the international markets, and how nature deals with the Island's crop. Prior to the consolidation of Dr. Fidel Castro's power, the fact that roughly 80 percent of Cuba's sugar went to the United States permitted the U.S. government and interests to affect greatly Cuba's internal and external political and economic policies. With the Soviet Union having displaced the United States as the major buyer, it now occupies the position of influence formerly held by the latter.

Should it ever be possible for Cuba to move into a position of greatly lessened dependence on the Soviet Union because of the resumption of limited sugar sales to the United States, the Island would have the option of tending toward a genuinely neutralist stance in the East-West rivalry. Such an evolution should be a desirable U.S. objective. It would be consistent with the security aspects embodied in the preamble of the Constitution, because a development of that nature would lessen Soviet leverage concerning the establishment in Cuba of increased military presence. But it is downright foolish to expect Cuba to weaken its economic lifeline to the USSR if no reasonably reliable alternative is available for its sugar.

A long-held Cuban aspiration, dating as far back as the first war of independence from Spain in 1868, is to be master of its destiny. Over the past century this desire has resulted in steadily increased nationalistic sentiments culminating in the present regime. In 1959–60 the actions taken against U.S. economic interests in the Island were initially somewhat

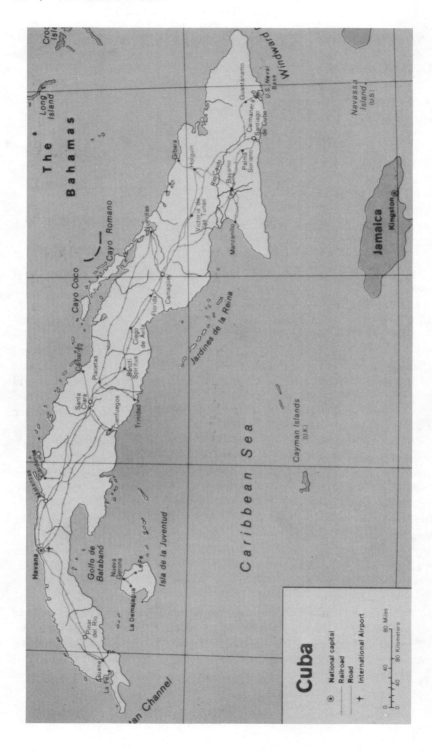

Cuba

less inspired by Marxist ideology than by a sense of exacerbated nationalism. Despite the emergence of Cuba as a rigid Communist nation somewhat in the image of the Soviet model, nationalist feelings are as intense as one would find in Poland or Mexico.

Despite the Cuban government's almost daily broadcast of its status as a "free" country, the reality of Cuba having swapped U.S. tutelage for Soviet patronage is a condition which misleads no one in or out of Cuba. From the Castro government's viewpoint the difference is that U.S. military forces are 90 miles from Cuba, and also in Guantanamo, while those of the Soviets are thousands of miles away. Hence the capability of the USSR to chastise Cuba militarily if it should step out of line is considered by the governing elite as an impossibility, despite the presence of a mechanized Soviet brigade in the island as of this writing. But Cuba's enormous dependence on the USSR for largesse and trade must perforce rankle with the island's leadership. It is no accident that the old pro-Moscow Communist faithful were long ago removed from positions of control within the country's Communist Party and top military command structure.

Another circumstance is Cuban concern that the Soviet-U.S. tug-of-war could involve the island in a holocaust if the Soviets should ever manage to place weaponry in the island aimed at the very heart of the United States. While there may be some rash souls in the Cuban governmental establishment driven by hate of the United States who are willing to run the risk, it is highly probable that the aging and now more experienced ex-guerrillas who control the governmental reins place the island's survival above narrow anti-U.S. government bias. They cannot be oblivious to the fact that the USSR, now going through a period of uneasy transition in its top leadership, might be misled by the various peace movements in the United States to believe in a lack of U.S. will to react vigorously or even violently, with Cuba as the net loser. We all came close to such a situation in the 1962 Missile Crisis. Hence, the extreme current dependence of Cuba on the USSR is a danger to both the United States and Cuba. The emergence of a neutralist Cuba would be a healthy development for the two countries and a loss in substantial yardage for the Soviets.

Obviously, the difficulties in the path of moving Cuba into a neutralist stance are fraught with obstacles. The USSR conceivably would not be happy with any Cuban slippage from its grasp and weakened leverage capabilities. But it is also possible that wiser heads in Moscow might welcome the economic relief which U.S. reentry into the Cuban picture might entail, as well as elimination of a potentially dangerous flashpoint. should meaningful arms control talks between the two superpowers end in positive results, a renewed East-West detente could emerge in which case some implicit agreement would develop concerning Cuba.

In the United States there would also be problems in the development of a policy leading toward a neutralist Cuba. Politically, given the nation's unwieldy foreign policy mechanism, combined with the passions of interest groups adhering to a "don't touch Castro with a ten foot pole" philosophy, it would be no easy task to evolve an important change in U.S. treatment of the Cuban issue. Economically, the major question would be the absorption of substantial quantities of Cuban sugar. The United States cannot very well cut out of the market countries which replaced Cuba as important suppliers and stood by the United States for at least two decades, not to mention the expansion of U.S. sugar production. Nevertheless, there are possible solutions even though difficult to develop. There have been suggestions that perhaps Japan could buy sugar from the Philippines, an important U.S. supplier, with Cuba as a replacement. How practical this approach would be is difficult at this point to assess.

With respect to Cuba, apart from the question of willingness, the government would have to reflect diplomatic finesse of a very high order and statesmanship. Furthermore, Dr. Fidel Castro's penchant for involvement in revolutionary activities around the globe would clearly be an occasional serious irritant. The best way to blunt Cuban enthusiasms for international meddling is to support vigorously whoever the opponents might be. This approach may sound logical. However, in light of Congressional restraint for U.S. counter-balancing actions in Angola, when in the 1970s Cuban troops landed for the purpose of supporting the pro-Communist regime, the suggestion is questionable unless Congress undergoes a change of heart.

With regard to Cuban international meddling, should the United States move in the direction of promoting the concept of a neutralist Cuba, a page should be taken out of the story of U.S. diplomacy in Egypt during President Gamal Abdul Nasser's regime. Nasser found it difficult to refrain from interfering in any of the Middle Eastern revolutions aimed at destabilizing traditionalist or pro-Western regimes. For example, in the early 1960s he landed over 60,000 Egyptian troops in North Yemen to support a group of Yemeni army officers who had dethroned the Imam. The Imam Badr with the help of Saudi Arabia for years waged a guerrilla war against the newly established Yemen republic and its Egyptian allies. This Egyptian action was as distasteful to the U.S. government as Castro's fiddling in Angola. Yet, the U.S. government not only maintained full diplomatic relations with the Nasser regime, but also furnished substantial economic assistance.

Soviet influence was at a peak in Cairo during that era resulting from help in the construction of the High Aswan Dam and arming of the

Egyptian military forces, obviously for use against Israel which the United States staunchly supported. Nevertheless, the United States skillfully kept its lines open to Egypt. In time Nasser's successor President Anwar Sadat expelled the Soviet military advisors from Egypt and the rest is history.

The U.S. Congress and senior policymakers should remember that in history personalities are transients while nations remain.

SUGAR AND FOREIGN TRADE

The position of Cuba among the world's leading sugar producers is indicated in Table 6.1, showing outputs for the six major countries in this industry. For purpose of clarification, it should be noted that Cuba relies on cane sugar, France and the Soviet Union on sugar beets, and the United States on both beets and cane.

Tables 6.2 and 6.3 show, respectively, Cuba's exports of principal commodities for the years 1965 and 1970–77; and imports for 1965 and 1970–76. From these tables, Cuba's continued heavy dependence on sugar is clearly evident.

The range of other leading exports is limited to nickel, tobacco, fish, and shellfish for a considerably smaller value. On the other hand, imports cover a broad variety of items from foodstuffs to machinery and fuel. An important result of this trade pattern is a marked excess of imports over exports. These serious deficits are reflected in Table 6.4, derived from the statistics in Tables 6.2 and 6.3.

For purpose of comparison, in 1958 the year before the Castro government assumed power, imports totaled $777 million and exports $734 million for a deficit of $43 million.[2] The pattern of trade imbalance did not originate with the post-Batista regime. Historically, except in extraordinary boom times of strong foreign demand and particularly high

TABLE 6.1. Leading Sugar Producers, 1978–80 (in metric tons)

	1978	1979	1980
Brazil	7,767	7,020	8,300
Cuba	7,457	8,048	6,787
France	4,065	4,313	4,250
India	7,018	6,367	4,300
Soviet Union	9,100	7,500	7,600
United States	5,353	6,096	5,207

Source: *Information Please Almanac*, 1983, (New York: A & W Publishers, 1983), page 136.

TABLE 6.2 Major Cuban Exports, FOB 1965–77 (in millions of U.S. $)

	1965	1970	1971	1972	1973	1974	1975	1976	1977[a]
Sugar	591	806	657	622	1,032	2,336	3,209	2,855	3,060
Nickel	40	173	136	124	182	167	164	193	NA
Tobacco	33	33	32	40	62	73	63	74	84
Fish and Shellfish	3	19	22	29	40	59	63	79	84
Other	24	19	14	25	56	72	73	83	441
Total	691	1,050	861	840	1,372	2,707	3,572	3,284	3,669

[a]Preliminary.

international sugar prices, Cuban exports generally cannot earn sufficient foreign exchange to cover essential and developmental needs. In the pre-Castro era, considerable U.S. tourist expenditures helped meet these deficits, as well as U.S. and other capital transfers from abroad for the establishment and operation of light industries.

U.S.-Cuban relations were severely strained throughout 1960 following mass nationalization of U.S. companies culminating in the announcement in October 1960 of a U.S. embargo on most exports to Cuba. Diplomatic relations were broken in January 1961. This development was followed by further U.S. measures which interrupted economic transactions between the two countries. This interruption is still in effect.

TABLE 6.3. Major Cuban Imports, CIF, 1970–77 (in millions of U.S. $)

	1961	1970	1971	1972	1973	1974	1975	1976	1977
Foodstuffs	205	263	316	324	411	684	718	723	—
Raw Materials and Intermediate goods	64	138	127	118	157	233	357	255	—
Fuel	85	114	127	163	194	241	377	423	—
Machinery and Transportation equipment	133	368	390	245	365	552	911	1,220	—
Manufacturers	153	131	138	149	215	341	465	399	—
Other	226	297	289	298	399	642	939	859	—
Total	866	1,311	1,387	1,297	1,741	2,693	3,767	3,879	

Source: From Tables 26 and 28, respectively, *The Cuban Economy, A Statistical Review—March 1981*. (Springfield, Virginia: National Technical Information Service, 1981): pages 29, 32.

TABLE 6.4. Cuban Merchandise Trade Deficits, 1965–76 (In Millions of U.S. $)

	1965	1970	1971	1972	1973	1974	1975	1976
Imports	806	1,311	1,387	1,297	1,741	2,693	3,767	3,879
Exports	691	1,050	861	840	1,372	2,707	3,572	3,284
Balance	−115	−261	−526	−457	−369	−986	−195	−595

Source: Same as Tables 6.2 and 6.3

Before looking further into the effects on Cuba's international balance of payments position arising from the shift in its major trading partner, a brief review might be helpful regarding imports and exports by major areas, comparing the pattern before and after Batista's flight. Table 6.5 sheds a light on the results of the change.

It will be seen from Table 6.5 that in 1957 of total exports valued at $818 million, non-Communist countries (principally the United States) accounted for $776 million while the Soviet Union's purchases totaled $42 million. By 1965 with the United States completely out of the trading picture, shipments to non-Communist buyers amounted to $162 million, in contrast to $323 million and $103 million exported, respectively, to the Soviet Union and Eastern Europe. An additional $103 million was also shipped to "Communist countries in the Far East," presumably China. At the end of 1978, the latter figures had become $3.320 billion and $397 million, respectively, for the Soviet Union and Eastern Europe, while the Communist Far East absorbed exports amounting to $138 million. Non-Communist buyers in 1978 purchased Cuban exports valued at $690 million.

However, in assessing the financial significance of the considerable difference in total export figures for the years covered in Table 6.5, consideration must be given to the fluctuations in the world prices for sugar, and to the special arrangements governing trade among the Soviet Union, Eastern Europe, and Cuba. Prices in the latter agreements have no direct relation to world market values. It is assumed that the "Far East Communist countries" probably purchased the Cuban products at open market prices. The data in Table 6.6 concerning world sugar prices, as well as those applicable to Cuba's trade with the Soviet Union, offer an explanation for the inflated value of shipments to the Soviet Union and Eastern European buyers, particularly from 1975 onward.

In 1980, world sugar prices rose sharply to slightly over $0.28 per pound, while the Soviet Union reportedly paid Cuba roughly $0.47 1/2 per pound. The combination afforded Cuba some relief for 1981, but the uncertainty of sugar prices raises havoc with an economy relying on a single crop for at least 80 percent of its foreign earnings.

TABLE 6.5. Cuban Foreign Trade by Major Areas, 1957–78 (in millions of U.S. $)

	1957	1965	1970	1971	1972	1973	1974	1975	1976	1977	1978
Communist countries	42	529	778	557	451	880	1,532	2,401	2,484	3,056	3,855
USSR	42	323	529	304	244	567	981	2,011	1,998	2,602	3,320
Eastern Europe	Negl	103	150	160	137	203	382	279	353	341	397
Far East	Negl	103	99	93	70	110	169	111	133	113	138
Non-communist countries	776	162	272	304	389	492	1,175	1,171	800	613	690
Total *exports*	818	691	1,050	861	840	1,372	2,707	3,572	3,284	3,669	4,545
Communist countries	2	649	905	969	997	1,236	1,631	1,935	2,267	2,887	3,769
USSR	Negl	428	691	731	779	965	1,240	1,513	1,818	2,341	3,083
Eastern Europe	2	98	125	143	126	149	208	304	356	452	537
Far East	Negl	123	85	95	92	122	183	118	93	94	149
Non-communist countries	893	217	406	418	300	505	1,062	1,832	1,612	1,401	963
Total *imports*	895	866	1,311	1,387	1,297	1,741	2,693	3,767	3,879	4,288	4,732
Communist countries	40	−120	−127	−412	−546	−356	−99	466	217	169	86
USSR	42	−105	−162	−427	−535	−398	−259	498	180	261	237
Eastern Europe	−2	5	25	17	11	54	174	−25	−3	−111	−140
Far East	Negl	−20	10	−2	−22	−12	−14	−7	40	19	−11
Non-communist countries	−117	−55	−134	−114	89	−13	113	−661	−812	−788	−273
Trade balance	−77	−175	−261	−526	−457	−369	14	−195	−595	−619	−187

Note: Negl indicates negligible.

Source: From Table 21, *The Cuban Economy, A Statistical Review—March 1981.* (Springfield, Virginia: National Technical Information Service, 1981): page 24.

TABLE 6.6 Cuban Sugar Export Prices (U.S. cents per pound)

Year	Soviet Union[a]	Eastern Europe[a]	China[a]	United States	Average World Market[b]
1957	5.4	5.4	[c]	5.3	5.0
1965	6.1	6.1	6.1	—	2.1
1970	6.1	5.6	6.1	—	3.8
1971	6.1	5.9	6.1	—	4.5
1972	6.1	6.1	6.1	—	7.4
1973	12.2	8.6	11.0	—	9.6
1974	19.6	19.6	17.0	—	30.0
1975	31.5	19.6	23.6	—	20.3
1976	30.2	19.6	21.3	—	11.6
1977	31.2	20.0	11.5	—	8.1
1978[c]	42.0	21.7	8.0	—	7.8
1979[c]	44.0	22.3	8.0	—	9.6

[a]Export prices for raw sugar, FOB under the trade protocols.
[b]Average annual export price, FOB Caribbean ports; actual price received by Cuba may differ because of seasonality of deliveries.
[c]Estimated.
Source: From Table 32, *The Cuban Economy, A Statistical Review—March 1981*, (Springfield, Virginia: National Technical Information Service): page 36.

With further reference to the data in Table 6.5, a summary shows adverse merchandise trade balances for Cuba with the non-Communist world for 1957, 1965, 1970, and 1971, favorable in 1972 and 1974, unfavorable in 1973, and massively adverse for the four years 1975–78. Cuba's balance with the Communist nations was positive in 1957, negative in 1965 and for the period 1970–74, but very favorable for the years 1975–78. Interestingly, in contrast with the 1975–78 adverse pattern of Cuba's commerce with the non-Communist areas, trade with the Communist nations reflected important surpluses in Cuba's favor. Since the terms of trade between Cuba and the Soviet Union have no relationship to world market prices, it is impossible to determine on the basis of available data the actual nature of the Cuban-Soviet equation, especially if substantial subsidies on Cuba's behalf are involved.

From the data reviewed there are several evident conclusions. The overwhelming economic reliance of Cuba on the Soviet bloc is so great that Cuba could collapse economically if the USSR were to suddenly interrupt trade relations. Within the Soviet bloc, industry has been unable to provide abundance of consumer goods due to internal political and economic structures, a system duplicated in Cuba. The Castro government likewise has not provided widely desired consumer goods, and is unlikely to do so if reliance continues on the Soviet Union for equipment and ideology.

Despite the extension of credits and loans by non-Communist nations, these have not been of the magnitude which would enable Cuba to achieve substantially improved economic levels. In fact, the total of Cuban hard currency indebtedness to its non-Communist suppliers has reached a point where the latter's inclination to continue indefinitely substantial financing must be in question. In this respect a news item published in *The Washington Post* on March 3, 1983 reported the following, a reflection of the creditors' concerns:

> Representatives of Cuba's creditor nations have agreed to recommend to their governments a major reorganization of its debts, according to a statement issued after a two-day meeting.
>
> Diplomatic sources said Cuba was seeking to reschedule a total of about $1,200,000,000, including bank debts of which between 70% and 80% was owed to governments.
>
> The statement yesterday said rescheduling would cover debt due between September 1, 1982 and December 31, 1983.
>
> It gave no details of the reorganization, but the diplomatic sources said Cuba had asked for a three-year moratorium on repayment of principal, followed by rescheduled payments over ten years. Cuba would continue paying interest throughout the period.[3]

What has happened in Cuba is that with only sugar as its main source for foreign exchange the country is gradually moving into an economic cul-de-sac. It may on occasion as in 1981 have a sharp internal spurt in its economy as new basic industries enter into production and sugar exports increase somewhat due to more extensive and efficient mechanization, but the balance of payments position remains in a critical situation. Only if for extraordinary reasons international-free market sugar prices were to shoot out of sight would relief be obtained. Alternatively, the USSR for geopolitical reasons may continue to bail out Cuba through extended and increased credits as it now does. But it is unlikely that the USSR would advance large sums of hard currency for Cuba to pay its western creditors. One thing is for the Russians to hand out armaments generously, but not cold cash.

Foreign trade data published in Table 6.7 of a report on Cuba for 1981 by the United Nations' Economic Commission for Latin America (E/ CEPAL/L.268/ADD.27, January 1983) reflect as continuing the negative pattern shown previously in Table 6.5. The U.N. data are based on information from official Cuban sources (*Anuarios Estadisticos de Cuba*) and the State Committee for Statistics (*Comite Estatal de Estadistica*). These are as follows in Table 6.7 in millions of Cuban pesos (One U.S. $ equals 1.20 pesos) for the years 1979–81.

To return to the matter of Cuba's foreign financial position, it is easy to see from Table 6.8 the extent to which the Island's hard currency foreign obligations have soared.

The cumulative debt (at year end) for the period 1970–78 grew steadily from $462 million to $2.319 billion.

Because of Cuba's chronic trade imbalance and substantial foreign debt, a brief look at Cuba's position with its non-Communist trading partners is of interest. Table 6.9 shows for the years 1975–77, by country, the total value of imports and exports, as well as the nature of the balance whether positive or negative.

It will be noted from Table 6.9 that Japan and Spain have emerged as Cuba's principal non-Communist partners both as to supply and purchase. However, the imbalance with Japan in the latter's favor was quite considerable for all three years, that with Spain positive for Cuba in 1975, but substantially negative for 1976 and 1977. Argentina is shown as a supplier but with zero purchases of Cuban exports. Negative balances were maintained with the other countries excepting Yugoslavia for 1975–

TABLE 6.7. Cuban Foreign Trade, 1979–81

	1979	1980	1981[a]
Soviet Union	2,370	2,253	2,455
Other communist countries	514	534	823
Non-communist countries	616	1,180	981
Total *exports*	3,500	3,967	4,259
Soviet Union	2,524	2,811	3,223
Other communist countries	534	699	877
Non-communist countries	629	999	981
Total *imports*	3,687	4,509	5,081
Soviet Union	−154	−558	−768
Other communist countries	−20	−165	−54
Non-communist countries	−13	181	—
Trade *balance*	−187	−542	−822

[a]Preliminary.

Source: United Nations, Consejo Economico y Social, *Estudio Economico de America Latina, 1981 Cuba* (New York: United Nations, 1983): 14.

TABLE 6.8. Cuban Hard Currency, 1970–78, Balance of Payments (in millions of U.S. $)

	1970	1971	1972	1973	1974	1975	1976	1977[a]	1978[a]
Trade balance	−134	−114	89	−13	113	−211	−612	−593	−148
Exports, FOB	272	304	389	492	1,175	1,621	1,000	808	815
Non-communist countries	272	304	389	492	1,175	1,171	800	613	690
USSR[b]	0	0	0	0	Negl	450	200	195	125
Imports, cost, insurance, and freight (CIF)	406	418	300	505	1,062	1,832	1,612	1,401	963
Interest payments	−26	−35	−40	−55	−70	−45	−55	−105	−190
Other current transactions[c]									
Current account balance	−140	−129	69	−43	68	−246	−642	−658	−276
Cumulative debt (year end)	462	591	522	565	497	743	1,385	2,043	2,319

[a]Estimated.
[b]Soviet hard currency purchases of Cuban sugar outside the Cuban-Soviet trade protocol at world market prices.
[c]Includes primarily receipts from tourism and ship chartering.
Source: From Table 33, The Cuban Economy, A Statistical Review—1981 (Springfield, Virginia: National Technical Information Service): page 37.

TABLE 6.9. Cuban Foreign Trade with Non-Communist Countries (in millions of U.S. $)

	1975			1976			1977[a]		
	Imports	Exports	Balance	Imports	Exports	Balance	Imports	Exports	Balance
Belgium-Luxemburg	24	8	−16	22	12	−10	97	11	−86
Canada	119	77	−42	126	69	−57	67	50	−17
France	127	21	−106	72	32	−40	83	28	−55
Italy	119	22	−97	79	26	−53	43	19	−24
Japan	437	269	−168	281	78	−203	357	54	−303
Mexico	33	1	−32	35	2	−33	36	3	−33
Morocco	—	47	47	—	42	42	—	NA	—
Netherlands	62	8	−54	50	4	−46	34	20	−14
Spain	184	273	89	227	123	−104	208	145	−63
Sweden	54	22	−32	43	54	11	42	10	−32
United Kingdom	155	16	−139	188	65	−123	57	20	−37
West Germany	169	6	−163	98	12	−86	74	10	−64
Yugoslavia	—	22	22	—	66	66	—	23	23
Argentina	127	—	−127	201	—	−201	144	—	−144
Other	222	379	157	190	215	25	159	220	61
Totals	1,832	1,171	−661	1,612	800	−812	1,401	613	−788

[a]Preliminary.

Note: Imports are CIF; Exports are FOB.

Source: From Tables 23 and 25, *The Cuban Economy, A Statistical Review—1981* (Springfield, Virginia: National Technical Information Service): pages 26, 28.

77, Morocco in 1975 and 1976, Sweden in 1976, but negative with this country in 1975 and 1977. There is no breakdown of the nations included under "other," an important item since balances positive for Cuba are reflected for all three years.

SOCIOECONOMIC CONSIDERATIONS

Apart from the importance of Cuba in the scheme of U.S. foreign alternatives in view of the Island's strategic location and close relationship with the Soviet Union, there is another aspect of the Cuban issue of profound interest to political scientists regardless of nationality or political coloration. Although the Cuban political and economic institutions are still in a consolidation stage, what is happening must still be considered as an experiment. Third World countries with a bent toward Marxism are observing the Cuban phenomenon carefully. What ultimately develops in the Island will affect thinking elsewhere. This leads to the hope that researchers in the U.S. policy establishment and in Congress study the events in Cuba both from a short-term and long-view perspective, and at the depth the issue warrants.

Regardless of the ideological basis from which the present form of Communist government evolved and the role of Soviet tutorship, Cuba moved quickly and until quite recently toward an extremely rigid Marxist-Leninist social, economic, political, and governmental structure. Given the reality of insufficient internal and foreign exchange resources, which would permit continuous economic growth, and the concomitant necessity of meeting inescapable, increasing costs related to Cuba's vast social programs, several crucial questions arise. Some of these relate exclusively to financial considerations. Others concern the sociopsychological consequences of the profound change in the traditional class structure, and the dramatic extension to the rural countryside of medical and educational facilities roughly equal to those in the urban centers. Indeed, the premise can be postulated that the ultimate fate of the Castro Revolution will hinge on these issues and what happens with inevitable changes in levels of expectation.

Unfortunately, sufficient data concerning the true situation of Cuba's fiscal position are not available to permit objective judgment regarding where the Island stands in this sense. Furthermore, without detailed explanations concerning Cuban methods for determining budgetary income and expenditures, as well as the preparation of gross domestic product estimates and projections, accurate interpretation of attainable figures is well nigh impossible. Hence, from an analyst's viewpoint, for the foreseeable future, reliance to a great extent on subjective judgments and spotty data is unavoidable. Cuba withdrew from the International Monetary Fund on April 2, 1964. It is not a member of the Inter-American Bank nor is it linked to the World Bank (IBRD). Thus, thoroughly detailed assessments ordinarily available from these institutions are nonexistent. Cuba does participate in the United Nation's Economic Commission for Latin America, but economic data obtainable from this source for Cuba are helpful but sparse. In recent years essential Cuban financial information does not appear in published material from the Organization of American States.

Cuba's population and growth rate are known factors. In 1965 the former totaled 7.810 million, about 9.336 million in 1975 and it is now estimated at a bit over 10 million. Annual growth rate for 1960–70 is reported at 2.0 percent, and 1.6 percent for the years 1971–77.[4] The substantial outflow of refugees in the early 1960s obviously affected both absolute figures and growth. It is roughly estimated that since the initial exodus between 800,000 and 1 million Cubans left the Island. Another factor that affects its demographic development is the success of the Castro government in the implementation of a nation-wide free health program. A decrease in infant mortality and increase in longevity are a result. Barring enormous flight from the Island, growth rate for the future may well average 2.0 percent annually, a percentage consistent with the average of 1.9 percent for the years 1953–58.[5]

Data are insufficient to permit construction of comparative tables for the past ten years, showing consequences of the drastic income redistribution policies following the departure of the high income entrepreneural and professional classes. With the exception of a small number of landowning farmers and a few pre-1959 physicians allowed to retain private practice, practically all other wage earners are employees of the government. With modest wage and salary lids affecting all employees, and limited possibility of spending cash surpluses, coupled with price controls and commodity allotments, it has been possible for the government to keep inflation under reasonable control. Availability of extensive sports and social facilities through a multitude of official organizations, free of charge, has helped distract the population from its Spartan living standards. Also, a type of widespread barter economy involving "goods for goods" or for services has emerged as a safety valve to remedy stringencies characteristic of the rigid social and economic structure. Although illegal, the government blinks at the practice. Restaurants are permitted to function and they afford an outlet for individual cash surpluses.

A basic objective of the Cuban government is avoidance of the development of a consumer-oriented society, with its strong demands for goods not produced in the Island and costly in foreign exchange to import. The purpose is to permit relatively scarce resources for use in the construction of basic industry and in the financing of essential goods, raw materials, and food which must come from abroad. The exodus of a major sector of the middle and upper income classes in the early 1960s removed the group which tended most toward consumerism, high standards of living, and constantly growing levels of expectation. Their emigration made it possible for the Castro regime to impose its austerity philosophy, since the lower income classes, which comprised the vast majority of the population led lives for the most part below or at present austerity levels, particularly if free medical service and nation-wide educational facilities are taken into account.

Castro's main support rested with the subsistence farming classes in the rural countryside from whom a limited diet was commonplace, as well as negligible educational and medical facilities. In the pre-Castro era illiteracy was very high among this *guajiro* (farming) element, and prospects for satisfying these two basic deficiencies were dim. The point to be stressed is that the aspirations of this rural group were so modest, that it has not been difficult for the government to meet them through crash programs. A benign climate made the task easier.

However, half of the Island's population was born after Castro came to power. Health and educational standards are now more or less uniform throughout the island, as a result of a mandate from the top. The nature of human beings being what it is, it is unlikely that an educated rural population with substantial technically trained cadres will be satisfied with the modest goals to which their parents aspired. The eventual evolution of Cuba's internal political and economic life probably will depend on the response to this point.

In the early days of revolutionary euphoria, material incentives were discouraged and idealistic motivation exalted. But time has shown that concrete rewards provide the spark for achievement of economic goals, and Cuban policies now recognize this fact of life.

The government appears to recognize increasingly the need to move away from the rigid dogmatism which has characterized the economy. A report, dateline Havana, by Marlise Simons, a *Washington Post* staff writer, and published in that newspaper on May 29, 1980, referred to "new rules imposed by the government including the sale of farm products in free markets and the issuance of licenses for craftsmen and entrepreneurs to go into business for themselves. State companies have been told their priority is to make profits rather than simply producing goods or providing jobs." The article further stated "it's like waking up the spirit of competition again one European observer said, . . . the absence of this, we've seen, has led to high costs, low productivity and boredom in the welfare states of socialism and capitalism alike."[6]

In short, as the Simons report indicated, "Now, like the Soviet Union and China before it, Cuba is unabashedly reestablishing the relationship between efforts and reward as a way to stir the sluggish economy." But the difference between Cuba and the two Communist superpowers is that these have vast internal natural resources, while Cuba is a mono-crop country with a chronic foreign balance of payments deficit, low capital formation rate, and a staggering government overhead. The situation is complicated by inefficiencies and miscalculations, a reality admitted by the government itself. In fact, conditions reached so critical a stage that a Havana *Prensa Latina* press agency report, carried in a UP dispatch from Mexico City, and published in *The Daily Progress* of Charlottesville, Virginia, on January 12, 1980, stated that "Cuban President Fidel Castro took direct control of Cuba's armed forces and reshuffled most of the government in an attempt to pull Marxist Cuba out of its economic slump since Castro's revolution."[7] Actually, economic conditions improved considerably in 1981 and 1982, but the Island's international balance of payments position has continued to worsen. But for the Soviet Union's and the bloc's help internal chaos would ensue. Will events move the Cuban government eventually toward a mixed economy of sorts? The constant drumming of attacks against capitalism, the "bourgeois states," extolment of Marx and socialist thinking of the Leninist variety emanating from Dr. Castro personally and from the official propaganda organs would appear to belie this possibility. Nevertheless, the prospect should not be ruled out. The Castro government would be perfectly capable of such a move if deemed necessary for survival and justify the shift by dubbing the development as a unique Cuban form of advanced socialism.

At this stage of affairs in Cuba the prospect seems unlikely. But overlooked are component elements of Cuban character. Despite the regimentation of Cuban youth in a disciplined school system, the government over the past 20 years or so has made determined efforts to encourage family cohesion. Hence, fundamental Cuban attitudes have been preserved. Dr. Castro's sharp gyrations in public and foreign policy, evidence of considerable pragmatism, which at times annoy his Soviet allies and disconcert our policymakers in Washington, are very much a Cuban trait. An adage frequently quoted in the island when abrupt changes of behavior occur in public or private behavior is that "it is wise to change one's views" (*Es sabio cambiar de parecer*). "To shift gears in midstream" is a predictable Cuban trait. While a sharp move toward capitalism within the relatively foreseeable future is definitely unlikely, an overnight transformation along the Hungarian, Roumanian, or Yugoslav models would be very much in Cuban character.

An important factor in Cuban cultural anthropology, crucial to understanding why abrupt and surprising shifts in personal and official behavior can occur with no apparent adverse consequences, concerns what is called in the island *relajo,* or *choteo.* There is no direct translation possible into the English language for these words. The trait is equally difficult to describe in socioanthropological terms. It even presents a problem in seeking a definition within the general context of broad Hispanic culture because as a behavioral phenomenon *relajo* or *choteo* is essentially a peculiarly Cuban trait. Some considerably milder form is found in Puerto Rico, the Dominican Republic, and possibly Vera Cruz in Mexico, but not to the extent of its prevalence in Cuba. Within the Island itself it is more pronounced in the Havana area than in the rest of the Republic.

Descriptively, *relajo* or *choteo* is a kind of "kidding the world" attitude. But it goes much beyond "leg pulling" in that it is the outward manifestation of a certain lightheartedness combined with a "what is to be is to be" philosophy which permits two important results. On one hand adversity cannot only be coped with resolutely, but humor can be seen even in tragic circumstances. On the other, abrupt changes of mind or spur of the moment judgments become acceptable *sans* loss of face with quick-witted explanations taken at face value expressed in all seriousness and gravity.

Some anthropologists, including Cuban scholars attribute the trait to an amalgam of the lightheartedness characteristic of the southern Spaniards who provided the early population base for the island, and a defensive social mechanism developed by the black slaves in dealing with arrogant Spanish upper classes.[8]

In the pre-Castro years many if not most Cubans who negotiated officially with people from the United States had been educated to some extent in the United States and instinctively understood U.S. thought processes and hence predictable behavior. In contrast, with very few exceptions, their U.S. counterparts had no conception of what made the Cuban negotiators tick. The bilingualism of the latter led official U.S. citizens to believe that they were dealing within the general framework of a familiar and common set of values. This frequently led to U.S. frustration when results panned out differently than anticipated. More importantly senior U.S. diplomatic officials at home and abroad were unable to grasp the basic thinking of Cuban negotiators. The situation was further aggravated by the near total lack of contact with the substratum of Cuban society not navigating in upper official and social circles. Hence, the intense nationalism and possibly envy underlying Cuban attitudes toward the United States as a nation was very imperfectly understood by U.S. policymakers, the understanding of which was all the more complicated by the dissimulation inherent in the *relajo* or *choteo* characteristic.

In the Castro years, the communications problem between U.S. officials and the revolutionary regime has become further complicated by the fact of diminished numbers of Cubans knowledgeable of basic U.S. thought processes and behavior. To the *relajo* or *choteo* component must be added the circumstances that in negotiations or assessment of developments, Cubans will tend to move to conclusions of a general nature as initial negotiating postures, with "filling of the pie" justifications following subsequently. In contrast, U.S. negotiations generally resort to a building blocks approach in most negotiations. The result are talks developing at different levels simultaneously leading inevitably to honest mutual confusions, frustrations, and resentment. The pressure on U.S. officials who negotiate with Dr. Castro and his officials is a double one. They must be in a position to translate for the benefit of senior Washington officials and concerned Congressmen what the Cubans really have in mind. They must also be in a position to translate U.S. thought in a fashion understandable by the Cubans. It should be remembered that language is only a means for the expression of substance, not the automatic reflection of value systems.

Implicit in the *relajo* or *choteo* context is a tinge of bluffing or exaggeration, combined with a tendency toward postulates designed to shock or surprise. However, when the hand is called, the principal figure involved for sake of *machismo* or face saving will on occasion stick by a daring, bizarre, or outrageous position advanced, even to the extent of an action phase. Within the Cuban ambience, the response, diffusing or unmasking procedure is to attempt cutting short recognizable *relajo* or *choteo* behavior by requesting it be stopped. The phraseology used is *dejate de relajo*, somewhat akin to our vernacular "quit that nonsense." However, it takes a thorough knowledge of Cuban culture to detect when *relajo* or *choteo*, or for that matter indirection, is part of a stance, a circumstance which puts at a negotiating disadvantage not only U.S. citizens, but also Spanish speaking negotitors from regimes or countries where *relajo* or *choteo* as a cultural trait is absent. As stated earlier, these tendencies are more pronounced in the Havana environment than in the rest of the Island, and is least in the rural sectors in the provinces of Santa Clara, Camaguey, and Oriente.

Since most of the guerrilla leaders controlling the government come from the eastern part of Cuba, their behavioral patterns, at least officially, are minimal in the reflection of traits inherent in *relajo* or *choteo* patterns. Nevertheless, despite Cuban attempts at justification for a military presence in remote places such as Angola, Ethiopia, and Aden on the basis of the regime's support for "liberation" movements, one cannot help but wonder if the quixotic thrust of these involvements had its genesis as a *relajo* spinoff of some undefinable sort. For U.S. official dealings with Cuba, however, the *relajo* or *choteo* factor should not be ignored. It may well come to pass in future years with regard to Cubans born after the Castro takeover that as one consequence of the humorless and rigid aspect of the Communist regime, *relajo* as a key cultural ingredient could undergo serious modification, even to the extent of disappearing altogether. But it is impossible to determine under present circumstances to what extent this process might have started already. At least for the time being, the country is governed by Castro's contemporaries all of whom were deeply exposed in their youth to the *relajo* aspect of Cuban mores.

STABILITY

Population control by the Cuban government relative to internal security is extraordinarily tight. The creation in the early 1960s of neighborhood vigilance units known as Committees for the Defense of the Revolution (*Comites de Defensa de la Revolución*), as an adjunct to the internal security apparatus, constitutes a thoroughly efficient counter-revolutionary suppressive mechanism. About half the population of the island reportedly belongs to these Committees. Whatever the real figure is, and the fact that the Committees now have considerably expanded social and political roles, the mechanism provides the authorities with the means of detecting rapidly any dissidence or potential threats to the regime.

If added to the Committee apparatus is the reality of a totally disarmed populace, the possibility of popular revolt for whatever the reason is an impossibility. Furthermore, despite a long history of Island revolts, there has been no instance of the urban public massively taking to the barricades, nor widespread uprisings of the peasantry. Even in the dramatic periods of the wars of independence (early 1800s) mass population active involvement in violent actions was absent. A similar phenomenon was observable after independence in the pre-Castro era. Revolts have been generally the work of a small middle or upper class group of dissidents. In fact that was the case in Castro's revolutionary activities. That the atmosphere in the island might have been, or was, favorable to the goals of revolutionaries is a different proposition from mass uprisings, such as those in Spain and other parts of Europe in the last and present centuries. By and large Cubans are not a violent people.

Another consideration is that the vast majority of Cubans over the past 250 years became enured to the concept of total power at the top. In the colonial period the Spanish governors were Captains General, authoritarian military men whose will, frequently capricious, was law. Many were personally corrupt and most were complacent on the issue of corruption in the colonial administration. Thus, Cuba entered the era of independence with a tradition of military despotism, corruption in government, its commerce and its plantations dominated mostly by Spaniards, Americans, Canadians, and other foreigners.

The two brief U.S. interventions at the turn of the century were also military with some governmental structures such as the health department and rural constabulary imposed from the top. While the U.S. presence was on the whole beneficial to the island in the sense of improved governmental administration, it was no lesson in democracy. With few exceptions, most Cuban presidents have been military men who functioned with a heavy hand, at times despotically as in the case of General Gerardo Machado and Fulgencio Batista in their second terms in office. The instances of civilian presidents were marked by either very brief stays in office or by widespread corruption.

Demands for democracy stemmed from intellectuals and self-seeking politicians who had a most imperfect understanding of its theory and practice. The great mass of Cubans were marginal factors in the political groups during the pre-Castro period. Neither by education, tradition, or a meaningful stake in the Cuban social and economic structure did they understand where and how democracy would fit into the Cuban scheme of things. Elections were frequent and equated in the popular mind to democracy. Their function as the mechanism by which a democracy expresses itself was never comprehended, including by most intellectuals agitating on its behalf. In short, absence of a tradition of democracy in the Western European and U.S. sense, and existence of a substantial rural nonlandowning peasantry, clouded the chances of democracy for success. It should be remembered that the highly respected Don Tomás Estrada Palma, the Republic's first president, attempted to institute fiscal integrity in government and respect for democracy. It ws not long before a revolution threw him out.

By the time Castro came to power, the Cuban government, after the sugar industry, was the Island's largest employer. A job in government was regarded by many Cubans as the only way to earn a living, because the private sector was too small to accommodate the educated surplus, including technical professionals such as engineers and agronomists; Castro's leap to making the government the sole employer caused few qualms. The more energetic of the middle and upper classes being committed to free private enterprise and desirous of efficient, democratic government left the Island. Urban based and constituting perhaps not more than 20 to 25 percent of the population, apathetic toward involvement in politics, its lack of cohesiveness could not stand in front of the juggernaut unleashed by Castro. The small remnant of middle income and affluent elements remaining were by no means going to run the risk of being singled out by the neighborhood Committee vigilantes as counter-revolutionaries. An important lesson to be derived from Castro's easy consolidation of power, and imposition of state control over all facets of

Cuban life, is that democracy can flourish only if a substantial urban and rural middle class exists. For the latter to be such it must be landowning, as in Costa Rica.

Dr. Fidel Castro's way of governing, in a fashion, is a regression to the pattern of exercise of power characteristic of the colonial Spanish Captains General, and mass Cuban reaction is as docile as it was in that era. Dr. Castro's main support seems to continue to be based on the rural peasantry, the urban lower income groups, and the members of the vast bureaucracy. The army, overwhelming with its presence and armed to the teeth, is the guarantor of Castro as supreme leader. Under the circumstances, the only dissidence which could surface as a threat to Dr. Castro's position would have to be from high ranking army echelons, an unlikely but not impossible prospect. If such were to develop it would stem from personal issues and not ideological causes.

From a U.S. policy viewpoint, despite possible internal Cuban modifications in its economic policies and foreign relations, for the long term, prospects are for the continuation of a monolithic Communist state. Only abandonment by the Soviet Union or total suspension of credits by non-Communist trading partners could introduce factors leading to internal chaos and collapse. And Cuban capacity for belt tightening is very considerable!

POLICIES, STRATEGIES, AND TACTICS

Time will be the arbiter of the dispute between the United States and Cuba. Eventually, the nearness of the vast U.S. market, the United States as a source of capital and internal Cuban economic necessities will be important factors in the solution of the present complex situation. With respect to the United States, realization is gradually developing that simplistic formulae, so dear to academic strategies and government "think" departments, will not apply to the Cuban question. Little by little both the public and leaders in the two major political parties are understanding that there are no quick answers to the problem, and that patience and greater sophistication are essential for successful U.S. diplomatic moves.

In connection with our diplomacy with regard to the Soviet Union, China, and the Middle East it took two generations for U.S. people to grasp the complexities of the issues and psychopolitical considerations involved. One dare say that the Central American mess, one which will be with us for a long time, will prove of tremendous educational value to the U.S. public and the nation's political leadership. The ultimate results will be a greater capability by the United States in dealing with the nations to our south.

But Cuba and the United States are close to the point where the beginning of easier relationships is possible. Unfortunately, Cuban and U.S. naiveness and miscalculations stemming largely from cross-cultural misreadings have hampered severely the evolution of working relationships. They have led to serious and dangerous Cuban over-dependence on the USSR, a peril to their national aspirations for true independence, and to the profound worry of the United States. It has even resulted in far-reaching political, economic, cultural, and demographic alterations in the important state of Florida.

Related to our future actions some basic assumptions must be established. The nature of our diplomacy will be dictated by their validity. If in error we will be no further down the road to solution than we now are. If correct, we can tread our way, warily, through a path plagued amply with quicksand.

1. Cuba's most serious fear is direct or indirect military action against it by the United States.
2. U.S. overriding concern is the use of Cuba by the USSR as a military threat to the United States and its interests in the Caribbean region.
3. Any successor regime in Cuba will be headed by another military figure with most State-controlled commercial, industrial, and political institutions remaining in place.
4. In the remote possibility of an internal Cuban collapse, with the USSR out of its support role, the annual cost to the United States for carrying Cuba on its back would be between $5 billion and $9 billion annually for an indefinite period. This load would no doubt be unacceptable to the U.S. public.
5. The Soviet Union will continue to bankroll Cuba as long as the island can be considered for its value as a military base 90 miles from Florida. Its influence in this sense over Cuba is tremendous.
6. Cuba will continue from time to time to furnish troops for overseas adventures of interest to the USSR. Financially these are advantageous as either host governments pay a sum per soldier as in the case of Angola, or the USSR increases its export credit line to Cuba. The operations permit Cuba to employ surplus labor, also to send out of the country army officers who because of a restless and ambitious temperament might cause problems among the military.
7. Cuba's penchant for meddling in Latin American turbid situations will surface on occasion to satisfy ideological yearnings and to annoy the United States. However, as Latin American explosions

are basically related to internal conditions, Cuban capabilities to be determinative will be sharply limited.

8. The United States will not invade Cuba, except under circumstances immediately related to a major military confrontation with the Soviet Union. Cubans are aware of this reality. Occasional threats from the United States, such as those former Secretary Alexander Haig formulated, merely help the Cuban regime to rally national support. Cubans are intensely nationalist first, Communists or whatever second.

9. Cuba does not believe any exile operation against it can succeed even if backed by clandestine U.S. support. But attempts are disturbing and distracting to the regime. With a well-trained army of some 227,000 officers and men, a good coastal navy, and an airforce consisting of over 200 combat jet planes, it would take a major invasion effort to secure even a firm beachhead.[9] The army's "perks" are very considerable and this force would not vanish into the horizon as did Fulgencio Batista's forces when confronted with Castro's handful of guerrillas. By and large it is unrealistic to expect the populace at large, particularly in rural sectors to cloak an invasion group viewed as wanting a return to the *ancien regime*.

10. While Cuba hurls diatribes at the successive administrations of the United States, it portrays the U.S. people as "good," and English is taught as a second language. This distinction is important for future Cuban-U.S. relations.

11. The present or successor Cuban regimes will continue to exercise tight control over the populace with regard to political activities. The media will remain as an instrument of the State.

12. A *modest* resurgence in U.S. tourist travel could in time develop, but would not for a decade at least equal the pre-Castro volume.

13. Despite Cuban legislation in March 1982 permitting the establishment of private or public companies owning as much as 49 percent, and facilities for remittance of profits, it is unlikely that there would be any large scale flow of U.S. capital to the island, if the United States economic embargo were lifted.

14. In time, Cuba may well move in the direction of the internal economic pattern characteristic of Yugoslavia. In fact, one suspects that technocrats within the regime would welcome such a policy.

15. Resumption of full but minimal Cuban-U.S. diplomatic relations which would include lifting of the U.S. trade embargo could result in time with an overall two-way trading figure of about $700 million to $800 million with exports mostly balancing imports.

From the assumptions and the detailed discussion earlier in the chapter with respect to Cuba's economic situation, it is readily apparent that no Cuban arrangement with the United States is possible which would put in jeopardy Cuba's current economic support by the USSR. Furthermore, under present circumstances the connection between the Soviet presence in Cuba and its financial help to the island is very obvious. Hence, U.S. demands for Cuban actions weakening fatally the Soviet link as a quid pro quo for resumption of full diplomatic ties and the lifting of economic sanctions are not realistic.

Neither is it pragmatic to suppose that Cuba would accept as *quid pro quo* abstention from mischief making elsewhere for the same price. The resulting loss of face among the more radical Third World countries would be too much for Cuban "machismo" to take. Given the intense distrust between the two governments, the Cubans would wonder whether the lifting of U.S. sanctions could constitute a Trojan horse.

President Jimmy Carter's imposition of a wheat embargo on shipments to the Soviet Union, and the removal of this measure not long after by President Ronald Reagan, and the about face of the Reagan Administration on the Soviet pipeline issue are examples of zigzags in U.S. foreign policy which throw both friends and foes alike into confusion. Thus, the Cuban regime is not going to put on the line its very existence by depending on U.S. foreign policy which could change at the drop of a hat through Presidential or Congressional whimsy.

That Cuba could be eventually weaned considerably away from the Soviet Union and from propensities to external adventurism is a distinct possibility. But first a thoroughly proven ground of mutual confidence must be established and this is not susceptible to a quick fix.

What is called for is identification as a long-term goal the encouragement of Cuba to move toward a genuinely neutral stance. Strategies and tactics should be designed to help Cuba achieve such a position. But it must be recognized publicly and officially that this aim is feasible because it is in the interest of Cuba to become truly independent, although not in the cards for the foreseeable future. Under an approach of this kind, the U.S. public and Congress and the Cubans would have a clear understanding of U.S. objectives for the Island. The Cubans, on the other hand, free from destabilizing threats predictably would discreetly cast about for ways to loosen gradually their implicit bondage to the USSR, as mutual trust emerges between the United States and Cuba.[10]

Critics of this open and fundamental approach, which probably would win quickly broad support in the United States, may argue that nearby nations might consider the U.S. action as rewarding Cuba for misbehavior. This thinking is not valid. All the nations in the northern rim of South America, the Isthmus, Mexico, and the Caribbean islands regard the Cuban-U.S. quarrel as destabilizing for the region, a thoroughly disagreeable situation. Their feeling is that if Cuba meddles in their affairs, the place to deal with it is at the place of interference. The larger nations such as Venezuela and Mexico feel confident to settle the meddler's hash in their own national territory. Venezuela has had troubles with Cuba before and has not hesitated to take appropriate action without carrying a perpetual grudge. If the small nations are in difficulties, usually because of internal abysmal social and economic conditions, as is now the case in El Salvador, the place to offset Cuban interference is there with U.S. or regional help if requested. A minor anti-Cuban action by the United States, or military bluff should have negligible effect.

Another aspect to consider is the doctrine or concept of "rewards" and "punishments" bandied about in the policy-making establishments, think tanks, and by academicians. The approach is puerile and untenable. Size does not make a nation eligible to be dealt with as a spoiled child. We do not own any of the nations that give us trouble and it is not our privilege to "reward" or "punish." The idea has even been applied to the USSR, i.e., the wheat embargo, and it always backfires. It should be dropped out of the vocabulary concerned with foreign policy.

Other theories which must be disposed of with regard to Cuba are "leverage" and "linkage" concepts. A high-risk regime that did not hesitate to turn its back on the U.S. sugar market as a result of nationalization policies in the 1960s, was angered by the Soviet missile removal in 1962, and has not hesitated to send troops half way across the globe, is not susceptible to real leverage or linkage concepts. What is required in U.S. diplomacy toward Cuba is a pragmatic and highly sophisticated approach with our eye ceaselessly set on the objective to move the regime eventually into a neutralist position.

The next question is obviously how does one get from here to there? The response is essentially to resort to a step-by-step approach with built-in modest *quid pro quos* of comparable relative importance, independent of occasional Cuban irritants. The exception to this strategy would be a Cuban action of the utmost gravity to the security of the United States, such as the positioning of Soviet intermediate missiles on the island with a five-minute delivery time to the U.S. mainland. Obviously, under those circumstances the option of military measures by the United States would undoubtedly come under review by the President and Congress, with relations totally broken off following a state of war if a decision to invade were reached.

Within the concept, the first step concerns the matter of the existing Interests Sections which we have in the Swiss Embassy in Havana and the Cubans in the Embassy of Czechoslovakia in Washington. Following this action in the Carter Administration, a sensible move concluded the several reciprocal agreements regarding tourist travel, fishing rights, hijacked planes, and business possibilities much to the benefit of the two nations. Cuban interference in Angola and later in Ethiopia threw the Carter Administration into a tizzy and relations deteriorated again.

Comment on what happened in the Carter overture is very much in order. The Carter Administration viewed the steps taken as inducement measures designed to entice the Cuban government away from foreign meddling. Overlooked by the Administration was the fact that the chain of events set off by the various agreements was as much to our benefit in general terms as it was to the Cubans. But not by the wildest stretch of imagination should it have been conceived that by themselves, combined somehow with a vague indication of things to come, the measures taken could offset Cuban actions elsewhere considered by them to be in their interest. The forward movement initiated by the Carter Administration should not have been interrupted. The place to wallop the Cuban action would have been in Angola by supporting their opponents to the hilt, sentiments obviously not held by Congress, since it prohibited in 1976 any military aid to the Union for the Total Independence of Angola (UNITA) rebels led by Joseph Savimbi against the regime supported by the Cubans.

Now, if the Cubans had not honored one of their specific agreements such as, say, those with respect to tourist travel, the United States would have been justified to have taken appropriate counteraction relative to Cuban visitors to the United States. The problem with the Carter Administration's diplomacy was that it viewed a few preliminary steps as though they were major instruments of crucial influence, a very thorough miscalculation.

Interests sections are useful devices to deal with basic consular services such as transmittal of documents requiring certification, minor travel difficulties, etc. They are not, and should not be, involved in diplomatic activities. There are several important reasons for this. The head of the section, although enjoying a diplomat's status, does not represent the president of the United States, who in our system is charged with the "conduct of foreign affairs." The lack of ambassadorial status places the section head also at a disadvantage with the Department of State, even though his personal status within the career service may be a very senior one. Accordingly, he does not enjoy full diplomatic respect in the foreign country and perforce by his very status is constrained to deal with opposites in the bureaucracy. He does not have access by virtue of his status to the chief executive of the nation to which he has been stationed.

Once a decision has been made to create an interests section, the move should be considered a preliminary and temporary one. Not long after, an exchange of ambassadors should take place. An ambassador as our president's representative has the right to demand audience with the head of a nation, and in the case in point with Dr. Fidel Castro himself. This permits the possibility of important dialogue because if need be, an ambassador can communicate directly with the president of the United States should a crucial matter be sidetracked in the Washington bureaucracy. While ambassadors almost always take their instructions from the secretary of state through his department's mechanism, the fact of his or her personal status and possibility of access to the president lends a respect for his or her views not otherwise accorded to the head of an interests section.

In the present situation with Cuba, it is very much to our advantage to designate an ambassador to Havana and resume minimal full diplomatic relations along the lines which govern our relations with Bulgaria. If for whatever reason we should be particularly unhappy with Cuba, a Chargé d'Affaires *ad interim* could look after the Embassy without the need of breaking off ties until matters cool off a bit. The Soviet Union has committed enough outrages in its foreign policy provocations to have warranted diplomatic interruptions many a time, yet we have rarely even pulled our ambassador out of the picture. Certainly Cuba's antics are no worse than those of the Soviet Union which is really behind much of their meddling mischief.

Furthermore, if unexpectedly the assumptions regarding the durability of the regime prove wrong, it would be most prudent for the United States to have on the spot an Embassy headed by a highly experienced chief and expert assistants. They would be in the best possible position to propose suitable courses of action. Under the present circumstances and arrangements there probably might well be as much confusion in Washington on what to do as there might be on the island.

To return to the step-by-step process, the question of an ambassador for Havana is crucial. Equally important are the qualifications of such a person, the composition of the Embassy staff, and the function of such an Embassy.

The probability of success or failure of a step-by-step approach in the rebuilding of Cuban-U.S. relations would hinge greatly on the performance of the ambassador designed to undertake the task. What is required for the job is someone with considerable experience in several Spanish-speaking countries, excellent command of the Spanish language, inexhaustible stock of patience, and temperament suited for a prolonged stay in an atmosphere of suspicion and hostility. He or she must enjoy the respect of peer groups within their own profession and be by virtue of age long past the stage of anxiety with regard to a career future.

Such a candidate can be found in the senior ranks of our career diplomats, in academe, and in the business world. Preferably, such an ambassador should have a scholarly bent of mind which would lead to a careful examination of the total Cuban environment. It may be that just as President Franklin D. Roosevelt very wisely drafted Dr. Carleton J.H. Hayes, a noted historian well known for his work on modern Europe, for service as ambassador to Madrid during World War II, a most delicate position, a similar selection might be in order. Within the Cuban context, there is much to be said in favor of an appointment outside the career service, particularly if the encumbent is personally known to the president and secretary of state. Knowledge that if need be the ambassador has ready direct access to the President would go a long way to avoidance of hampering bureaucratic pettifoggery.

Equally important as the ambassadorial position is the nature of the Embassy's staff. With 33 or so Washington agencies having a finger in the foreign policy pie, most of them will want to get into the Cuban act. This is one reason why we have in many places absurdly large and unwieldy Embassy staffs. It would be hoped that the President puts his foot down firmly on any such prospect and insists that the staff size and composition be strictly what is needed for the accomplishment of U.S. diplomatic objectives.

Basically, the staff should consist of a senior foreign service officer to serve as deputy chief of mission, one who would double as political analyst, an experienced economist drawn from the foreign service, a cultural affairs expert from the U.S. Information Agency, a Department of Agriculture specialist with an agricultural engineering background, two career consular officers, a foreign service career administrative officer, and proportionate support personnel. All should have a good command of Spanish and fairly broad experience elsewhere in Latin America or Spain. Given the paranoia of the Cuban government about the U.S. intelligence services, under no circumstances should anyone from these agencies be assigned to Havana. All attached to the Embassy should have credentials easily available which show that they are what they claim to be. The question of a possible military attache would be the subject of exploration with the Cubans. If the Cuban government proves amenable, the appointment should be limited to one officer and a clerical assistant. As can be seen the group would be small and highly knowledgeable, and should be kept that way.

The main role of the Embassy, and the Cubans should so be told, is to obtain firsthand data of what is happening in the Island without resort to clandestine or obscure sources, but by functioning within a traditional diplomatic context. The purpose would be to explore where the two countries can find common ground for cooperation in specific detail and in what fashion. Low-key exploratory negotiations could be initiated relative to a number of outstanding matters such as compensation for nationalized

U.S. properties, the question of the return to Cuba of criminals who formed part of the Mariel exodus, drug traffic issues, etc.* The pace of negotiations should be devoid of urgency and every instance of agreement with crystal clear quid pro quo aspects. "Flaps" that would arise from time to time because of U.S. or Cuban international activities should in no way be permitted to affect the measured rhythm established by the Embassy in line with the guidelines suggested. The ultimate target of a genuinely independent Cuba should always be overriding, without regard to what happens within or outside the Island.

Considerable attention has been devoted to some of the basic aspects of the mechanism for implementation of the step-by-step approach, because time and again excellent U.S. foreign policy formulations have been adversely affected, mortally at times, through faulty strategic and tactical follow-up measures.

Establishment of minimal full diplomatic relations with Cuba "a la Bulgarian formula" does not imply in the least either approval of the Castro regime or basic displeasure of what it stands for, any more than U.S. attitudes toward the Moscow or Polish governments are altered by the fact of diplomatic recognition. And one could argue that in the absence of a diplomatic relations mechanism with these two countries, the danger of military confrontation with the Soviets would increase, and Poles might be worse off.

In March 1977 passport facilities for travel to Cuba were lifted, as well as certain restrictions affecting currency transfers or expenditures relative to travel, by the U.S. government. A consequence was that starting in 1978 over 100,000 Cuban exiles visited the Island before President Carter reimposed travel restrictions following Dr. Castro's military meddling abroad. The impact of these visits had the result of reminding Cubans how bad off they were as compared to the exiles in the United States. These visits culminated in the Mariel exodus of more than 125,000 new exiles.

The fact is that prolonged Cuban-U.S. travel will not be of such a volume as to remedy Castro's financial problems, but would prod some liberalizing little by little. Furthermore, it would permit word of mouth description of events in the United States and outside world to an extent probably more significant than any special broadcasts from the United States. In short, the renewal of contact between Cuban-Americans and Cubans in the homeland is good for all concerned, except for Dr. Castro who must fear the liberal effect of contact with outsiders not in sympathy with the dictatorship in the island and its police state trappings.

---

*In December, 1984, the U.S. and Cuba reached an agreement for the return to Cuba of over 2000 Cuban criminals.

Renewal of full diplomatic relations with Cuba would carry inherently the assumption of revitalized travel facilities between the two countries. To allow such travel for U.S. citizens without the modicum of protection which the presence of an ambassador affords is foolish and dangerous. The Castro regime would be far more inhibited from perpetrating outrageous treatment of U.S. visitors on some flimsy or trumped up charges if the price carried with it the danger of a new breakoff in whatever relations had been established. This added protective need is particularly important for naturalized Cuban-Americans, since the Cuban government follows the practice of considering as nationals those born in the island regardless of foreign naturalization.

For the United States there is, however, a potential problem. Estimates of Cubans wanting to leave the island range between 600,000 and 1 million and Dr. Castro might be tempted to unload these discontented elements on the United States, as he did once before.

SUMMARY

Cuba's genuine long unfulfilled aspiration for true independence, combined with a need for a formula, designed to ease its economic dependence on the Soviet Union, offer an opportunity for U.S. diplomacy to influence the island's future. We once had the opportunity of assisting Cuba develop a democracy concerned with respect for individual human rights, freedom of the press, preeminence of private enterprise, and so forth. We failed, mostly because of the existence of a large nonland-owning, culturally and economically deprived rural peasantry. Perhaps, it as beyond our power and capacity to overcome the destructive and selfish heritage of the colonial period. Who knows? But this is water over the dam.

It may be that unwittingly Dr. Fidel Castro may have planted the seeds for the evolution of the type of "bourgeois" society he publicly excoriates. The unquestionable success of the regime in the mass education of the island's youth could very well, in time, engender an irresistible movement in the direction of a free society. The possibility brings to mind Ernest Hemingway's *The Old Man and the Sea*. Will the old guerrillas' dependence on Communism and a police state eventually be gobbled up by educated man's eternal yearning for freedom?

7

CONCLUSIONS AND SUGGESTIONS

Happy the man whose treasure-trove
is wisdom, who is rich in discernment;
silver and gold are less profitable
in the handling. More rare is it
than all things else; no prize thou
covetest can match it.

Proverbs 3, 13–16

The biblical injunction has no truer application than in foreign affairs. To the extent that we as a nation and our leaders in particular are knowledgeable about the ways of other nations and our relations with them, so will our international dealings be smooth or troublesome. If we see phantasms where there are none, lack the sensitivity to detect dangers to our well-being or base our decisions and policies on utopian considerations we will pay a price, sometimes awesome in dimensions.

It is astonishing at times in a nation such as ours where no responsible industrial or commercial enterprise would settle in a new area, or open new domestic markets, without thorough surveys and careful choice of personnel, to find our foreign responsibilities entrusted to officials new to diplomacy. It would be unthinkable for General Motors or one of its peer corporations to assign as general sales manager someone with no automobile merchandising experience. In fact it is basic personnel policy in the United States to select for regional responsibilities individuals whose personalities and awareness of particular "territories" will minimize failures. Yet, somehow the sentiment has prevailed in administration after administration that because someone has been an outstanding success in merchandising, engineering, corporate legal practice, the legal profession in general, politics, but to name a few of the activities from which policy-making officials are frequently appointed, that an individual can transfer such experiences to the complex field of diplomacy and foreign affairs. On occasion the exception proves the general rule, but more often than not failure is the result.

As a consequence of this problem, architects for successful foreign policy must include the following among other obvious attributes:

common sense, reasonable fluency in the language of the country or region within their responsibility and thorough knowledge of the cultural mores and thinking processes of the people to be dealt with, as well as of their history, and close familiarity with the U.S. political process and foreign policy mechanisms.

What is intended in this chapter is to look into how our present policies for the areas reviewed adhere to the national interest in terms of the Preamble of the Constitution, and *quid pro quo* considerations. In situations where we feel there are weaknesses, we will suggest remedies.

Overlooked by successive administrations is that what presidents say to the public through the press or media can be only as convincing as the key presidential advisors can make it be. Franklin D. Roosevelt was able to project effectively the Good Neighbor policy concept because he had A.A. Berle, Sumner Welles and other career experts behind him. In an attempt at emulation, President Kennedy announced the Alliance for Progress. The rhetoric was there but the substance was not, for the simple reason that his advisors in the White House lacked the necessary depth of knowledge about Latin America that the situation required. Initial distrust of the career Foreign Service precluded reliance on their judgment, a phenomenon more or less characteristic of new administrations since the 1930s. Confidence in the career officials develops after the first flush of experimentation shows fallacies of preconceived notions.

If the public and Congress perceive the key figure in policy formulation for a particular geographic area, or function such as arms control, to be an expert in his or her field, in addition to a proven record of experience in diplomacy, widespread bipartisan support will be forthcoming. In an age when the media has reached a high level of sophistication and developed a marked investigative inclination, it is not long before the press tumbles to the qualifications of a policymaker for a particular responsibility. If found wanting, all the presidential statements will not generate confidence in what is said to the public. Confusion and congressional bitter debate will result to the detriment of national policy. These situations have occurred time and again in administration after administration. It is puzzling that White House aides, sensitive as they are to public sentiment and political winds, have not accepted as a basic fact of life, that for key foreign affairs jobs in the White House and Department of State only truly qualified and experienced people should hold those positions. It is also a pity that the Senate does not insist that such be the case, since it holds the whip hand through the confirmation process for most appointments at the level considered, at least with regard to the Department of State.

THE ISLAND REPUBLICS

In any attempt to assess the common sense or efficacy of U.S. foreign policy with respect to the island republics in the Caribbean, the activities of the United States in that region during the past 80 years or so must be very much taken into account. The whole area could be grouped as an apparently homogenous bit of geography for which some basic policy might suffice; in reality the only common thread applicable to most is dependence on a few products for export which does not cover the cost of badly needed economic development. If the United States wishes to maintain a strong influence in the area based on a defense of the Caribbean doctrine, it must reconcile itself for a long haul involving direct budgetary and balance-of-payment support for several of the independent islands. Tourism, one-way free import duty facilities, private U.S. investment, long-term loans by the international banking system, technical assistance, are all crucial to their existence. But, the need for U.S. subsidy in certain cases, for at least a decade, is an inescapable fact of life if stability and progress are to be achieved. These imply security for the United States.

Paramount U.S. interest in the Caribbean since the construction of the Panama Canal has been its protection. This consideration is as valid today as it was in President Theodore Roosevelt's era. It is complicated by the fact that military technology has advanced to the point that any of the islands in a potential enemy's hands can pose an unacceptable threat to the U.S. mainland. Furthermore, it is the sealane for a major portion of U.S. supplies and trade.

Throughout this century in the Dominican Republic and in Haiti, the United States has imposed custom house intervention to assure payment to U.S. banks and foreign creditors in order to forestall European encroachment. The United States has tried gunboat diplomacy, dollar diplomacy, treaty diplomacy, the occupation of Haiti by U.S. military forces from 1915 to 1934, and in the neighboring Dominican Republic from 1916 to 1934. At the turn of the century the United States worried about the Germans and British. At present, officials are concerned about the Soviet Union.

Behind the history of the various attempts at intervention lay always a hope that internal stability would ensue, combined with fiscal sobriety thus eliminating any excuse for an outside power to collect by force what they felt was due them or their citizens. Always Washington expressed the hope that the development of a U.S. brand of democracy would take root and bring about the virtues of peace, prosperity, and natural growth. A Spanish inheritance of despotic and corrupt administrations, lack of capital formation, authoritarian cultural patterns, and total absence of a tradition of democracy combined with a landless peasantry, rendered the prospect impossible for the Dominicans. In Haiti, independent since 1804 after expelling the French, preservation of an African agricultural way of life (characteristic of the early years of the last century), overpopulation relative to inadequate natural resources, and an interminable succession of brutal rulers have created a terribly baffling human problem. In recent years we have witnessed the desperate attempts of the Haitian "boat people" to reach refuge on Florida's shores.

If the brief economic comments provided for these two republics, which share ancient Hispaniola, as reflected in Chapter 5, are combined with the observations included above, the question of a U.S. subsidy is unavoidable. If Puerto Rico, with its high educational standards, escape valve to the mainland for excess population, and free import duty entry for products of an impressive industrial complex, still requires massive U.S. subsidies in the form of food stamps and other federal assistance, how can anyone anticipate peace and quiet in its island neighbor?

The United States simply must face up to the necessity of developing expensive policies not only for the two republics discussed, but for other islands in the Caribbean. This is self-evident from the details reviewed. Otherwise, Washington will have to face periodic brush fires until someday a charismatic leader prone to high risk taking will seize the advantage of the Soviet-U.S. tug-of-war *a la Castro*.

A few additional comments are in order regarding Jamaica, Barbados, Grenada, and Trinidad-Tonago. Jamaica became independent on August 6, 1962 but it still maintains a nominal linkage with Great Britain. Queen Elizabeth II is acknowledged as sovereign and a Governor General is resident in the island. But though the latter appoints the island's prime minister, the ceremony is really *proforma*. Jamaica has a working democracy which determines actually who will lead the country as Prime Minister.

Though the British help Jamaica to the extent of their very limited capability, the latter needs easier access to the U.S. markets, increased private investment from abroad, and expanded tourism. No direct U.S. budgetary support appears to be warranted.

Barbados acquired its independence on November 30, 1966, but has preserved close ties to Great Britain much along the same lines as Jamaica. No direct budgetary aid seems required for Barbados either. Grenada became independent on February 7, 1974 and despite the fact that it has preserved its nominal ties to Great Britain, it may be in the interest of the United States to provide direct budgetary support provided Grenada reduces its dealings with Cuba to minimal diplomatic levels. Last, Trinidad-Tobago acquired independence on August 1, 1976, and has maintained only the most tenuous of connections with Great Britain through the Commonwealth of Nations Organization. It does not appear to require U.S. economic subsidy.

CUBA

The Cuban situation was discussed in some detail in Chapter 6. There is little to add at this point. However, measured against the defense reference in the Preamble to the Constitution of the United States, it is obvious that U.S. policies toward Cuba for the past 20 years or so have failed. That the Castro phenomenon may be considered as an accident of history is a defensible thesis, but that does not alter the fact of the island becoming an advanced beachhead in the Caribbean benefitting Soviet objectives in the Basin. Both the Soviet presence in Cuba and the arming of the Cuban military forces also represent a direct threat to U.S. security. If anything, U.S. policies of successive administrations from Kennedy to Reagan have merely served to push Cuba deeper into the Soviet's camp.

Common sense would indicate a change in fundamental posture toward Cuba. One alternative is a military assault on the island. But, the nature of the present military threat to the United States does not seem to warrant a costly operation of this kind, especially taking into account repercussions in Latin America in particular. Furthermore, the prospect of carrying a hostile Cuba well into an indefinite future at a cost of $5 to $9 billion annually would be utterly distressing to the U.S. taxpayer.

The alternative would be to seek an accommodation with Cuba for the objective of slowly enabling that country, with or without Castro (since dictators are also mortal), in the direction of genuine independence. That aim would serve as the basis for eventually developing comfortable *quid pro quo* relations resting on a growing degree of mutual trust and understanding.

Another possibility is to preserve the status quo and let Cuba "stew in its own juice." The appeal for this approach rests on the assumption that the agreement between the United States and the Soviet Union, reached after the 1962 missile crisis, has the effect of providing a security mantle for the United States. The contention has merit and certainly warrants serious consideration.

However, the "status quo" approach would appear to reflect several serious weaknesses. It would depend on the Soviet Union honoring a commitment made more than 20 years ago, when it was definitely at a disadvantage relative to sea power. That is not the situation today. In fact, it was precisely because of the 1962 crisis that the Soviet Union embarked on a far-reaching build-up of its naval strength.

The record of the Soviet Union in honoring commitments unless forced to do so by circumstances or self-interest is anything but reassuring (i.e., Helsinki accords). Soviet direct military interference in Afghanistan, indirect military support for pro-Marxist revolutions in Africa, and more recently in Central America is consistent with Soviet behavioral patterns or support for the use of force to achieve its objectives.

More recently, the destruction of a Korean civilian airliner in September 1983 with the total loss of 269 men, women, and children, when the latter strayed off its course and wandered over Soviet territory, was extraordinarily revealing in several vital aspects. It showed clearly ascendency of the Soviet military over civilian authority in matters regarded by the former as relating to Soviet security regardless of impact abroad. The prolonged stonewalling of the Soviet Union before admitting to the destruction of the Korean plane, deliberate lying about the circumstances and violation of international civilian airline doctrine continued to raise grave doubts about Soviet willingness to honor commitments.

The Berlin blockade in President Harry S. Truman's era, the 1962 missile crisis, the invasion of Afghanistan, and the shooting down of the Korean airliner also consistently reflect Soviet miscalculation of U.S. public and official reactions. If to this trait there is added the volatility and adventurism of Dr. Fidel Castro, the continued presence in Cuba of a Soviet brigade and availability of Cuban ports to Soviet naval forces, it is very much in the interest of U.S. security to develop a policy which in time would neutralize the Soviet threat in the Caribbean. The proposal to move Cuba into a neutralist position is thus advocated as a U.S. security policy, not as a bailout for Cuba. The intent is based on a fundamental national Cuban aspiration for genuine independence and our desire for Caribbean security.

It can be argued that Dr. Castro would not move toward a neutralist position, and merely take advantage of benefits derived from entry into the U.S. market, much in the way that President Gamal Abdul Nasser would not budge from his linkage with the Soviet Union. But men are not eternal. Cuba will be where it is after Dr. Castro and his immediate group are claimed inevitably by the scythe of time. Skillful diplomacy like expert chess, calls for moves that ultimately result in the winning of much desired objectives. But, also like chess, meaningful diplomacy is a slow process because it concerns the involvement of human temperament. The question is whether successive U.S. administrations, Congress, and the U.S. people can sustain a prolonged course in the absence of events which raise national passion.

One can cite as precedent President Nixon's approach to China. It took a great deal of common sense and political courage to take that step.

One would be put at a loss to find many today who would chide that move.

It cannot be denied that the present state of affairs between the United States and Cuba is extremely unsatisfactory. An action on our part to restore minimal diplomatic relations at an ambassadorial level would not be interpreted either at home or abroad generally as a sign of U.S. weakness. Our enormous military strength belies such an assumption. Rather the initiative would be considered as evidence of U.S. maturity.

Last, for optimum success, should both nations exchange ambassadors and Washington lift diplomatic and economic sanctions, and if a decision also has been taken to revitalize the Central American Common Market, the timing of both approaches should coincide. Two consequences would flow from the coordination. On one hand Cuba would find it in its own interest to begin focusing on the new situation. On the other, anti-Marxist elements in Nicaragua and El Salvador would take heart and act appropriately in reducing or eliminating the influence of the Marxist-Leninist groupings, militarily or otherwise.

CENTRAL AMERICA

With regard to Central America, there are a number of recurrent patterns in the region's history of importance to U.S. policymakers. One persistent inclination is to recur to the conference table, as the result of third party urging, when an intraregional conflict threatens gravely the survival of a state or particular regime. A treaty that is more like a formal truce generally results wiping the slate clean. A new tableau emerges.

In the current crisis since the United States is a part of the situation, the third party urging comes from Mexico, Panama, Venezuela, and Colombia (Contadora Group). Frequently in the past the United States has played the prodder's role. On occasion the Organization of American States has performed the service. In the current problem it would have been wiser to inspire the Organization of American States to lead the cooling off effort, rather than the Contadora Group!

None of the four in this group have the slightest interest in the primary concern of the United States in the matter. Mexico has serious internal problems of its own to contend with. Conditions in southern Mexico are not too different from those in most of Central America and constitute a powder keg. Furthermore, Mexico has traditionally regarded Guatemala with suspicion, precisely because of unsettled circumstances in the border area. Whatever Mexico officially says or does is largely for internal consumption. Colombia has a chronic internal security problem, reflecting some of the characteristics of the one confronting El Salvador.

Panama has its own axe to grind. Probably, Venezuela is the only one of the four which would pursue and objective solution.

During the past four years the growing intensity of conflict in Central America and sharply increased U.S. involvement through military and economic aid programs, with the side effects of debate within the administration, Congress, academia, and news coverage, all have led to a greater understanding in the United States of the problems of the area. While the Kissinger report did not advocate the specifics of an overall program, it helped place the issues within an interdisciplinary framework, a far cry from former Secretary of State Alexander Haig's apparent view of the problem through strictly military binoculars, almost four years ago.

Gradual stabilization of the overt political process in El Salvador through the swearing in as president of José Napoleon Duarte in mid-May 1984, a political moderate committed to civilian rule, further reforms, and civil rights and well regarded by both the U.S. Congress and the Reagan Administration, represents considerable progress for the region. The conviction in late May 1984 of five former Salvadoran National Guardsmen accused of murdering four U.S. Catholic churchwomen three and a half years earlier is also clear evidence of the evolution of respect for civil rights in El Salvador and willingness of the government to stand up to the extreme right in the country.

In the diplomatic arena, the fact of Secretary of State George P. Shultz's unexpected visit to Nicaragua on June 1, 1984 even if probably prompted by a nudge from President Miguel de la Madrid of Mexico during the latter's visit to the White House in mid-May, represented intensified high level U.S. interest in the prospects of diplomacy for peace in the region. This development is consistent with Central America's penchant for treaty diplomacy as a solution to regional conflicts.

In terms of persistent patterns of behavior, the probability is that the present crisis will go the conference table, via the peace treaty route. If such be the case, the United States will herald the result as a great forward step for regional peace. It will actually be another truce-like arrangement apt to be broken, if there is no solid forward movement in the direction of correcting economic and social ills.

Another facet of Central American life repeatedly surfacing in its history and to which the United States should be extremely sensitive is the perpetual yearning, in vain perhaps, for unified regional actvities hopefully leading one day to political union. While the overall hope may represent wishful thinking, the inclination to work together is always there. This realization should be a keystone in U.S. policy toward the area. It obviously calls for great skill in blending together bilateral and regional support policy, strategies, and tactics. U.S. diplomacy in the area rarely has shown that distinction, mainly because of too rapid a change in senior officials setting and implementing policy. Frequently, lack of firsthand knowledge of the region and of its history, and recurrent patterns of behavior, account for U.S. "spinning of wheels" approaches in the region.

Another aspect of impediments to common attacks on the economic and social ills of the area, crucial if peace, prosperity, and stability are ever to come to Central America, concerns the leaders of those countries. Too often exaggerated individualism accompanied by excessive vainglory has prevented the give-and-take essential for the successful melding of divergent interests. U.S. encouragement for common approaches will meet the frustrating intransigence which the two traits mentioned imply, but patience combined with a sense of humor should enable U.S. policy-makers and implementers at home and in the region to cope with these idiosyncrasies. Anyone who has dealt with both federal and state bureaucracies in the United States is fully aware that the two character-istics flagged are no monopoly of the politicians south of the border! But, in a nation as large as ours with a well-oiled democratic process, countervailing actions can be set in motion to deal with federal or state intransigence. Except in Costa Rica, there are no mechanisms in being which permit the challenge of maximum authority within an orderly process. Therein lies one of the causes for the frequency of armed revolt.

The thrust of the authors' contention is that it is fundamental for the prospect of stability in Central America that strong U.S. support be developed for regional approaches to economic problems. U.S. policy-makers tend to concentrate on five different policies for five different countries and discount coordinated regional efforts, alleging failure in the past. Nevertheless, in the heyday of the Alliance for Progress program the outstanding success, possibly the only true one within the context of the Alliance, was the performance of the Central American Common Market. This vehicle should be revitalized with strong emphasis for the develop-ment of "integrated" industries, that is those which would have access to the entire region as a market. In the early days of the Alliance, as will be recalled from previous comment in this study, there was U.S. opposition to the "integration" concept due to concern over possible ill effects for U.S. factories. Subsequently, this opposition ebbed and some attempts at "integration" went forward.

From our own industrial experience and that of Europe, we know that labor will migrate to where the jobs are. When this kind of situation arises and domestic labor reserves are inadequate, governments are the first to encourage immigration as a solution. One need only witness the large scale movement of Italian, Turkish, and Spanish workers in Europe following the success of the Marshall Plan. The region as a whole has ample room for population expansion. If under a revived Common Market, the five countries allow the free movement of labor across national frontiers, a highly explosive situation will have been defused. The present connection between El Salvador's internal strife and overpopulation is inescapable.

The matter of the nature of U.S. financial assistance to the Central American republics warrants serious comment. A program of loans from U.S. official sources, private U.S. and other foreign banks, multinational lending institutions such as Inter-American Development Bank, World Bank, and other similar bodies is most proper with respect to the financing of private industry and government constructed infrastructural facilities (dams, roads, etc.).

But loans for the purpose of covering balance of payments deficits either from private or official U.S. sources is a mistake. Funds of this kind must eventually be repaid. If the terms of trade worsen for the few exports that account for the bulk of foreign exchange income, instability will inevitably ensue as forward internal economic momentum bogs down in these terribly fragile economies. The possibility of default on the loans looms as a probability. Further lending is curtailed and the cycle of internal civil war once more becomes a sad reality. As time goes on and this pattern becomes more frequent, aggravated by population imbalance, the opportunity opens for Marxist-Leninists to warble siren songs crying for repudiation of international debts and confiscation of foreign properties without compensation. Carried far enough the situation eventually becomes very tense with the United States, true to basic instincts in similar situations, with implicit congressional approval, will resort at least to economic coercive measures. A major crisis could then be in the making once more.

In the course of time, the Central American countries will develop economies strong enough to have surpluses for domestic capital formation even in times of international recession. But that prospect is a good deal down the road. What follows from this brief analysis is an argument for food grants and direct budgetary support by the United States for the purpose of preventing balance of payments deficits. Currently U.S. policy provides for the former but not the latter. Congress initially recoils from this sort of approach, but on reflection the bite is not particularly high compared to overall world aid program costs for the United States. It would be highly justifiable in terms of security because of the contribution such a policy would make toward the region's stability. It would certainly be a great deal cheaper than having periodically to ship expensive military supplies and incur related expenditures, plus the complication which special costly U.S. military maneuvers entail. One may call such budgetary support an aspect of "crisis prevention diplomacy."

Central Americans do not stand in front of the capitol in Washington with their hat held out for such type of aid. There will be critics at home and in Central America alleging that this aid constitutes a step in heightened dependence on the United States tantamount to semicolonial status. Marxist-Leninist proponents would be alarmed at the approach because of its contribution toward stability. Actually, a program of the kind envisaged, combined with solid support both bilateral and Common Market oriented, would offer the best prospects for these countries to move away from the need for balance of payments support, in measure to the growth of their economies.

Probably, Castro's best appeal to the isthmian states is the relative success his government has enjoyed in raising health and educational standards quite substantially in the Cuban countryside. It would be in the interest of the U.S. government and the nations in the region if a plan were developed, including help from Puerto Rico, and stemming from Central American concrete proposals to not only meet the levels achieved by Castro but to surpass them. The implementations would have dramatic impact from one end of South America to the other. These are the only two fields, other than raising disorder here and there, in which the Castro experiment has a point-with-pride case. Housing fell short of expectations and Cuba's economy is a mess and will continue to be so, as long as the island stays on the present rigid Marxist-Leninist track. Furthermore, as Thomas Jefferson wisely indicated in support of public education, democracy is impossible or cannot survive without an educated electorate. It may be stated categorically that there will be no stability in Central America as long as the rural masses remain in abysmally low health and educational levels. The resources of these countries are insufficient as of now to remedy this potentially dangerous condition.

The relationship of rural landownership to the creation of middle classes essential to the functioning of democracy, since most of the population is rural, has already been discussed. Aid programs should relate to the kind of social and political order desired. One does not see the Soviet Union sponsoring economic assistance policies developed in a fashion which would strengthen middle classes anywhere! The process would be slow in any event because education has a bearing on the capabilities of farmers to manage their properties effectively, within or outside of cooperative establishments. But this is a workable approach. Furthermore, the development of such a program should under no circumstance jeopardize possibilities of increased food production.

Admittedly, the task outlined would be difficult for both the United States and the Central Americans to achieve, if only because of cross-cultural problems. But the plan can succeed because it must do so. U.S. aid programs within the concept discussed must clearly be limited in scope and confined to the specific goals determined by the Central Americans themselves. The buckshot approaches historically characteristic of U.S.

economic assistance have no place in Central America. They help preserve status quo situations, an undesirable objective for the isthmian region.

Probably, the major obstacle to the development of a long-term policy for Central America lies in the problem of persuading Congress and the U.S. people to underwrite the approach as an extended commitment. With respect to the Middle East, East Asia, Europe, Japan, and Soviet-U.S. relations, there is a common understanding of the issues, ergo the need to support heavy expenditures and, particularly regarding Europe and Japan, have agreed to difficult compromises in the past. But it took several terrible wars for the U.S. public and their representatives to reach the necessary level of understanding characteristic of our attitudes today. That kind of understanding is absent regarding the Caribbean Basin. Can we develop a common sense approach to the vitally important Caribbean Basin, without having to undergo the trauma of massive military or emotional involvement? Or, are we and our political system so constituted that we can only learn the hard way?

The question naturally arises concerning how a rural middle class can develop in Central America, particularly in overpopulated El Salvador. The point is especially valid because land reform in that country is the focus of considerable attention. Obviously, continued breakup of large estates will lead to diminished production as earlier Mexican experience with the *ejidos* demonstrated. Furthermore, in time inheritance would result in widespread uneconomic *minifundia* giving rise to persistent poverty as landholdings become too small to support families. Nevertheless, there is ample historical and contemporary evidence concerning the evolution of rural labor into middle income status, as a result of the establishment of industry in the midst of agricultural districts. Furthermore, there need be no connection with the availability with wood products or agricultural produce as raw material for processing or manufacturing, even though such development is always desirable.

An interesting example to flag because of its Spanish connection was the development of the textile industry in Catalonia, Spain. The fierce dynastic civil war which raged in the Basque provinces, Navarra, and Catalonia from 1833 to 1839, over the respective claims to the Spanish throne of the Regent Maria Cristina on behalf of her daughter, Isabela, following the death of Ferdinand VII, her husband and father of the infant Isabela, and his brother Don Carlos, left Catalonia's agricultural areas in a difficult condition. However, the importation from England of modern equipment and the manufacture in Barcelona of steam-powered machinery lent considerable impulse after the conflict to the development of Catalonia's eventual important textile industry. Although, in the early 1800s there already existed the nucleus of a cotton industry in the region employing some 2,000 workers, by the mid-1800s, these numbers had increased dramatically, many located in rural communities.

Catalan geographer Dr. Joan (John) Vila Valenti in his book *El Mon Rural A Catalunya* (Barcelona, 1973), in a discussion of the establishment of the textile and other industries in Catalonia touches upon the effect of the former, in particular, in rural areas. He explains how the industry owed much of its success to the fact that rural women entered the textile labor force in a ratio of three or four to one over men. The added income supplemented that of their fathers, husbands, and sons allowing the male members of the famly to devote full efforts to agriculture. Vila further stated that the industry established training centers at Tarrasa in the Province of Barcelona for the purpose of teaching necessary skills to women from strictly rural areas such as "Mura, Talamanca, Rocafort, Calders, et cetera."[1]

There are conclusions that can be drawn from the Catalan experience in the last century applicable to the development of light industry in rural El Salvador. In such event, farmers could own small rural property enjoying limited economic prospects, while they or their families earned wages in industry. Property ownership combined with industrial jobs would lay the foundation for a rural middle class, probably reflecting values somewhat like those characteristic in rural Catalonia, Costa Rica, and agricultural counties in the U.S. South.

With adequate roads and basic physical infrastructure financed by the Salvadoran government, assisted financially by the international banking system such as the World Bank, Inter-American Bank, etc., for which there is ample precedent, the creation of light industry and supporting service sectors, the latter two financed by internal private capital, could become a distinct possibility if encouraged by Central American national policies.

In the determination of what industries could be established much could be learned from the rapid initial development of the Central American Common Market. In an exhaustive and objective analysis of the economic integration experience in Central America (sponsored jointly by the Brookings Institution, Washington, D.C., and the Secretariat of Economic Integration of Central America, Guatemala City, published in 1978, and financed by the U.S. Agency for International Development through its Regional Office for Central America and Panama, and edited by William R. Cline and Enrique Delgado, respectively, senior fellow in the Brookings Foreign Policy Studies program and director of Central American Studies of Integration and Development in the Secretariat of Economic Integration of Central America, Guatemala City), the viability of the integration concept is apparent, despite internal contention, and tensions arising from the evolution of the Common Market movement. To quote from the Brookings study: "the CACM (Central American Common

Market) may be seen as a success case that should provide important evidence on the potential for economic benefits of such integration."[2]

The Brookings work did not examine the possibility of industrial development in the rural sectors. Its approach to agricultural economics concerned primarily marketing and pricing complexities and the consequences of liberalization of agricultural trade, within the CACM, on welfare and employment. Nevertheless, from the massive amount of data and discussions at depth covered in the study, there appears to be no reason why a program calling also for the location of industries in purely agricultural areas cannot be successfully implemented.

But, it should be further postulated that success for such a program would hinge among other important considerations on a revitalized Central American Common Market and free mobility of labor throughout the region. One consequence of the effort could be decongestion of excessively populated areas. Another may well be an increase of labor availability in areas where the latter is insufficient. The long-term effect would be gradual emergence of a rural middle income class. Since it is also assumed that educational and health facilities would accompany the creation of industry in the agricultural areas, in time families would be reduced in size, a characteristic of middle class social outlook as evident from census data in Western Europe and the United States.

With respect to the United States, the movement during the past 25 years of industry to nonmetropolitan areas is a well-established fact. The literature on the subject is vast and growing. In fact by the middle of the 1960s "there were about 14,000 local organizations in the United States whose primary goal was that of recruiting additional nonfarm industry, a majority of which were in rural areas."[3] In addition at the federal level the Economic Development Administration, the Small Business Administration, and the Farmers' Home Administration all have programs of support for the establishment of industry in the rural sectors of the nation, to which must be added to state agencies concerned with such promotion.

The significance of the availability of data concerning the movement out of metropolitan areas into rural United States, as well as the social and economic consequences, is that the variety of experiences is so great that there are ample models which can be examined for the benefit of what is proposed for rural Central America.

To narrow examples further, in Orange County, Virginia, the gradual increase over the past 20 years of feed prices, agricultural equipment, higher taxes caused by rising land values, and more recently increased fuel costs, combined with periodic declining or stagnant beef cattle prices made the operation of many family farms under 200 acres generally uneconomic. Further problems arose when adverse weather conditions affected corn and hay production in these farms. Thus, the margin which would permit safely to draw on bank loans to tide over tight moments was either wiped out or became dangerously narrow. The livelihood of hundreds of workers to whom farming had been the only way of life was severely threatened.

Beginning in the 1960s efforts to bring industry to Orange were increasingly intensified. The net result some 20 years later is that change in acreage devoted to farming has shown little variation. From two or three factories, there are now some 17 industries and a healthy county economy. What has happened is that many farm owners have full-time jobs in industry while still maintaining farming operations. Altnernatively, many a farmer's wife has a job in commerce or industry which provides the economic safety net for difficult market or weather caused problems. Per capita income for the county has risen sharply because industry pays higher wages and the competition for labor has forced large and well-financed farms to pay increased rates. Had Orange County failed in its efforts to attract industry, in time there would have been points of similarity with El Salvador's rural sections.[4]

In short, the answer to the development of a middle class in rural El Salvador, and other Central American countries, lies in the establishment of industry in the countryside, particularly in the most impoverished sections. If this objective is adopted as national policy throughout Central America in conjunction with regional economic aims tied to a revitalized Common Market, supported by U.S. aid policy, it would not be long before the horizon for Central America brightens. Naturally, there will be difficulties such as those related to import substitution and complicated public and private negotiations. But these can be surmounted through perseverance and a clear view of the future.

While conditions in the United States relative to industrialization in rural areas obviously would be drastically different from those which would obtain in Central America, especially since objectives in the latter would be both economic and political, these are nevertheless conclusions drawn from some aspects of the U.S. experience tentatively applicable to particular situations in Central America. In this respect the following comments included in *A Synthesis, How New Manufacturing Industry Affects Rural Areas*, prepared under the direction of Professors Eldon D. Smith, University of Kentucky and Gene F. Summers, University of Wisconsin-Madison with the assistance of ten experts from the Universities of Kentucky, Alabama, A. & M., Tennessee, Oklahoma State University, the United States Department of Agriculture Federal Extension Service, and the Kentucky Department of Commerce, are apropos of the approach suggested for Central America:

> Operators of smaller farms may obtain full-time work off the farm while continuing their farming operation, at least for some time. At first, they

may continue their farming operation as is, then begin to change by dropping various enterprises and by hiring more labor. Finally, as they become familiar with nonfarm work and are better able to realize job satisfaction and a good income or feel relatively secure in their nonfarm employment, they are likely to quit farming completely, although they may continue to live in a rural area (Scott, 1968).

For the continuing commercial farmers, the higher wage rate and tighter labor market mean a higher cost for hired labor and a more accelerated reorganization of their businesses in the same trend that has existed for some time—greater substitution of capital for labor. This also means that grain farming, where capital substitution has been the greatest, will receive still greater emphasis.

Changes toward more off-farm work by farmers are likely to increase conflict between landlords and tenants regarding leasing arrangements and the tenants' use of their time. The greatest conflict will be between tenants and landlords whose farms are large enough to fall into the low end of the commercial farming segment, but may not be large enough to continue as a single operating unit without additional income from the tenant. Conflict is also likely to increase on farms with livestock leases (Scott, 1968).

Operators who are fully employed with good incomes on farms of medium to large size which do not hire much extra labor are the least likely to change farm operations or to be attracted by off-farm jobs. Large farms are more likely to make adjustments in operations because they hire substantial amounts of labor. A higher labor wage will probably slow down the trend to larger farms unless new labor-saving technologies are invented or developed (Scott and Chen, 1973).

There is some evidence that under the impact of industrialization income has increased for smaller farms and decreased for larger farms. Moreover, the total income in the farm sector has increased (Scott, 1968). *Most of the increased income to the farm sector during industrialization, other than capital sales of land, comes from off-farm wage sources.*[5]

A fact of life is that, as mini-nations, the Central American republics would encounter increasing difficulties in the achievement of long-term individual economic viability. Their only hope to do so is within a revitalized Common Market concept. Predictably there will arise among the republics contention with respect to the integration of industries. The role of the United States would be in such situations to help mediate the differences.

Historically, the development of rural middle classes is undoubtedly difficult and of slow evolution. Nevertheless, with hope and a U.S. helping hand, successive Central American generations would remain sustained in their efforts. In time these would acquire a momentum of their own.

What the authors suggest as a first step is that the U.S. Agency for International Development establish a consultants' commission comprised of experts on the U.S. experience. This commission would be consulted on how best to develop a program calling for a two-month study visit by Central American experts to rural areas in the United States, where industry has been attracted in recent years. The Central American visitors would then be in a position to incorporate into policy, strategies, and tactics those of their findings adaptable to Central American conditions. That is, assuming that it became U.S. policy to support a revitalized Central American Common Market, and that the Central Americans opted to go that route.

The next phase would involve two aspects. The first concerns identification by Central American experts of specific desirable new industries, location, study of internal credit availabilities, costing, marketing prospects, and relation to import substitution. The other points to infrastructural requirements underpinning proposed new industries, such as power plants, sewer and water facilities, roads and their tentative costing. The third phase would lead to negotiations among the Central American nations to implement the previous stage. The role of the United States as mediator would be crucial as intraregional differences surface from time to time.

Finally, one other point should be made. It has been said that he who does not read history will be doomed to relive it. While we cannot expect the U.S. public to take a crash course on the history and culture of the Caribbean Basin, we can expect our representatives in Congress, with the help of their aides, to master at some depth the story of the nations concerned and be familiar with our diplomacy toward them during the last century at least. One can also insist that policymakers be people with a background of direct experience in the areas for which they are responsible, and that senior officials in the White House respect their judgment. We can also require that our area policymakers be sensitive to the concerns and aspirations of the U.S. people in the United States, since no policy can succeed without their support.

NOTES

PREFACE

1. Letter from Ambassador Robert F. Woodward to authors, September 6, 1983.

CHAPTER ONE

1. Department of State, *GIST*, May 1982, "US Interests in the Caribbean Basin."

2. *Ibid.*

3. J. Roland Pennock, *Democratic Political Theory* (Princeton: Princeton University Press, 1979), pp. 230–232; Bruce M. Russett, "Inequality and Instability: The Relation of Land Tenure to Politics," *World Politics* 16 (1964): 442–454; Bruce M. Russett *et al., World Handbook of Political and Social Indicators* (New Haven: Yale University Press, 1964), pp. 153–157, 245.

4. For an introduction to these concepts see Alfred G. Meyer, *Leninism* (New York: Praeger, 1962), pp. 57–77, 235–257; Robert C. Tucker, *The Soviet Political Mind* (New York: Praeger, 1963): p. 152, *passim.*

5. The characteristics of totalitarian governments in general can be seen in Hannah Arendt, *The Origins of Totalitarianism* (New York: Harcourt, Brace Jovanovich, 1951), and for many useful insights into twentieth century authoritarian regimes see Stanley G. Payne, *Fascism: Comparison and Definition* (Madison: University of Wisconsin Press, 1980).

6. Reinhold Niebuhr and Paul E. Sigmund, *The Democratic Experience: Past and Prospects* (New York: Praeger, 1969), pp. 74–75, 120, 139.

7. Felix Gilbert, *To The Farewell Address: Ideas of Early American Foreign Policy* (Princeton, N.J.: Princeton University Press, 1961), pp. 89–104.

8. F.S. Northedge and M.J. Grieve, *A Hundred Years of International Relations* (New York: Praeger, 1971), p. 369; their conclusions are neatly detailed in a final essay, pp. 351–369.

CHAPTER TWO

1. *The American College Dictionary* (New York: Random House, 1958).

2. U.S. Congress, *Legislation on Foreign Relations Through 1982, February 1983*, vol. I: *Current Legislation and Related Executive Orders* (Washington, D.C.: Government Printing Office, 1983), "Foreign Assistance Act of 1961, Part 1, Chapter 1, Section 116," p. 32.

3. *Ibid.*, "Foreign Assistance Act of 1961, Part 3, Chapter 1, Section 502B," p. 97.

4. Department of State, *Report on Human Rights Practices in Countries Receiving U.S. Aid. Report Submitted to the Committee on Foreign Relations, U.S. Senate, and Committee on Foreign Affairs, U.S. House of Representatives by the Department of State. February 8, 1979* (Washington, D.C.: Government Printing Office, 1979).

5. *Ibid.*, 2–3.

6. Department of State, *Country Reports on Human Rights Practices for 1982. Report Submitted to the Committee on Foreign Relations, U.S. Senate, and Committee on Foreign Affairs, U.S. House of Representatives by the Department of State, February 1983* (Washington, D.C.: Government Printing Office, 1983).

7. U.S. Congress, *Legislation on Foreign Relations*, "Foreign Assistance Act of 1961, Part 1, Chapter 1, Section 101," pp. 12–13.

8. *Ibid.*, "Part 1, Chapter 2, Title IV, Section 231," p. 50.

9. *Ibid.*, "Part 3, Chapter 1, Section 620 (e)," p. 136.

10. *Ibid.*, "Part 1, Chapter 1, Section 101," p. 12.

11. *Ibid.*, "Part 1, Chapter 1, Section 101," pp. 13–14.

12. *U.S. Federal Register*, vol. 40, Nos. 91–109 (Washington D.C.: Government Printing Office, 1975): 20263.

CHAPTER THREE

1. Samuel Flagg Bemis, *The Latin American Policy of the United States* (New York: Harcourt, Brace Jovanovich, 1943), pp. 146–147.

2. U.S. Congress, Senate, *Second International Congress. Senate Document No. 330. Message From the President of the United States Transmitting A Report with Accompanying Papers, of the Delegates of the United States, Held at the City of Mexico from October 22, 1901 to January 22, 1902* (Washington, D.C.: Government Printing Office, 1902):31.

3. *Ibid.,*32.

4. *Ibid.,*32–33.

5. U.S. Congress, *Report of the Delegates of the United States to the Third International Conference of the American States, Held at Rio de Janeiro, Brazil, July 21 to August 26, 1906* (Washington, D.C.: Government Printing Office, 1906):62.

6. *Ibid.,*62.

7. *Ibid.,*64.

8. These views are briefly summarized in Hubert Herring, *A History of Latin America* (New York: Alfred A. Knopf, 1972), pp. 731–732. For a full treatment of Argentina see Thomas F. McGann, *Argentina, the United States, and the Interamerican System, 1880–1914* (Cambridge: Harvard University Press, 1957).

9. Conversation between James N. Cortada and Jaime A. Cortada during the late 1930s. The elder Cortada exported U.S. products to Latin America prior to World War I.

10. U.S. Department of State, *Foreign Relations of the United States, December 2, 1902* (Washington, D.C.: Government Printing Office, 1903):881–883. (Hereafter cited FRUS and year in title).

11. *Ibid.*, 883.

12. *FRUS, 1904*, 351.

13. *Ibid.*, 351–352.

14. *Ibid.*, footnote 2, 37.

15. *FRUS, 1906*, 837.

16. *Ibid.*, 848. Appendix II of our book reproduces the treaty negotiated on the USS *Marblehead.*

17. *Ibid.*, 854.

18. The San Jose Treaty of 1906 is reprinted below as Appendix III.

19. Manuel Vidal, *Nociones de historia de Centro America (Especial de El Salvador)* (San Salvador: n.p., 1935); 234.

20. *Ibid.*, 235.

21. *Idem.*

22. *Idem.*

23. World Peace Foundation, Pamphlet Series, *The New Pan Americanism*, Part III. *Central American League of Nations*, vol. 7, No. 1 (Boston: World Peace Foundation, February 1917): 123.

24. *FRUS, 1907,* 628–629.

25. *Ibid.,* 629.

26. The Amapala Treaty is reprinted below as Appendix IV.

27. *FRUS, 1907,* 644.

28. *Ibid.,* 661.

29. *Ibid.,* 673–674.

30. *Ibid.,* 674–675. For a full report by William I. Buchanan see 665–727.

31. The treaty is reprinted below as Appendix V.

32. Samuel Flagg Bemis, *The Latin American Policy of the United States,* footnote 1, p. 162.

33. Dana G. Munro, *Intervention and Dollar Diplomacy in the Caribbean* (Princeton, N.J.: Princeton University Press, 1964), pp. 160–161.

34. *Idem.*

35. Samuel Flagg Bemis, *The Latin American Policy of the United States,* pp. 165–166.

36. Isaac Joslin Cox, *Nicaragua and the United States* (Boston: World Peace Foundation, 1927), p. 708.

CHAPTER FOUR

1. Department of State, *Conference on Central American Affairs, Washington D.C., December 4, 1922–February 7, 1923* (Washington, D.C.: Government Printing Office, 1923): Article Sixth, 8. The Tacoma Agreement is published below as Appendix VI.

2. *Ibid.,* 22.

3. *Ibid.,* 24.

4. *Idem.*

5. Samuel Flagg Bemis, *The Latin American Policy of the United States,* pp. 207–208.

6. *FRUS, 1923, passim.*

7. Lester D. Langely, *The United States and the Caribbean in the Twentieth Century* (Athens, GA.: The University of Georgia Press, 1982), p. 107.

8. Department of State, *Report of the Delegates of the United States of America to the Sixth International Conference of American States, Held at Havana, Cuba, January 16 to February 20, 1928* (Wshington, D.C.: Government Printing Office, 1928): 228–230.

9. Lester D. Langely, *The United States and the Caribbean,* footnote 6, p. 136.

10. Samuel Flagg Bemis, *The Latin American Policy of the United States,* p. 434.

11. U.S. Department of State, *Report of the Delegation of the United States* (Washington, D.C.: GPO, 1948), *passim.*

12. Lester D. Langely, *The United States and the Caribbean,* footnote 6, p. 181.

13. Ambassador Robert F. Woodward to the authors, September 6, 1983.

14. John Bartlow Martin, *U.S. Policy in the Caribbean* (Boulder, Colo.: Westview Press, 1978), p. 45.

15. *Ibid.,* pp. 268–70.

CHAPTER FIVE

1. Department of State, *GIST,* February 1979, "The Caribbean Basin Initiative."

2. Organization of American States, *Statistical Bulletin* (Washington, D.C.: Organization of American States, 1982), 4: 26.

3. Richard C. Brown, "Liberation Theology in Latin America: Its Challenge to the United States," *Conflict* 4 No. 1 (1983): 21–58.

4. Fredrick B. Pike and Thomas Stritch (eds.), *The New Corporatism* (Notre Dame: University of Notre Dame Press, 1974), p. 6.

5. *Ibid.*, pp. 54–55.

6. Brown, "Liberation Theology in Latin America," p. 27.

7. *Ibid.*, p. 32.

8. Fredrick B. Pike, *Spanish America, 1900–1970* (New York: Norton, 1973): p. 141.

9. Organization of American States, *Statistical Bulletin*, p. 26.

10. *Idem.*

11. *Idem.*

12. *Idem.*

13. *Idem.*

14. *Idem.*

CHAPTER SIX

1. See Hugh Thomas, *Cuba: The Pursuit of Freedom* (New York: Harper & Row, 1971), pp. 27–41, 109–127 for a summary of early developments in Cuba's sugar industry.

2. *Area Handbook for Cuba* (Washington, D.C.: Government Printing Office, 1971), p. 387.

3. *Washington Post*, March 3, 1983, p. A-1, 21.

4. *The Cuban Economy—A Statistical Review, March 1981* (Springfield, Va.: National Technical Information Service, 1981), from Tables 37 and 49, pp. 41, 46.

5. *Area Handbook for Cuba* (Washington, D.C.: Government Printing Office, 1976), p. 63.

6. *Washington Post*, May 29, 1980, p. A-15.

7. *The Daily Progress*, January 12, 1980, p. A-2.

8. For further discussion of Cuban character traits see Wyatt MacGaffey and Clifford R. Barnett, *Twentieth Century Cuba* (New York: Anchor Books, 1965), pp. 108–124; and Elias José Entralgo, "El Caracter Cubano," *Revista Bimestro Cubana*, 27 (March–April, 1931): 267–294.

9. For a discussion of Cuba's military status see Edward Gonzalez, *A Strategy for Dealing with Cuba in the 1980s* (Santa Monica, Cal.: Rand Corporation. [R-2954-DOS/AF], 1982): 6–9.

10. For intriguing *quid pro quo* strategies applicable to American policy alternatives for Cuba, see *Ibid., passim*.

CHAPTER SEVEN

1. Joan Vila Valenti, *El Mon Rural a Catalunya* (Barcelona: Curial, 1973):147.

2. William R. Cline and Enrique Delgado (eds.)., *Economic Integration in Central America* (Washington, D.C.: Brookings Institution, 1978), p. 5.

3. Tennessee Agricultural Experiment Station, *Industrial Location and Growth in Submetro Tennessee and Kentucky Communities* (Knoxville, University of Tennessee, 1975(?)):7.

4. Observed first-hand by the authors in their home county of Orange, Virginia, between 1962 and 1983.

5. *A Synthesis. How New Manufacturing Industry Affects Rural Areas*. Rural Development Series No. 1A (Rural Development Center, State of Mississippi, September 1978):1–2.

BIBLIOGRAPHIC ESSAY

FOREIGN POLICY TOOLS

For readers who wish to look further into the question of national interest, the presidential memoirs and those of their senior advisors shed considerable light on their perceptions of the national interest and rationale for the foreign policy in their respective administrations.

Of particular interest in connection with initial U.S. aid to Greece, emergence of the Marshall Plan, creation of NATO, and the Korean conflict, see Harry S. Truman, *Year of Decisions* (New York: Doubleday, 1955) volume 1, and also his second volume, *Years of Trial and Hope* (New York: Doubleday, 1956). President Truman's actions represented a sharp departure from traditional isolationist tinted U.S. policy. It will be noted that Truman related his decisions to the security needs of the United States, one of the considerations in the Preamble of the Constitution.

See Lyndon B. Johnson, *The Vantage Point* (New York: Holt, Rinehart and Winston, 1971) for justification of his Viet Nam policy on the basis of the national interest. This point comes through very clearly at the bottom of page 505 in which his instruction is quoted as given to the U.S. delegation traveling to Paris in 1968 to negotiate with representatives from Hanoi.

President Johnson reflected concern for the proliferation of our aid programs, which he indicated was a matter of worry in the nation. Still he also felt that they related to the security, prosperity, and tranquility of the United States when he expressed concurrence with the thoughts on the interdependence of nations contained in a memorandum prepared by Secretary of State Dean Rusk (page 347).

For a drastic departure from the security considerations underlying the Truman and Johnson positions, one may turn to President Jimmy Carter's idealistic conception of human rights as a key factor for our foreign policy. In this respect see Jimmy Carter, *Keeping Faith* (New York: Bantam Books, Inc., 1982), pp. 141–51.

The difference in the two visions of the nation's foreign policy role personified by Messrs. Truman and Johnson on one hand and Mr. Carter on the other reflects two basic schools of thought which emerged after World War II among scholars and diplomatists. One calls for realism in our policies and the other stresses idealism or utopic considerations. George F. Kennan, *Realities of American Foreign Policy* (Princeton, N.J.: Princeton University Press, 1954), and his two volume memoirs both published in

Boston, Massachusetts by Little, Brown in 1967 and 1972, respectively, argue for the realism approach.

For a scholarly treatment of the two approaches, see Donald Brandon, *American Foreign Policy: Beyond Utopianism and Realism* (East Norwalk, Conn.: Appleton-Century-Crofts, 1966).

For a thoughtful discussion of foreign policy instruments, mechanics of the process, and related substantive considerations see Thomas A. Bailey, *The Art of Diplomacy* (New York, Appleton-Century-Crofts, 1968). Another very good book on the same general subject, particularly if read in conjunction with the Bailey work is Burton M. Sapin, *The Making of United States Foreign Policy* (New York: published for the Brookings Institution by Praeger, 1966). Although somewhat dated because of some internal changes within the structure of the Department of State, Sapin's book is still very useful.

As the president of the United States has the definitive responsibility for the conduct of our foreign policy and the Department of State is by law the principal means for implementation, the relationship between the president and his secretary of state is an extremely important matter. For the Truman-Acheson equation see Dean Acheson, *Present at the Creation* (New York: Signet non-fiction series published by The American Library, Inc., 1970). An interesting book, which reflects the late President John F. Kennedy's personal penchant to direct foreign policy and how he viewed the Secretary of State and his Department, is Arthur M. Schlesinger, Jr., *A Thousand Days* (Boston: Houghton Mifflin, 1965). Recently published is Cyrus Vance, *Hard Choices* (New York: Simon and Schuster, 1983). Apart from this book's value as a reflection of the views of Mr. Carter's Secretary of State, it highlights the complications which arise when the National Security Council is headed by an aggressive chief, in this case Dr. Zbigniew Brezinski, and the Secretary is dealt out in important foreign policy issues.

CENTRAL AMERICA

For an outstanding bibliography regarding U.S. diplomacy and relations with Latin America in general, and the Caribbean Basin in particular, see the recently published *Guide to American Foreign Relations*, edited by Richard Dean Burns (The Society of Historians of American Foreign Relations); Santa Barbara, Calif. and Oxford, England, ABC-Clio, Inc., 1983. Although worldwide in scope the Guide is divided into sections by time periods, topics, and geographic areas. As such it is an invaluable reference tool, containing also the names of other bibliographies and an index of authors.

Two helpful books for an overview of U.S. diplomacy within a historical context and rich in detailed information are: Thomas A. Bailey, *A Diplomatic History of the American People*, 10th edition (Englewood Cliffs, N.J.: Prentice-Hall, 1980), and Julius W. Pratt, Vincent P. De Santis, and Joseph M. Siracusa, *A History of United States Foreign Policy*, 4th edition (Englewood Cliffs, N.J.: Prentice-Hall, 1980).

Recommended standard works concerning United States-Latin American relations are: Samuel Flagg Bemis, *The Latin American Policy of the United States* (New York: Harcourt, Brace, 1943); J. Lloyd Mecham, *A Survey of United States-Latin American Relations* (Boston: Houghton Mifflin, 1965); Graham H. Stuart and James L. Tigner, *Latin America and the United States*, 6th edition (Englewood Cliffs, N.J.: Prentice-Hall, 1975).

For a critical work of U.S. foreign policy in Latin America reflecting the exploitation theme, see Alonso Aguilar Monteverde, *Pan Americanism from Monroe to the Present: A View from the Other Side*, translated by Asa Zatz (New York: Monthly Review Press, 1969).

Helpful in the understanding of cross-cultural impacts on U.S. relations with Latin America is Morell Heald, and Lawrence S. Kaplan, *Culture and Diplomacy. The American Experience* (Westport, Conn.: Greenwood Press, 1977). Although not written with Latin America as a focal point, it includes two excellent chapters related to different historical periods. They reflect perceptions of how the views and actions of the United States and Latin America impinge on each other, particularly outside officialdom.

Dependency as a factor derived from the Spanish colonial period is covered in Stanley J. Stein and Barbara Stein, *The Colonial Heritage of Latin America, Essays on Economic Dependence in Perspective* (New York: Oxford University Press, 1970).

Concerning geographic considerations, see E. Preston James, *Latin America*, 4th edition (Indianapolis: Odyssey Press [Bobbs-Merrill], 1969).

For a discussion of the economic development issues, see Celso Furtado (well-known Brazilian economist), *Economic Development of Latin America: Historical Background and Contemporary Problems*, 2nd edition, (London, Cambridge University Press, 1977); Karel Holbik *et al.*, *Trade and Industrialization in the Central America Common Market* (Austin: University of Texas Press, 1972); William R. Cline and Enrique Delgado (eds.), *Economic Integration in Central America* (Washington, D.C.: The Brookings Institution, 1978).

From a cultural viewpoint, recommended reading is: Charles Wagley, *The Latin American Tradition: Essays on the Unity and Diversity of Latin American Culture* (New York: Columbia University Press, 1968).

Three books which deal with other Latin American aspects and which complement the preceding suggestions are: Claudio Velez, *The Centralist*

Tradition of Latin America (New Jersey: Princeton University Press, 1980): Howard Wiarda, ed., *Politics and Social Change in Latin America: The Distant Tradition,* 2nd revised edition (Amherst, Mass.: University of Massachusetts Press, 1982); Luigi Binaudi, *et al., Arms Transfer to Latin America, Toward a Policy of Mutual Respect* (Santa Monica, Calif.: Rand Corporation, 1973).

The above listings concentrate on overall Latin American topics because they are somewhat essential, or at a minimum useful, in the understanding of Central American and Caribbean Island social, economic, and political phenomena, as they are part of the whole picture south of the Rio Grande.

For interesting and useful overview studies of the Central American region the following are suggested: Thomas L. Karnes, *The Failure of Union: Central America 1824–1960* (Chapel Hill: University of North Carolina Press, 1961); F. D. Parker, *The Central American Republics;* Ralph J. Woodward, *Central America: A Nation Divided* (New York: Oxford University Press, 1976). For a fine comprehensive study of U.S. involvement in Central America through the start of the Reagan era see Walter Lefeber, *Inevitable Revolutions: The United States in Central America* (New York: Norton, 1983).

Highly recommended to be read in conjunction with overview studies is A. Curtis Wilgus, ed., *The Caribbean: The Central American Area* (Gainesvile: University of Florida Press, 1961). This book is a collection of short essays prepared by outstanding specialists dealing with a broad range of Central American topics from archaeology to international relations.

For deeper investigation regarding the region's Indian cultures see Richard N. Adams, *Cultural Surveys of Panama, Nicaragua, Guatemala, El Salvador, Honduras* (Detroit: Blaine Ethridge Books, 1976 [Reprint of 1957 edition]).

For an interpretive and succinct survey of U.S. foreign policy in the Caribbean Basin the following three books are suggested to be read in sequence all by Lester D. Langely, *Struggle for the American Mediterranean, United States-European Rivalry in the Gulf-Caribbean 1776–1904* (Athens, Ga.: University of Georgia Press, 1976); *The United States and the Caribbean in the Twentieth Century* (Athens, Ga.: University of Georgia Press, 1982); *Banana Wars: An Inner History of American Empire, 1900–1934* (Lexington: University of Kentucky Press, 1983).

Also in connection with with foreign policy matters, see Harold Eugene Davis, John J. Finan, and F. Taylor Peck, *Latin American Diplomatic History, An Introduction* (Baton Rouge: Louisiana State University Press, 1977), and former Ambassador John Bartlow Martin's *U. S. Policy in the Caribbean* (Boulder, Colo., Westview Press, 1978).

For discussion related to the economic integration issues see Jeffrey B. Nugent, *Economic Integration in Central America, Empirical Investigations,*

(Baltimore, Md.: Johns Hopkins University Press, 1975); William R. Cline and Enrique Delgado, eds., *Economic Integration in Central America: A Study* (Washington: Brookings Institution, 1978); Royce Q. Shaw, *Central America: Regional Integration and National Political Development,* (Boulder, Colo.: Westview Press, 1978).

An interesting study concerned with the problem of overpopulation relative to resources is William H. Durham, *Scarcity and Survival in Central America, Ecological Origins of the Soccer War* (Stanford: Stanford University Press, 1979).

With respect to economic data for the Caribbean Islands and Central America, most useful is the *Statistical Bulletin of the Organization of American States,* issued quarterly by that Organization. Also helpful is the *Statistical Yearbook for Latin America,* Economic Commission for Latin America, United Nations Publications, New York City. For business opportunities and prospects in the Caribbean Basin, particularly useful are the various publications of Caribbean/Central American Action, Suite 1010, 1333 New Hampshire Avenue, NW, Washington, D.C., and those of the United States Department of Commerce, Washington, D.C..

There are available for each of the Central American countries and most of the Caribbean Island Republics Area Handbooks, prepared by the Foreign Area Studies Division of American University, Washington, D.C. These may be ordered from the U.S. Government Printing Office, Washington, D.C.

For movement of industry to rural areas in the United States see Gene F. Summers *et al., Industrial Invasion of Nonmetropolitan America* (New York: Praeger, 1976); Richard E. Lonsdale and H.L. Seyler, *Nonmetropolitan Industrialization* (Washington, D.C.: Winston & Sons, 1979); another volume by Gene F. Summers with Arne Selick (eds.), *Nonmetropolitan Industrial Growth and Community Change* (Lexington, Mass.: D.C. Heath, 1979); *Industrialization of Rural Areas, Rural Development Bibliography Series No. 1* (Mississippi State, Southern Rural Development Center, Box 5406, Mississippi State, MS 39762).

Three other books are useful on political affairs in Central America. For the impact of the OAS see G. Pope Atkins, *Latin America in the International Political System* (New York: Free Press, 1977). On the role played by the United States in Guatemala during the 1950s see Richard H. Immerman, *The CIA in Guatemala: The Foreign Policy of Intervention* (Austin: University of Texas Press, 1982). On the Sandinista government in Nicaragua see Thomas W. Walker (ed.), *Nicaragua in Revolution* (New York: Praeger, 1982). The Kissinger report is also an important document on the politics of the region, Henry A. Kissinger, *Report of the National Bipartisan Commission on Central America, January 1984,* Washington, D.C., U.S. Government Printing Office, 1984. Of related interest is *Changing Course:*

Blueprint for Peace in Central America and the Caribbean (Washington, D.C., Institute for Policy Studies, 1984).

CUBA

The suggested readings concerning Cuba are mainly for the non-specialist. This clarification is necessary because the volume of primary and secondary source material regarding Cuba's history in the nineteenth and early part of the twentieth centuries, in fact up to Dr. Fidel Castro's takeover, is considerable. Review of some of this material is essential for expert analysis of events leading to the 1959 development. Since the establishment of the Castro regime some fine books have been published concerning the background of the island's history and its relation to the situation which made the Castro phenomenon possible.

The interruption of diplomatic relations between the United States and Cuba, and the economic blockade instituted against the island by Washington has resulted in a sharply diminished flow of data from Cuba, particularly of a technical nature. Even if recourse is adopted in obtaining publications originating in Havana in third countries, the quality and reliability raise serious questions, so much is tinged with a view to propaganda, let alone absence of detailed explanation regarding methodologies used. This is particularly true for economic studies.

For an understanding of what has happened and why, there are three books which warrant careful study. The *Area Handbook for Cuba* (Washington, D.C.: American University [Foreign Area Studies], U. S. Government Printing Office, 1976) is a good starting point. It is a concise birds-eye overview of Cuba from the discovery period to the mid-1970s, including comment on social, political, and economic evolution.

The *Handbook* may profitably be followed by Wyatt MacGaffey and Clifford R. Barnett (in collaboration with Jean Haiken and Mildred Vreeland), *Twentieth-Century Cuba* (formerly published in 1962 as *Cuba*) (New York: Anchor Books, 1965). The MacGaffey-Barnett work is a scholarly and thorough treatment of key facets in Cuba's development from the colonial era well into the Castro period. Both authors are anthropologists and their skills are evident in what nevertheless is a historical treatment of the subject. Of special interest because of the role of middle classes in political development, or lack of participation as the case may be, is the chapter on "Ethnic Influences and Social Patterns," pp. 34–67, and that on "Competition for Status," pp. 108–124. Also helpful is an extensive bibliography.

Hugh Thomas, *Cuba: The Pursuit of Freedom* (New York: Harper & Row, 1971), which consists of some 1700 pages is in effect an encyclopedic approach to Cuba's background and in this sense is a useful book. It also has a very extensive bibliography with pertinent notations for specific works.

For the period immediately preceding the advent of Dr. Castro to power and consolidation of his position with respect to Cuban-American diplomatic relations see Philip W. Bonsal, *Cuba, Castro and the United States* (Pittsburgh: University of Pittsburgh Press, 1971). Mr. Bonsal was a career diplomat and ambassador to Cuba in the crucial years of 1957–1960. Peter Wyden, *Bay of Pigs* (New York: Simon and Schuster, 1979), is probably the best treatment of the subject.

For a good account of Cuba's leap into the world scene recommended reading is Cole Blasier, and Carmelo Mesa-Lago, eds., *Cuba in the World* (Pittsburgh: University of Pittsburgh Press, 1978). The use of Cuba within Soviet strategic considerations is ably dealt with in Jacques Levesque, *The USSR and the Cuban Revolution: Soviet Ideological and Strategic Perspective* (New York: Praeger, 1978).

A thoughtful study of the limits to the effects of Castro's personality on Cuba is Edward Gonzalez, *Cuba Under Castro: The Limits of Charisma* (Boston: Houghton Mifflin, 1974). Also by the same author is *A Strategy for Dealing with Cuba in the 1980s* (Santa Monica, Calif.: The Rand Corporation, 1982). This book includes a very good statement concerning Cuba's military capability and possible consequences for the United States. It also contains perceptive assumptions concerning Cuba as a basis for U.S. policy and proposes some intriguing approaches for the United States.

For a glimpse of the sense of nationalism among Cubans long before Dr. Castro appeared on the scene the works of several highly respected Cuban authors, written in Spanish, makes interesting reading. Resentment against the United States runs through these studies which help explain in part why it was relatively easy for Castro to mobilize support for his anti-U.S. sentiment.

The first Cuban war of independence lasted from 1868 to 1878. It was a long hard bitter fight and contributed enormously to the formation of Cuban nationalistic sentiments. For an account of the war see Ramiro Guerra y Sanchez, *Guerra de los Diez Años*, 1868–1878. 2 vols. (Havana: Editorial de Ciencias Sociales, 1972, [2nd edition 1960]).

For an excellent account of Cuban relations with Spain and the United States from a pre-Castro Cuban viewpoint recommended reading is Herminio Portell Vila, *Historia de Cuba en sus relaciones con los Estados y España*, 4 vols. (Havana, 1938).

With regard to the War of Independence in 1895–1898, a view of the Cuban effort may be obtained from B. Souza, *Biografia de un regimiento mambi: el regimiento Calixto Garcia* (Havana: 1899), and by the same author *Maximo Gomez, el generalisimo* (Havana: 1936). On the same theme see

Orestes Ferrara, *Mis relaciones con Maximo Gomez* (Havana: 1942). In English consult Philip S. Foner, *The Spanish-Cuban-American War and the Birth of American Imperialism, 1895–1902.* 2 vols. (New York: Monthly Review Press, 1972).

For economic statistical data for Cuba the following are useful: *Estudio Económico de America Latina, Cuba 1981,* New York, Comisión Económica para America Latina, United Nations, 1983; *Statistical Yearbook for Latin America,* Economic Commission for Latin America, United Nations, 1980; and *The Cuban Economy, A Statistical Review March, 1981,* National Technical Information Service, Springfield, Virginia.

For an excellent survey of U.S. policy regarding Cuba within the framework of early U.S. interest in the island, the evolution of that concern up to Castro's regime and the consequences stemming from the latter's anti-U.S. policies and tactics, see Lester D. Langley, *The Cuban Policy of the United States: A Brief History (1776–1962)* (New York: Wiley, 1968).

On studies concerning the Cuban character traits there is Wyatt MacGaffey and R. Barnett Wyatt, *Twentieth Century Cuba* (New York: Anchor Books, 1965), pp. 108–124. The most detailed work was done many years earlier: Elias José Entralgo, "El Caracter Cubano," *Revista Bimestre Cubana,* 27 (March–April 1931):267–294; Calixto Maso y Vazquez, *El Caracter Cubano* (Havana: 1941); Fernando Ortíz, *Entre Cubanos* (Paris: 1914); José Antonio Ramos, *Manual del Perfecto Fulanista* (Havana: 1916); Fernando Ortíz, *Los Negros Esclavos* (Havana: 1916); Fernando Ortíz, *La Decadencia Cubana* (Havana: 1924); and José Antonio Saco, *La Vagancia en Cuba* (Havana: 1946).

THE CARIBBEAN ISLANDS

The amount of literature concerning basic developments in the Caribbean Islands is somewhat limited, particularly with regard to specific aspects. For a grasp of the overall situation in these islands, the following books are suggested: John Macpherson, *Caribbean Lands* (New York: Longman, 1980) (a good geography); David Lowenthal, *West Indian Societies* (New York: Oxford University Press, 1972); Malcolm Cross, *Urbanization and Urban Growth in the Caribbean* (New York: Cambridge University Press, 1980); Harold P. Mitchell, *Caribbean Patterns: A Political and Economic Study of the Contemporary Caribbean* (New York: Halstead Press, 1972); Ransford W. Palmer, *Caribbean Dependence on the United States Economy* (New York: Praeger, 1979).

For the history of the Caribbean, it is suggested that *From Columbus to Castro: The History of the Caribbean* (New York: Harper & Row, 1971), by the noted West Indies historian and former Prime Minister of Trinidad Eric Williams be read, followed by what may be considered an update: P.M. Sherlock, *West Indian Nations: A New History* (London: Macmillan, 1973).

Regarding Haiti, the following is very helpful in assessing its prospects: Vera Rubin and Richard Schaedel, (eds.), *The Haitian Potential, Research and Resources of Haiti* (New York: Teacher's College Press, 1975).

For the Dominican Republic see Howard J. Wiarda, *Dictatorship, Development and Disintegration: Political and Social Change in the Dominican Republic* (Ann Arbor, Mich.: Xerox University Microfilms, 1975) (3 vols.).

APPENDIXES

APPENDIX I

CENTRAL AMERICAN TREATY OF PEACE*

The Governments of Nicaragua, Salvador, Honduras, and Costa Rica, desirous of contributing by all means in their power to the maintenance of the peace and good harmony that exists and should exist among them, have agreed to celebrate a convention of peace and obligatory arbitration, and to that effect have named as their respective plenipotentiaries:

The Government of Nicaragua, his excellency Señor Doctor Don Fernando Sanchez, minister of foreign relations;

The Government of Salvador, his excellency Señor Doctor Don Salvador Rodríguez, subsecretary of foreign relations;

The Government of Honduras, his excellency Señor Doctor Don Cesar Bonilla, minister of foreign relations;

The Government of Costa Rica, his excellency Señor Don Leonidas Pacheco, minister of foreign relations;

Who, after having presented their credentials and the same being found in good and due form, have agreed upon the following covenant:

Article I. It is declared that the present convention has for object the incorporation in form of public treaty the conclusions to which have arrived their excellencies, the Presidents, General Don J. Santos Zelaya, General Don Tomas Regalado, General Don Terencio Sierra, and Don Rafael Iglesias, in the several conferences that have been held in this port with the sole object of maintaining and assuring, by all possible means, the peace of Central America.

Article 2. The contracting Governments establish the principle of obligatory arbitration, in order to adjust every difficulty or question that might present itself between the contracting parties, binding themselves in consequence to submit them to a tribunal of Central American arbitrators.

Article 3. Each one of the contracting parties shall name an arbitrator and a substitute to constitute the tribunal. The terms of the arbitrators shall be for one year, counting from their acceptance, and then they may be reelected.

---

*"Enclosure-From *El Comercio*, Managua, Nicaragua, January 30, 1902.-Translation," *FRUS* 1902, Part I; 881–883.

Article 4. The arbitrators of those states among whom exists the disagreement shall not form part of the tribunal for the consideration of the concrete case, this remaining entirely with the arbitrator or arbitrators of the remaining states.

Article 5. If, through pairing, there should be no decision, the tribunal shall select a third among the substitutes. The third should necessarily adhere to one of the views given out.

Article 6. As soon as a difficulty or question presents itself between two or more states, their respective Governments shall advise the remaining signers of the present convention.

Article 7. The contracting Governments establish and recognize the right of each one of them to offer without delay, singly or conjointly, their good offices to the Governments of the states that are in disagreement, even without previous acceptance by them, and though they should not have notified them of the difficulty or question pending.

Article 8. The friendly offices exhausted without satisfactory result, the government or governments that would have exercised them shall notify the others, declaring at the proper time arbitration proceedings. This declaration shall be communicated with the greatest possible brevity to the member of the tribunal corresponding to the president of same, with the object that within a period not exceeding fifteen days the tribunal that is to know and decide the case comes together. The installation of the tribunal shall be communicated by telegraph to the signing governments, demanding from the contending parties the presentation of their claims within the fifteen days following.

Article 9. The tribunal will give its judgment within five days following the expiration of the term spoken of.

Article 10. The difficulties which may arise through questions of pending limits, or through interpretation, or execution of treaties of limits, shall be submitted by the governments interested to the knowledge and decision of a foreign arbitrator of American nationality.

Article 11. The Governments of the states in dispute solemnly agree not to execute any hostile act, warlike preparations, or mobilization of forces, with the object of not impeding the arrangement of the difficulty or question through the means established by the present agreement.

Article 12. The presidency of the arbitration tribunal shall be held alternately, for annual periods by each one of the members, following the alphabetical order of the states represented, the first year corresponding to the Costa Rican arbitrator, the second to that of Salvador, and so on. When in the event foreseen in Article 4, the member filling the presidency of the tribunal shall be prohibited from acting the temporary presidency for the case in question shall be filled by an arbitrator that may be available according to precedence established in the foregoing paragraph. The tribunal shall be held in the capital of the state to which the arbitrator belongs, who should preside.

Article 13. The arbitation tribunal shall dictate all those rational dispositions that it considers necessary to fully carry out the high mission which is conferred upon it by this treaty.

Article 14. With the object of preventing those abuses that might be committed in a state by political emigrants from another against the public peace and tranquility of this, the contracting Governments agree to send to the frontier those emigrants with respect to whom a petition should be made by the Governments interested.

Article 15. With the object of harmonizing as much as possible the ideas and tendencies of the Governments signing, in all that relates to the maintenance and strengthening the bonds of Central American friendship and good understanding among them, while for such ends there are not established permanent legations among the contracting States, the nomination of consuls-general be recommended from each one in the other States, who shall have at the same time the character of confidential agents from their respective Governments.

Article 16. The present convention shall be submitted to the ratification of the respective congresses as soon as possible and once ratified by them all will enter into force thirty days after without the need of exchange.

Article 17. For the installation of the arbitration tribunal established by this agreement, the 15th of September of the current year, anniversay of the independence of Central America, is named.

Article 18. In the desire that the present convention may unite all the States of the Central American family, the signing Governments shall invite, jointly or separately, the Government of the Republic of Guatemala to adhere to its stipulations if it shall be possible.

In witness hereof we sign four copies of the same tenor in the port of Corinto, Republic of Nicaragua, the 20th day of January, 1902.

Fernando Sanchez
Salvador Rodríguez
Cesar Bonilla
Leonidas Pacheco

The present treaty being drawn up in accordance with instructions to that effect, the president of the Republic resolves to give it his approval.

Zelaya

National Palace, Managua, January 28, 1902. Sanchez, Minister of Foreign Relations.

APPENDIX II

TEXT OF THE CONVENTION OF PEACE CELEBRATED ON BOARD
THE CRUISER *MARBLEHEAD*, OF THE NAVY OF THE UNITED
STATES OF AMERICA (TRANSLATION)

The friendly initiative of Their Excellencies Theodore Roosevelt, the President of the United States of America, and General Porfirio Diaz, President of the United States of Mexico, having been accepted by the Governments of the Republics of El Salvador, Guatemala, and Honduras to discuss the bases upon which peace, unfortunately interrupted between the three Republics, is to be established, and to assure as far as possible the permanent enjoyment of its benefits, Messrs. Jose Rosa Pacas and Salvador Gallegos, delegates from the Republic of El Salvador, Francisco Bertrand, delegate from the Republic of Honduras, and Arturo Ubico, Jose Pinto, Juan Barrios M. and Manuel Cabral, delegates from the Republic of Guatemala, assembled on board the cruiser *Marblehead* of the United States Navy, and after examining their respective credentials and fully deliberating on the object of the conference, under the honorary presidency of Their Excellencies William Lawrence Merry and Leslie Combs, ministers plenipotentiary of the United States to the Republics of El Salvador, Guatemala, and Honduras, and of His Excellency Frederico Gamboa, minister plenipotentiary of the United States of Mexico, the first named being, besides, the special delegate from the Republic of Costa Rica to the conference of peace, to which also attended in the same capacity Mr. Modesto Barrios, for the Republic of Nicaragua; they have agreed upon the following terms:

First. The Republics of El Salvador and Honduras return to a state of peace with the Republic of Gautemala, relegating to oblivion their past differences. Consequently, they will concentrate their respective armies within three days counted from that following the signing of the present Convention, and will disarm them within the subsequent eight days, leaving only the garrisons ordinarily maintained in their cities and the movable detachments serving on police duty.

Second. The contracting parties will reciprocally deliver the prisoners of war and will care for, free of charge, the wounded who may be in their respective territories, until they may be able to return to their homes or may be demanded by their respective Governments. In the same manner all political prisoners now held shall at once be placed at liberty; and each delegation shall recommend to its respective Government that a general amnesty be decreed as soon as possible.

Third. The high contracting parties bind themselves to concentrate the political refugees who are in or may come to their respective territories, as also to exercise surveillance over their conduct in order to prevent their taking improper advantage of their asylum and their machinations against the tranquility and public order of the country whence they may have emigrated.

Fourth. Within two months from this date the contracting parties shall celebrate a general treaty of peace, amity, and navigation, and the capital of the Republic of Costa Rica is hereby designated for the meeting of the representatives of the three Governments fully authorized and for their negotiations.

In the meantime it is agreed that all international stipulations binding the contracting parties shall remain in force, and specially those of the Second Pan-American Conference assembled at Mexico.

Fifth. If, contrary to expectations, any one of the high contracting parties shall fail in the future in any of the points agreed upon in this treaty, or should give cause for new differences, these shall be submitted to arbitration, Their Excellencies the Presidents of the United States of America and of the United States of Mexico being hereby designated as arbitrators, to which arbitration shall also be submitted the recent actual difficulties between Guatemala, El Salvador and Honduras.

The present convention remains under the guarantee of the loyalty of the Governments interested and of the moral sanction of the Governments of the mediating and participating nations.

Without prejudice to the immediate execution of this treaty, the exchange of the ratifications shall take place by exchange of notes in the cities of Guatemala, San Salvador and Tegucigalpa, at the latest on the thirtieth of the current month.

In witness whereof we sign and seal the present on board the American cruiser *Marblehead,* this twentieth day of the month of July in the year one thousand nine hundred and six.

> J. R. Pacas
> Salvador Gallegos
> F. Bertrand
> Arturo Ubico
> J. Pinto
> Juan Barrios M.
> Manuel Cabral

Honorary presidents:
  William Lawrence Merry.
  Leslie Combs.
  F. Gamboa.
  Modesto Barrios.
At the invitation of the legations:
  R. T. Mulligan
    Commander, U.S.N., Commanding *Marblehead*

By appointment from Minister William L. Merry, as the representative of the Government of Costa Rica.

Salvador Gallegos.

Source: FRUS, 1909, Part I: 851–852.

APPENDIX III

General Treaty of Peace and Amity, Arbitration, Commerce, Etc., Between the Republics of Costa Rica, Salvador, Guatemala, and Honduras.

The Governments of the Republics of Salvador, Guatemala and Honduras in conformity with the stipulations of the treaty of July 20th of the current year, concluded on board of the American cruiser *Marblehead*, and the Republic of Costa Rica acting on invitation of said countries, and desirous to be present at this act which concerns the entire Central American Fatherland, for the purpose of establishing peace on firm and stable foundations and binding closer their family relations and the ties which must unite them because of their common destiny, through the delegates hereafter to be named, have held various meetings in conference spreading upon the several minutes of the Protocol thus formed the conclusions reached on such an important subject; and all being desirous to give said agreements a more solemn form, they have concluded to embody them in a general treaty.

The representatives were, on behalf of the Republic of Costa Rica, His Excellency, Licentiate Don Luis Anderson; on behalf of Salvador, their Excellencies, Drs. Don Salvador Gallegos and Don Salvador Rodriguez Gonzalez; on behalf of Guatemala, their Excellencies, Dr. Francisco Anguiano and Licentiate Don Jose Flamenco, and on behalf of Honduras, His Excellency, General Sotero Barahona, who after having presented their respective Full Powers, found to be in good and due form, have agreed to the following articles:

ARTICLE 1.

There shall be perpetual peace and a frank, loyal and sincere friendship among the Republics of Costa Rica, Salvador, Guatemala, and Honduras, each and every one of the aforesaid Governments being in duty bound to consider as one of their principal obligations the maintenance of such peace and the preservation of such friendship, by endeavoring to contribute every means to procure the desired end, and to remove, as far as lies in their power, any obstacles, whatever their nature, which might prevent it. In order to secure such ends, they shall always unite when the importance of the case demands it, to foster their moral, intellectual, and industrial progress, thus making their interests one and the same, as it becomes sister countries.

ARTICLE 2.

In the event, which is not to be expected, that any of the high contracting parties should fail to comply with or cause any deviation from any of the subjects agreed to in the present treaty, such event, as well as any particular difficulty which may arise between them, shall necessarily be settled by the civilized means of arbitration.

ARTICLE 3.

The Governments of Salvador, Guatemala, and Honduras, in conformity with the stipulations of the treaty executed on board the *Marblehead*, hereby appoint as umpires, Their Excellencies the Presidents of the United States of America and of the United Mexican States, to whom all particular difficulties arising among said Governments shall be submitted for arbitration.

For the purpose of agreeing on the manner to effect such arbitration, the above-mentioned Repbulics shall accredit, at the latest within three months from this date, their respective legations near the Governments of the United States of America and Mexico, and in the meanwhile arbitration shall be ruled according to the stipulations of the treaty of compulsory arbitration concluded in Mexico on the 20th of January, 1902.

ARTICLE 4.

Guatemala not having subscribed to the Corinto convention of January 20, 1902, Costa Rica, Salvador, and Honduras do hereby respectively declare, that said Corinto convention is to continue in force, and that any particular difference which may arise among them shall be settled in conformity with the aforesaid convention and with the regulations established by the Central American court of arbitration on the 9th of October of that year.

ARTICLE 5.

Citizens of any of the high contracting parties, resident in the territory of any of the other parties, shall enjoy the same civil rights as native citizens, and shall be considered as naturalized citizens of the country of residence, provided they possess the qualifications required by the respective constitutional laws and have declared before the respective departmental authorities their intention of becoming citizens; or that they accept any public office or charge, in which case such intention is presumed. Nonnaturalized citizens shall be exempt from obligatory military service, either by sea or land, and from all forced loans, levies, or military requisitions, and under no circumstances shall they be obliged to pay more assessments, ordinary or extraordinary taxes, than those to which native citizens are subject.

ARTICLE 6.

The diplomatic agents of each of the high contracting parties shall exercise their good offices in order that due justice shall be administered their fellow citizens. It is well understood, however, that in the defense and protection of their rights and interests, and in their claims and complaints against the nation or private individuals, no other proceedings shall be resorted to than those which the laws of each signatory Republic may provide for their respective citizens, and they must conform to the final decision of the courts of justice.

ARTICLE 7.

Those who may have acquired a professional, literary, artistic, or industrial title in any of the contracting Republics shall be free to practice in any of the other countries, without any restraint whatever, their respective professions, arts, or trades, in conformity with the laws of the country of their residence, and without any other previous requirements than the presentation of the proper title or diploma, duly authenticated, and, in case of need, to establish the identity of the person and to obtain the approval of the executive power in case the law should so require.

Scientific or literary studies made in the universities, technical schools, Institutes of secondary education in any of the contracting countries, shall also be valid after presentation of the proper authenticated documents certifying to such studies and corresponding identification.

ARTICLE 8.

Citizens of any of the signatory countries residing within the territory of any of the others, shall enjoy the right of literary, artistic, or industrial property (copyright) on the same terms and subject to the same requirements as those applying to their native-born citizens.

ARTICLE 9.

Commerce between the republics of Salvador, Guatemala, and Honduras of articles of their growth, produce, or manufacture, whether by sea, or through their land frontiers, shall be exempt from all fiscal duties, and shall not be burdened with any local or municipal import dues. In case of Salvador and Guatemala this exemption does not apply to their export duties. Products manufactured in the country with foreign raw material are excepted, and they shall only pay 50 per cent of the duty assessed upon them on their reciprocal importation from one country to another.

Notwithstanding the stipulations contained in the foregoing paragraph, the governments of the high contracting parties shall frame, of common accord, all such measures as may tend to prevent fraud under the exceptions herein stipulated.

ARTICLE 10.

In order that such national products, either natural or manufactured, may enjoy the exemption aforesaid, the political authority from the country of origin shall be required to certify to the origin of said article; and customhouse collectors, at the port of shipment, shall certify in a similar manner, that such product is a natural product of the respective country and that its origin is genuine.

ARTICLE 11.

The exemptions contained in the foregoing article shall not apply—
1. In respect to Guatemala and Salvador, to salt and sugar.
2. To the natural or manufactured products the monopoly of which actually is or may hereafter be established in each of the contracting republics for the benefit of the state.
3. To articles of illicit commerce and, in general, to all such articles that the governments may agree to exempt.

ARTICLE 12.

Whosoever in any manner defraud, or intend to defraud, the public treasury of any of the contracting parties under cover of any of the provisions of this treaty shall be prosecuted and punished as the fiscal laws of the respective countries may prescribe.

ARTICLE 13.

In respect to the commercial relations between the above-mentioned republics and Costa Rica, it is agreed, as a general proposition, that free importation shall be limited, for the present, only to such national products as can not be obtained in any of the other countries in quantities sufficient to meet the necessities of consumption, such articles to be freely designated and the extent of the exemptions established for each year by correspondence between the respective departments during the next preceding year.

ARTICLE 14.

The merchant vessels of any of the four contracting parties shall be regarded as national (home) vessels while on the seas, coasts, and ports of any of the other countries. They shall enjoy the same exemptions, franchises, and concessions accorded to such vessels, and shall pay no other dues, nor be burdened with other charges than those affecting vessels of the respective countries.

ARTICLE 15.

Diplomatic and consular agents of the contracting republics in foreign cities towns, or ports shall extend to the persons, vessels, and other property of the citizens of any of the aforesaid republics the same protection due to the persons, vessels, and other property of their respective fellow-citizens, and they shall not ask for such services, any other, or higher fees than those usually charged in the case of their own fellow-citizens.

ARTICLE 16.

With a view to encourage commerce among the contracting republics, their respective governments shall take the necessary steps tending to an agreement for the establishment of a national merchant marine for the coastwise trade, or to make contracts with, or grant subsidies to the steamship companies carrying on the trade between San Francisco, Cal., and Panama, and between Colon and Puerto Barrios.

ARTICLE 17.

The high contracting parties, recognizing the necessity and great advantage of promoting and supporting the establishment of the best means of communication between the respective States, hereby agree to grant, as each country may determine within its own territory, the necessary concessions for the construction of railroads and the establishment of new submarine cables and wireless telegraph stations.

They equally bind themselves to improve as much as possible their telegraphic and telephonic means of communication, it being agreed that telegraphic communication shall not be subject to any higher rates than those established by the respective tariffs for interior service in each republic.

ARTICLE 18.

There shall exist among the contracting governments a complete and regular exchange of official publications of all kinds. This exchange also applies to all scientific and literary publications made within their respective territories by private individuals and to this end every publisher, and owner of a printing establishment, shall be bound to supply their respective department of foreign relations, immediately after publication, with the necessary copies for the exchange. For the purpose of due preservation and easy consultation, each government shall deposit one copy of said publications in such public library as it is deemed convenient.

ARTICLE 19.

Public instruments delivered in one of the contracting republics shall be valid in the others, when duly authenticated and made in accordance with the laws of the republic where they originate.

ARTICLE 20.

The judicial authorities of the contracting republics shall execute all requisitions in civil, commercial, or criminal matters relating to summons, examinations, and other legal proceedings.

Other judicial acts in civil or commercial matters growing out of personal actions shall have within the territory of any of the high contracting parties the same force as in the respective local courts, and shall be executed as in the latter when duly authorized by the supreme tribunal of the republic wherein they are to be executed. Such authorization exists when the essential conditions required by each particular legislation, as well as the rules governing in each country the execution of sentences, have been complied with.

ARTICLE 21.

The contracting republics, desirous that crimes and offenses committed within their respective territories shall not be left unpunished, and in order to prevent that criminal responsibility should be evaded by the escape of the offender, do hereby agree reciprocally to surrender persons seeking refuge within their respective territories, charged with, or convicted of, having committed in any of the countries, either as principals or as accessories, any of the following crimes, to wit: Homicide, arson, robbery, piracy, embezzlement, abigeat (cattle stealing), counterfeiting of money, forgery of public documents, breach of trust, malversation of public funds, fraudulent bankruptcy, perjury, and, in general, any crime or offense that can be prosecuted without the necessity of a formal accusation, and which the common penal code of the country wherein the crime was committed punishes by imprisonment for a period exceeding two years, even when the penalty for that particular crime is less, or different, in the country where the criminal has taken refuge.

ARTICLE 22.

The penalty of two years' imprisonment establishes the nature of the extraditable crime or offense when such extradition is requested during the judicial proceedings, but does not limit the effects of the proceedings if, either by extenuating circumstances or other evidence favorable to the accused person, he will be condemned to a lighter penalty.

Should extradition be requested by virtue of the sentence of a court, the accused person shall be surrendered in case the penalty inflicted be no less than imprisonment for one year.

ARTICLE 23.

No extradition shall be granted in the case of a person under sentence for, or charged with a political crime, or offense, even when such crime or offense may have been committed in connection with another crime or offense calling for extradition.

It develops upon the courts of justice of the republic where the fugitive is found to determine the nature of political crimes or offenses.

The person surrendered cannot be tried or condemned for political crimes or offenses, or other acts in connection thereof, committed prior to the extradition.

ARTICLE 24.

Extradition shall not be granted:

1. If the offender whose extradition is requested has already been tried and sentenced for the same act committed in the republic where he resides.

2. If the act for which extradition is demanded is not considered as a crime or offense in the republic where he resides; and

3. If in conformity with the laws of the claiming republic, or that of refuge, the action or penalty has prescribed.

If the person whose extradition is requested has been charged with or condemned in the country of refuge for an offense or crime committed within its territory, he shall not be surrendered until acquitted by sentence of the court, or, in case of having been condemned, not until such sentence has been filled, or he has been pardoned. In case of urgency, temporary detention of the accused may be requested by telegraphic or postal communication to the minister of foreign relations, or through the respective diplomatic agent or consul, in default of the former. Such temporary arrest shall conform with the rules established by the laws of the country, but, if within a month, reckoned from the day when the arrest was effected, no formal demand of the prisoner has been made, such temporary arrest shall cease.

ARTICLE 25.

The high contracting parties are not bound to surrender their respective citizens, but they shall prosecute them for violations of the penal code committed in any of the other republics, and the government in whose territory such violation was committed shall transmit to that of the nationality of the accused all such proceedings, information, and documents in the case, as well as the objects constituting the corpus delicti, and all other evidence necessary to establish the guilt and to expedite the action of the court. This being done, the trial shall proceed to its end, and the government of the country of trial shall inform the other interested governments of the final disposition of the case.

ARTICLE 26.

Extradition shall always be granted, even in case the alleged offender may fail, because of his surrender, to discharge contractual obligations. In such cases the interested parties shall have the right to bring the proper action before the competent judicial authorities.

ARTICLE 27.

The surrender shall always be made on condition that if the penalty attached to the crime or offense for which the extradition is requested is not the same in the claiming nation as in the nation of refuge, the lower penalty shall be applied to the offender, and in no case the death penalty.

ARTICLE 28.

If the accused or condemned person whose extradition is requested should be equally claimed by one or more of the governments for crimes committed by him within their respective jurisdication, he shall be surrendered in preference to the government having first demanded his extradition.

ARTICLE 29.

For the extradition of criminals the respective signatory governments shall negotiate either directly or through diplomatic channels. In submitting the request for extradition specification shall be made of the evidence or the principle on which the proof that, in accordance with the laws of the republic where the offense or crime was committed is sufficient to justify the arrest and trial of the accused.

The sentence, accusation, warrant of arrest, or any other equivalent legal proceedings shall also be submitted, stating the nature and gravity of the alleged offenses and the penal dispositions applicable thereto. In case of escape of the offender after sentence has been passed, or before the penalty has been fully completed, the requisition shall relate such circumstances and be accomplished only by the sentence.

ARTICLE 30.

In order to facilitate proof of ownership of the property stolen or taken from one of the republics to any of the others, the authorization and authentication of the property documents may be made by the highest political authorities of the department wherein the crime has been committed, and pending the appearance of the interested parties the judicial authority of the country where such property is found shall direct it to be deposited, and to this end a telegraphic request from any of the authorities above mentioned shall be sufficient. Upon the establishment of the right ownership of said property it shall be delivered to the proper owners, even when the offender is not amenable to extradition, or when such extradition has not been decreed.

ARTICLE 31.

In all cases when the detention of the fugitive is demanded, he shall be informed within twenty-four hours that extradition proceedings shall be instituted against him, and that within the peremptory term of three days from notification he may oppose such extradition by alleging—

1. That he is not the person whose extradition is requested;
2. Any material defects that may exist in the submitted documents; and
3. That the request for extradition is contrary to law.

ARTICLE 32.

In case the proof of the alleged facts is needed, proceedings shall be had in accordance with the prescriptions contained in the laws of procedure of the republic to which the request has been made.

When the proof has been established, judgment shall be passed, without further proceedings within ten days, establishing whether extradition shall be granted or not.

Against such decision, and within three days following its notification, the legal remedy granted by the laws of the country where the fugitive is found shall be granted, but five days at the latest, after the expiration of this term, final judgment shall be passed.

ARTICLE 33.

Expenses incurred by reason of the arrest, support, and transportation of the person whose surrender is requested, as well as the expenses incurred in the delivery and transportation of the property to be returned or forwarded because of its connection with the crime of offense, shall be defrayed by the republic making the request.

ARTICLE 34.

The high contracting parties do hereby solemnly declare that they do not hold themselves, nor do they hold the other Central American Republics, as foreign nations, and that they shall continuously endeavor to preserve among them all their family ties and the greatest cordiality in their reciprocal relations, uniting in a common cause in case of war or difficulties with foreign nations, and amicably and fraternally mediating in case of private disturbances.

ARTICLE 35.

In their endeavor to maintain peace and to forestall one of the most frequent causes of disturbances in the interior of the republics and of restlessness and distrust among the Central American people the con-tracting governments shall not allow the leaders of principal chiefs of political emigrations, nor their agents to reside near the frontier of the countries whose peace they seek to disturb. Neither shall they employ in their respective armies emigrants from any of the other republics and, should the interested governments so request, such emigrants shall be concentrated at one point. Should the political emigrants resident in any of the contracting republics incite or encourage revolutionary work against any of the other republics, they shall forthwith be exiled from the respective territory. All these measures shall be enforced irrespective of the nationality of the person against whom issued; but any government issuing such orders shall weigh the burden of the proof submitted or the evidence obtained by such government.

ARTICLE 36.

The present treaty is of a perpetual nature and always obligatory as regards peace, friendship, and arbitration, but as regards commerce, extradition, and other stipulations it shall remain in full force for a term of ten years from the date of exchange of the ratifications. If, however, one year before the expiration of such term none of the high contracting parties should have officially notified the others of its intention to terminate the treaty as stated, it shall continue to be obligatory for one year after the said notification.

ARTICLE 37.

This treaty shall be ratified and the ratifications exchanged in the city of San Salvador within two months from date of the last ratification.

ARTICLE 38.

As the principal stipulations contained in the treaties made heretofore between the contracting countries are condensed or properly modified in the foregoing treaty, it is hereby declared that all such former treaties shall remain without effect and be abrogated when the present treaty is duly approved and the exchange of ratifications has been made.

In faith whereof the respective plenipotentiaries have signed and sealed the foregoing treaty in the city of San Jose de Costa Rica on the twenty-fifth day of the month of September, one thousand nine hundred and six.

(Signed) Luis Anderson
(Signed) Salvador Gallidos
(Signed) Salvador Rodríguez G.
(Signed) F. Anguiano
(Signed) Jose Flamenco
(Signed) Sotero Barahona

Source: FRUS, 1909, Part I; 857–865.

APPENDIX IV

Treaty of Peace Between Nicaragua and Salvador, Signed in Amapala, April 23, 1907.

The undersigned, José Dolores Gamez, minister for foreign affairs of the Republic of Nicaragua, and Ramón Garcia González, minister for foreign affairs of the Republic of El Salvador, each in the representation of his respective Government, and fully authorized according to the full powers exhibited and which were found to be in good and due form, after extensive discussion and with the friendly mediation of Mr. Philip Brown, charge d'affaires of the United States near the Government of the Republic of Honduras, have agreed to celebrate the treaty of peace, friendship, and commerce contained in the following clauses:

I.

The good harmony and friendly relations existing between the signatory Governments having been altered in consequence of the late war between Nicaragua and Honduras, in which the Government of El Salvador found itself obliged to intervene on account of its alliance with the Government of Honduras that was presided over by General Manuel Bonilla, and taking in consideration powerful reasons of the necessity and convenience to restore peace between both countries and after protracted discussions they have mutually agreed to reestablish the friendly relations which were temporarily interrupted on the base of the best good faith that ought to rule in the friendly understanding of two sister Republics.

II.

Peace being reestablished by the present treaty, the signatory Governments herewith agree that the Government of Nicaragua is to issue an invitation to the other Governments of Central America to attend a Central-American Congress that will be held at Corinto, pursuant to the propositions made by the representatives of the Governments of these Republics conjointly with the American Secretary of State in Washington, this congress will be composed of representatives of the five sister Republics, who will have full powers to conclude a general treaty of peace and friendship having for a base obligatory arbitration, to replace the former treaties of the same nature, celebrated at Corinto and at San Jose of Costa Rica, with the purpose of avoiding in the future armed conflicts between sister Republics. The representatives of the five Republics will moreover be able to conclude arrangements in reference to commerce, navigation, and any other questions that they may judge profitable to Central American interests.

III.

While the disposition of the foregoing clause is being complied with it remains stipulated herewith that any difference that may arise in the future between El Salvador and Nicaragua that might alter their good relations shall be adjusted by means of the obligatory arbitration of the Presidents of the United States and Mexico, conjointly, who shall have the power in case of not arriving at an agreement, to name a third person, whose decision shall be definite. The President of Mexico will have the right to delegate his faculties as arbitrator upon the person of the Mexican ambassador at Washington or on the person that he may designate.

IV.

As a manifestation of the sincerity with which the signatory Governments have proceeded and also of the confidence that they have in the fulfillment of all the clauses of this treaty, they offer with the best good will to issue in their respective countries a decree of unconditional and ample amnesty in favour of their countrymen who may have taken opposite sides in the last events of Honduras.

V.

El Salvador and Nicaragua solemnly pledge themselves to celebrate a treaty of commerce on the base of interchange.

VI.

The present treaty shall be ratified and the ratifications shall be exchanged in the city of Managua or at San Salvador, a month after the last ratification or before that time if possible.

In witness whereof, the negotiators have signed the present treaty in triplicate, conjointly with Mr. Philip Brown, charge d'affaires of the United States near the Governments of Honduras and Guatemala, who has interposed his good offices and the moral authority of the country which he represents. Done at Amapala this twenty-third day of April in the year one thousand nine hundred and seven.

> Ramón Garcia González
> José D. Gamez
> Philip Brown

Source: FRUS, 1907, Part II: 633–34.

APPENDIX V

GENERAL TREATY OF PEACE AND AMITY

The Governments of the Republics of Costa Rica, Guatemala, Honduras, Nicaragua and Salvador, being desirous of establishing the foundations which fix the general relations of said countries, have seen fit to conclude a general Treaty of Peace and Amity which will attain said end, and for that purpose have named as Delegates:

COSTA RICA: Their Excellencies Doctor Don Luis Anderson and Don Joaquin B. Calvo;

GUATEMALA: Their Excellencies Doctor Don Antonio Batres Jauregui, Doctor Don Luis Toledo Herrarte, and Don Victor Sanchez Ocaña;

HONDURAS: Their Excellencies Doctor Don Policarpo Bonilla, Doctor Don Angel Ugarte, and Don E. Constantino Fiallos;

NICARAGUA: Their Excellencies Doctors Don José Madriz and Don Luis F. Corea; and

SALVADOR: Their Excellencies Doctor Don Salvador Gallegos, Doctor Don Salvador Rodriguez Gonzalez, and Don Federico Mejia.

By virtue of the invitation sent in accordance with Article II of the protocol signed at Washington on September 17, 1907, by the Plenipotentiary Representatives of the five Central American Republics, their excellencies, the Representative of the Government of the United Mexican States, Ambassador Don Enrique C. Creel, and the representative of the Government of the United States of America, Mr. William I. Buchanan, were present at all the deliberations.

The Delegates, assembled in the Central American Peace Conference at Washington, after having communicated to one another their respective full powers, which they found to be in due form, have agreed to carry out the said purpose in the following manner:

ARTICLE I.

The Republics of Central America consider as one of their first duties, in their mutual relations, the maintenance of peace; and they bind themselves always to observe the most complete harmony, and decide every difference or difficulty that may arise amongst them, of whatsoever nature it may be, by means of the Central American Court of Justice, created by the Convention which they have concluded for that purpose on this date.

ARTICLE II.

Desiring to secure in the Republics of Central America the benefits which are derived from the maintenance of their institutions, and to contribute at the same time in strengthening their stability and the prestige with which they ought to be surrounded, it is declared that every disposition or measure which may tend to alter the constitutional organization in any of them is to be deemed a menace to the peace of said Republics.

ARTICLE III.

Taking into account the central geographic position of Honduras and the facilities which owing to this circumstance have made its territory most often the theater of Central American conflicts, Honduras declares from now on its absolute neutrality in event of any conflict between the other Republics; and the latter, in their turn, provided such neutrality be observed, bind themselves to respect it and in no case to violate the Honduranean territory.

ARTICLE IV.

Bearing in mind the advantages which must be gained from the creation of Central American institutions for the development of their most vital interests, besides the Pedagogical Institute and the International Central American Bureau which are to be established according to the Conventions concluded to that end by this Conference, the creation of a practical Agricultural School in the Republic of Salvador, one of Mines and Mechanics in that of Honduras, and another of Arts and Trades in that of Nicaragua, is especially recommended to the Governments.

ARTICLE V.

In order to cultivate the relations between the States, the contracting Parties obligate themselves each to accredit to the others a permanent Legation.

ARTICLE VI.

The citizens of one of the contracting Parties, residing in the territory of any of the others, shall enjoy the same civil rights as are enjoyed by nationals, and shall be considered as citizens in the country of their residence if they fulfil the conditions which the respective constituent laws provide. Those that are not naturalized shall be exempt from obligatory military service, either on sea or land, and from every forced loan or military requisition, and they shall not be obliged on any account to pay greater contributions or ordinary or extraordinary imposts than those which natives pay.

ARTICLE VII.

The individuals who have acquired a professional degree in any of the contracting Republics, may, without special exaction, practice their professions, in accordance with the respective laws, in any one of the others, without other requirements than those of presenting the respective degree or diploma properly authenticated and of proving, in case of necessity, their personal identity and of obtaining a permit from the Executive Power where the law so requires.

In like manner shall validity attach to the scientific studies pursued in the universities, professional schools, and the schools of higher education of any one of the contracting countries, provided the documents which evidence such studies have been authenticated, and the identity of the person proved.

ARTICLE VIII.

Citizens of the signatory countries who reside in the territory of the others shall enjoy the right of literary, artistic, or industrial property in the same manner and subject to the same requirements as natives.

ARTICLE IX.

The merchant ships of the signatory countries shall be considered upon the sea, along the coasts, and in the ports of said countries as national vessels; they shall enjoy the same exemptions, immunities, and concessions as the latter, and shall not pay other dues nor be subject to further taxes than those imposed upon and paid by the vessels of the country.

ARTICLE X.

The Governments of the contracting Republics bind themselves to respect the inviolability of the right of asylum aboard the merchant vessels of whatsoever nationality anchored in their ports. Therefore, only persons accused of common crimes can be taken from them after due legal procedure and by order of the competent judge. Those prosecuted on account of political crimes or common crimes in connection with political ones, can only be taken therefrom in case they have embarked in a port of the State which claims them, during their stay in its jurisdictional waters, and after the requirements hereinbefore set forth in the case of common crimes have been fulfilled.

ARTICLE XI.

The Diplomatic and Consular Agents of the contracting Reublics in foreign cities, towns, and ports shall afford to the persons, vessels, and other property of the citizens of any one of them, the same protection as to the persons, ships, and other properties of their compatriots, without demanding for their services other or higher charges than those usually made with respect to their nationals.

ARTICLE XII.

In the desire of promoting commerce between the contracting Republics, their respective Governments shall agree upon the establish-ment of national merchant marines engaged in coastwise commerce and the arrangements to be made with and the subsidies to be granted to steamship companies engaged in the trade between national and foreign ports.

ARTICLE XIII.

There shall be a complete and regular exchange of every class of official publications between the contracting Parties.

ARTICLE XIV.

Public instruments executed in one of the contracting Republics shall be valid in the others, provided they shall have been properly authenti-cated and in their execution the laws of the Republic whence they issue shall have been observed.

ARTICLE XV.

The judicial authorities of the contracting Republics shall carry out the judicial commissions and warrants in civil, commercial, or criminal matters, with regard to citations, interrogatories, and other acts of procedure or judicial function.

Other judicial acts, in civil or commercial matters, arising out of a personal suit, shall have in the territory of any one of the contracting Parties equal force with those of the local tribunals and shall be executed in the same manner, provided always that they shall first have been declared executory by the Supreme Tribunal of the Republic wherein they are to be executed, which shall be done if they meet the essential requirements of their respective legislation and they shall be carried out in accordance with the laws enacted in each country for the execution of judgments.

ARTICLE XVI.

Desiring to prevent one of the most frequent causes of disturbances in the Republics, the contracting Governments shall not permit the leaders or principal chiefs of political refugees, nor their agents, to reside in the departments bordering on the countries whose peace they might disturb.

Those who may have established their permanent residence in a frontier department may remain in the place of their residence under the immediate surveillance of the Government affording them an asylum, but from the moment when they become a menace to public order, they shall be included in the rule of the preceding paragraph.

ARTICLE XVII.

Every person, no matter what his nationality, who, within the territory of one of the contracting Parties, shall initiate or foster revolutionary movements against any of the others, shall be immediately brought to the capital of the Republic, where he shall be submitted to trial according to law.

ARTICLE XVIII.

With respect to the Bureau of Central American Republics which shall be established in Guatemala, and with respect to the Pedagogical Institute which is to be created in Costa Rica, the Conventions celebrated to that end shall be observed, and those that refer to Extradition, Communications, and Annual Conferences shall remain in full force for the unification of Central American interests.

ARTICLE XIX.

The present Treaty shall remain in force for the term of ten years counted from the day of the exchange of ratifications. Nevertheless, if one year before the expiration of said term none of the contracting Parties shall have given special notice to the others concerning its intention to terminate it, it shall remain in force until one year after such notification shall have been made.

ARTICLE XX.

The stipulations of the Treaties heretofore concluded among the contracting Countries, being comprised or suitably modified in this, it is declared that all stipulations remain void and revoked by the present, after final approval and exchange of ratifications.

ARTICLE XXI.

The exchange of ratifications of the present Treaty, as well as that of the other Conventions of this date, shall be made by means of communications which are to be addressed by the Governments to that of Costa Rica, in order that the latter shall notify the other contracting States. The Government of Costa Rica shall also communicate its ratification if it affects it.

Signed at the city of Washington on the twentieth day of December, one thousand nine hundred and seven.

> Luis Anderson
> J. B. Calvo
> Antonio Batres Jauregui
> Luis Toledo Herrarte
> Victor Sanchez O.
> Policarpo Bonilla
> Angel Ugarte
> E. Constantino Fiallos
> José Madriz
> Luis F. Corea
> Salvador Gallegos
> Salvador Rodríguez G.
> F. Mejia

Convention for the Establishment of a Central American Court of Justice.

The Governments of the Republics of Costa Rica, Guatemala, Honduras, Nicaragua, and Salvador, for the purpose of efficaciously guaranteeing their rights and maintaining peace and harmony inalterably in their relations, without being obliged to resort in any case to the employment of force, have agreed to conclude a Convention for the constitution of a Court of Justice charged with accomplishing such high aims, and, to that end, have named as Delegates:

COSTA RICA.—Their Excellencies Doctor Don Luis Anderson and Don Joaquin B. Calvo;

GUATEMALA.—Their Excellencies Doctor Don Antonio Batres Jauregui, Doctor Don Luis Toledo Herrarte, and Don Victor Sanchez Ocana;

HONDURAS.—Their Excellencies Doctor Don Policarpo Bonilla, Doctor Don Angel Ugarte, and Don E. Constantino Fiallos;

NICARAGUA.—Their Excellencies Doctors Don José Madriz and Don Luis F. Corea; and

SALVADOR:—Their Excellencies Doctor Don Salvador Gallegos, Doctor Don Salvador Rodríguez Gonzelez, and Don Federico Mejia.

By virtue of the invitation sent in accordance with Article II of the protocol signed at Washington on September 17, 1907, by the Plenipotentiary Representatives of the five Central American Republics, their excellencies, the Representative of the Government of the United Mexican States, Ambassador Don Enrique C. Creel, and the Representative of the Government of the United States of America, Mr. William I. Buchanan, were present at all the deliberations.

The Delegates, assembled in the Central American Peace Conference at Washington, after having communicated to one another their respective full powers, which they found to be in due form, have agreed to carry out the said purpose in the following manner:

ARTICLE I.

The High Contracting Parties agree by the present Convention to constitute and maintain a permanent tribunal which shall be called the "Central American Court of Justice," to which they bind themselves to submit all controversies or questions which may arise among them, of whatsoever nature and no matter what their origin may be, in case the respective Departments of Foreign Affairs should not have been able to reach an understanding.

ARTICLE II.

This court shall also take cognizance of the questions which individuals of one Central American country may raise against any of the other contracting Governments, because of the violation of treaties or conventions, and other cases of an international character; no matter whether their own Government supports said claim or not; and provided that the remedies which the laws of the respective country provide against such violation shall have been exhausted or that denial of justice shall have been shown.

ARTICLE III.

It shall also take cognizance of the cases which by common accord the contracting Governments may submit to it, no matter whether they arise between two or more of them or between one of said Governments and individuals.

ARTICLE IV.

The Court can likewise take cognizance of the international questions which by special agreement any one of the Central American Governments and a foreign Government may have determined to submit to it.

ARTICLE V.

The Central American Court of Justice shall sit at the City of Cartago in the Republic of Costa Rica, but it may temporarily transfer its residence to another point in Central America whenever it deems to be expedient for reasons of health, or in order to insure the exercise of its functions, or of the personal safety of its members.

ARTICLE VI.

The Central American Court of Justice shall consist of five Justices, one being appointed by each Republic and selected from among the jurists who possess the qualifications which the laws of each country prescribe for the exercise of high judicial office, and who enjoy the highest consideration, both because of their moral character and their professional ability.

Vacancies shall be filled by substitute Justices, named at the same time and in the same manner as the regular Justices, and who shall unite the same qualifications as the latter.

The attendance of the five justices who constitute the Tribunal is indispensable in order to make a legal quorum in the decisions of the Court.

ARTICLE VII.

The Legislative Power of each one of the five contracting Republics shall appoint their respective Justices, one regular and two substitutes.

The salary of each Justice shall be eight thousand dollars, gold, per annum, which shall be paid them by the Treasury of the Court. The salary of the Justice of the country where the Court resides shall be fixed by the Government thereof. Furthermore each State shall contribute two thousand dollars, gold, annually toward the ordinary and extraordinary expenses of the Tribunal. The Governments of the contracting Republics bind themselves to include their respective contributions in their estimates of expenses and to remit quarterly in advance to the Treasury of the Court the share they may have to bear on account of such services.

ARTICLE VIII.

The regular and substitute Justices shall be appointed for a term of five years, which shall be counted from the day on which they assume the duties of their office, and they may be reelected.

In case of death, resignation, or permanent incapacity of any of them, the vacancy shall be filled by the respective Legislature, and the Justice elected shall complete the term of his predecessor.

ARTICLE IX.

The regular and substitute Justices shall take oath or make affirmation prescribed by law before the authority that may have appointed them, and from that moment they shall enjoy the immunities and prerogatives which the present Convention confers upon them. The regular Justices shall likewise enjoy thenceforth the salary fixed in Article VII.

ARTICLE X.

Whilst they remain in the country of their appointment the regular and substitute Justices shall enjoy the personal immunity which the respective laws grant to the magistrates of the Supreme Court of Justice, and in the other contracting Republics they shall have the privileges and immunities of Diplomatic Agents.

ARTICLE XI.

The office of Justice whilst held is incompatible with the exercise of his profession, and with the holding of public office. The same incompatibility applies to the substitute Justices so long as they may actually perform their duties.

ARTICLE XII.

At its first annual session the Court shall elect from among its own members a President and Vice-President; it shall organize the personnel of its office by designating a Clerk, a Treasurer, and such other subordinate employees as it may deem necessary, and it shall draw up the estimate of its expenses.

ARTICLE XIII.

The Central American Court of Justice represents the national conscience of Central America, wherefore the Justices who compose the Tribunal shall not consider themselves barred from the discharge of their duties because of the interest which the Republics, to which they owe their appointment, may have in any case or question. With regard to allegations of personal interest, the rules of procedure which the Court may fix shall make proper provision.

ARTICLE XIV.

When differences or questions subject to the jurisdiction of the Tribunal arise, the interested party shall present a complaint which shall comprise all the points of fact and law relative to the matter, and all pertinent evidence. The Tribunal shall communicate without loss of time a copy of the complaint to the Governments or individuals interested, and shall invite them to furnish their allegations and evidence within the term that it may designate to them, which, in no case, shall exceed sixty days counted from the date of notice of the complaint.

ARTICLE XV.

If the term designated shall have expired without answer having been made to the complaint, the Court shall require the complainant or complainants to do so within a further term not to exceed twenty days, after the expiration of which and in view of the evidence presented and of such evidence as it may *ex officio* have seen fit to obtain, the Tribunal shall render its decision in the case, which decision shall be final.

ARTICLE XVI.

If the Government, Governments, or individuals sued shall have appeared in time before the Court, presenting their allegations and evidence, the Court shall decide the matter within thirty days following, without further process or proceedings; but if a new term for the presentation of evidence be solicited, the Court shall decide whether or not there is occasion to grant it; and in the affirmative it shall fix therefore a reasonable time. Upon the expiration of such term, the Court shall pronounce its final judgment within thirty days.

ARTICLE XVII.

Each one of the Governments or individuals directly concerned in the questions to be considered by the Court has the right to be represented before it by a trustworthy person or persons, who shall present evidence, formulate arguments, and shall, within the terms fixed by this Convention and by the rules of the Court of Justice do everything that in their judgment shall be beneficial to the defense of the rights they represent.

ARTICLE XVIII.

From the moment in which any suit is instituted against any one or more governments up to that in which a final decision has been pronounced, the court may at the solicitation of any one of the parties fix the situation in which the contending parties must remain, to the end that the difficulty shall not be aggravated and that things shall be conserved in *statu quo* pending a final decision.

ARTICLE XIX.

For all the effects of this Convention the Central American Court of Justice may address itself to the Governments or tribunals of justice of the contracting States, through the medium of the Ministry of Foreign Relations or the office of the Clerk of the Supreme Court of Justice of the respective country, according to the nature of the requisite proceedings, in order to have the measures that it may dictate within the scope of its jurisdiction carried out.

ARTICLE XX.

It may also appoint special commissioners to carry out the formalities above referred to, when it deems it expedient for their better fulfillment. In such case, it shall ask of the Government where the proceeding is to be had, its cooperation and assistance, in order that the Commissioner may fulfill his mission. The contracting Governments formerly bind themselves to obey and to enforce the orders of the Court, furnishing all the assistance that may be necessary for their best and most expeditious fulfillment.

ARTICLE XXI.

In deciding points of fact that may be raised before it, the Central American Court of Justice shall be governed by its free judgment, and with respect to points of law, by the principles of International Law. The final judgment shall cover each one of the points in litigation.

ARTICLE XXII.

The Court is competent to determine its jurisdiction, interpreting the Treaties and Conventions germane to the matter in dispute, and applying the principles of international law.

ARTICLE XXIII.

Every final or interlocutory decision shall be rendered with the concurrence of at least three of the Justices of the Court. In case of disagreement, one of the substitute Justices shall be chosen by lot, and if still a majority of three be not thus obtained other Justices shall be successively chosen by lot until three uniform votes shall have been obtained.

ARTICLE XXIV.

The decisions must be in writing and shall contain a statement of the reasons upon which they are based. They must be signed by all the Justices of the Court and countersigned by the Clerk. Once they have been notified they can not be altered on any account; but at the request of any of the parties, the Tribunal may declare the interpretation which must be given to its judgments.

ARTICLE XXV.

The judgments of the Court shall be communicated to the five Governments of the contracting Republics. The interested parties solemnly bind themselves to submit to said judgments, and all agree to lend all moral support that may be necessary in order that they may be properly fulfilled, thereby constituting a real and positive guarantee of respect for this Convention and for the Central American Court of Justice.

ARTICLE XXVI.

The Court is empowered to make its rules, to formulate the rules of procedure which may be necessary, and to determine the forms and terms not prescribed in the present Convention. All the decisions which may be rendered in this respect shall be communicated immediately to the High Contracting Parties.

ARTICLE XXVII.

The High Contracting Parties solemnly declare that on no ground nor in any case will they consider the present Convention as void; and that, therefore, they will consider it as being always in force during the term of ten years counted from the last ratification. In the event of the change or alteration of the political status of one or more of the Contracting Republics, the functions of the Central American Court of Justice created by this Convention shall be suspended *ipso facto*; and a conference to adjust the constitution of said Court to the new order of things shall be forthwith convoked by the respective Governments; in case they do not unanimously agree the present Convention shall be considered as rescinded.

ARTICLE XXVIII.

The exchange of ratifications of the present Convention shall be made in accordance with Article XXI of the General Treaty of Peace and Amity concluded on this date.

PROVISIONAL ARTICLE.

As recommended by the five Delegations an Article is annexed which contains an amplification of the jurisdiction of the Central American Court of Justice, in order that the Legislatures may, if they see fit, include it in this Convention upon ratifying it.

ANNEXED ARTICLE.

The Central American Court of Justice shall also have jursidiction over the conflicts which may arise between the Legislative, Executive, and Judicial Powers, and when as a matter of fact the judicial decisions and resolutions of the National Congress are not respected.

Signed at the city of Washington on the twentieth day of December, one thousand nine hundred and seven.

Luis Anderson
J. B. Calvo
Antonio Batres Jauregui
Luis Toledo Herrarte
Victor Sanchez O.
Policarpo Bonilla
Angel Ugarte
E. Constantino Fiallos
José Madriz
Luis F. Corea
Salvador Gallegos
Salvador Rodríguez G.
F. Mejia

APPENDIX VI

TACOMA AGREEMENT

Agreement Between the Presidents of Honduras, Salvador, and Nicaragua, Signed August 20, 1922, on Board the U. S. S. *"Tacoma."*

In the waters of the Gulf of Fonseca, aboard the *Tacoma,* a war vessel of the United States of America, on the 20th day of the month of August of the year 1922, the undersigned Presidents of Republics: Of Honduras, His Excellency Señor don Rafael Lopez Gutierrez; of Salvador, His Excellency Señor don Jorge Melendez; and of Nicaragua, His Excellency Señor don Diego Manuel Chamorro, who have assembled in this conference moved by the desire to seek the most efficacious friendly means to remove all of the causes which may have caused the unrest which has disturbed Central America in recent years, after a frank discussion of all matters relating to the political conditions in the three countries and to their other vital interests; in the presence of Their Excellencies: the Honorable Franklin E. Morales, Minister of the United States of America to Honduras; the Hondorable Montgomery Schuyler, Minister of the United States of America to Salvador; the Honorable John E. Ramer, Minister of the United States of America to Nicaragua, who on this occasion represent the Goverment of the United States of America, in evidence of the deep interest felt by that friendly Republic in having the lofty aims of this convention attained so as to cement actual and lasting peace,

AGREED:

First. In view of the differences of opinion which have arisen as to the General Treaty of Peace and Amity signed in Washington by the five Republics of Central America on December 20, 1907, being in force, and pending a revision of that said Treaty, they declare that beginning from this date, the three States over which they preside shall regard the said Treaty as being in force in everything that affects the relations maintained by the three Republics.

Second. The three Presidents promise one another not to permit the political refugees from any one of the Republics to prepare in the territory

---

Source: *FRUS,* 1927: Part I, 422–425.

of the others any armed invasion whatsoever of the other contracting States or to threaten the public peace in any other manner; and for that purpose they agree to apply rigorously Article XVI of the General Treaty of Peace and Amity mentioned in the preceding clause, binding themselves also to guard their respective frontiers in order to prevent the said invasions.

Third. In case that any one of the States should be actually invaded from one of the other two signatories of this Convention, the Government of the State in whose territory the invasion was prepared shall be obligated immediately to send forces to the disturbed frontier for the purpose of cooperating within its territory to the reestablishment of normal conditions, and to that end shall capture and disarm the offenders to whom Clause XVII of the General Treaty of Peace and Amity above mentioned shall be rigorously applied. They undertake, also, without any other restrictions than those flowing from the constitutions of the respective countries, to expel from their territory, in case of such invasions, the guilty leaders of the invasions, provided it be requested by the Government of the Republic which may be invaded. It is understood that this provision shall be applied even to invasions which may have taken place previously in any one of the three Republics and caused the unrest which has brought about this conference.

Fourth. The three signatory Presidents agree not to accept in the armies of their respective Governments the political refugees of any of the other Republics, nor to appoint them to any office that may carry military authority. They assume the same obligation with respect to the nationals of the three Republics or other individuals who may have incited invasions even though they may not be political refugees. If the State's own nationals are involved, the guilt must be proved in a satisfactory manner by the offended Government, in order to obligate the others.

Fifth. The three signatory Presidents desiring further to promote *rapprochement* between those countries in the sense of a practicable way which may lead to the ideal of the Central American Union, cherished by all three, will call a conference to be attended by the respective plenipotentiaries of the five Governments of Central America for the purpose of deciding upon measures, such as free trade, unification of currency, unification of the tariff systems, ways of communication and other measures guaranteed by treaties aiming to draw them closer to one another, which would tend to make really practicable, in a future thus prepared, the political unification of Central America. For that purpose the month of December next is fixed for a preliminary conference, the object of which will be to determine what form studies made in each country shall take relative to the realization of the above-mentioned measures. The place where this preliminary conference will be held shall be decided upon by agreement made among the Foreign Offices of the Central American Republics. The purposes of this conference shall not be modified except for unanimous consent of the contracting parties.

Sixth. The Presidents of Nicaragua and Salvador agree to endeavor to secure from their respective Governments the granting of free trade in the natural products of their respective States and also in goods therein manufactured from their own raw materials. Whatever may be accomplished on this point shall be by way of experiment and an effort will be made to establish the system of free trade on January 1st of the coming year 1923 for a period of one year.

Seventh. Actuated always by the same spirit of concord which has inspired this Convention and in order to make effective their purpose of maintaining peace in Central America, putting aside all differences of opinion which might turn into keen causes of trouble, the signatory Presidents agree to submit to arbitration all disputes now existing, or which may arise among the signatory Republics, over boundary questions, the interpretation of treaties, and any other matters which may give or have given rise to discussions or dissension among them. The preliminary conference of the plenipotentiaries referred to in Clause V shall establish the form and organization of the arbitration. The boundary question between Honduras and Nicaragua is excepted from the stipulations contained in this clause, each one of the interested parties reserving the right to maintain the legal position it has thus far maintained.

Eighth. In their desire that the benefits of assured peace which may be derived from this conference shall extent to all of Central America the three contracting Presidents shall invite the Presidents of the Republics of Costa Rica and Guatemala to adhere to this Convention. The mere notice from either one of the two Presidents referred to, of Costa Rica and Guatemala, that he has accepted this Convention shall be held sufficient to make him a signer of and party to it.

As recording the whole covenant they now sign six identical copies with the assistance of their respective Secretaries of State for Foreign Affairs and in company with Their Excellencies the Ministers of the

United States of America to Nicaragua, Salvador and Honduas above named.

R. Lopez G.
Jorge Melendez
Diego M. Chamorro
Franklin E. Morales
Montgomery Schuyler
John E. Ramer
F. Bueso
Arturo R. Avila
Carlos Cuadra Pasos

INDEX

ABOUT THE AUTHORS

James N. Cortada spent 28 years in the U.S. Foreign Service. He served in Cuba and Spain and throughout the Middle East, and rose to the rank of Foreign Service Officer Class One. He is a graduate of the Havana Business University and taught for one year at U.C.L.A. as Diplomat in Residence. He is the author of several hundred newspaper and magazine articles on foreign policy. He lives in Orange, Virginia where he currently is preparing a book on democracy in the Hispanic world.

James W. Cortada works for IBM. He earned his Ph.D. from Florida State University and is the author of fourteen books, the majority dealing with U.S.-Spanish relations, and some 50 academic articles. His most recent books include *Spain and the American Civil War, An Historical Dictionary of the Spanish Civil War, 1936–1939,* and *Spain in the Twentieth Century World.* He currently is co-authoring a book on democracy in the Hispanic world with his father.